VISUAL FRIENDLIES, TALLY TARGET: HOW CLOSE AIR SUPPORT IN THE WAR ON TERROR CHANGED THE WAY AMERICA MADE WAR

VISUAL FRIENDLIES, TALLY TARGET: HOW CLOSE AIR SUPPORT IN THE WAR ON TERROR CHANGED THE WAY AMERICA MADE WAR

Volume I: Invasions

ETHAN BROWN

Pennsylvania & Yorkshire

Published in the United States of America and Great Britain in 2024 by
CASEMATE PUBLISHERS
1950 Lawrence Road, Havertown, PA 19083
and
47 Church Street, Barnsley, S70 2AS, UK

Copyright 2024 © Ethan Brown

Hardback Edition: ISBN 978-1-63624-422-8
Digital Edition: ISBN 978-1-63624-423-5

A CIP record for this book is available from the British Library

All rights reserved. No part of this book may be reproduced or transmitted in any form or by any means, electronic or mechanical including photocopying, recording or by any information storage and retrieval system, without permission from the publisher in writing.

Printed and bound in the United Kingdom by CPI Group (UK) Ltd, Croydon, CR0 4YY

Typeset in India by Lapiz Digital Services, Chennai.

For a complete list of Casemate titles, please contact:

CASEMATE PUBLISHERS (US)
Telephone (610) 853-9131
Fax (610) 853-9146
Email: casemate@casematepublishers.com
www.casematepublishers.com

CASEMATE PUBLISHERS (UK)
Telephone (0)1226 734350
Email: casemate@casemateuk.com
www.casemateuk.com

The views expressed in this publication are those of the author and do not necessarily reflect the official policy or position of the Department of Defense or the U.S. Government. The public release clearance of this publication by the Department of Defense does not imply Department of Defense endorsement or factual accuracy of the material.

Use of names, locations, events and other contextual information is intended for historical purposes and has been vetted to the maximum possible extent by the author using available resources.

This work, and those that follow, is dedicated to all the forward air controllers who gave their all, in defense of our way of life, who paid the ultimate sacrifice so we may live under unfettered skies, and not under the burden of tyranny.

As this work is about the men who controlled the machines above for the ones below, particular, and specific, dedication for Book I is to the following TACPs:

SSgt Andre Berkley, Killed in training, July 19, 1989
SSgt Brian Daly, Killed in training, September 4, 1996
SSgt Jason Faley, Killed in training, March 12, 2001
Maj. Gregory Stone, Killed in action, March 25, 2003
SSgt Jacob Frazier, Killed in action, March 29, 2003
A1C Ray Losano, Killed in action, April 25, 2003
MSgt Steve Auchman, Killed in action, November 9, 2004
CW2 Dennis Hay, Killed in action, August 29, 2005
SrA Bradley Smith, Killed in action, January 3, 2010
Maj. David Gray, Killed in action, August 8, 2012
MSgt Joshua Gavulic, Killed in training, February 21, 2014
TSgt Timothy Officer, Killed in training, August 3, 2015
TSgt Wesley Kubie, Killed in training, June 8, 2021

You are gone, but never forgotten.

"Good morning, Men!"
"Gung ho!"
"What are you?"
"Gung ho!"
"How far?"
"All the way, every day!"
"What's the word?"
"The strong shall stand, the weak will fall by the wayside …"

Daily opening remarks, parade deck, TACP assessment and selection.

Contents

Author's Note and Thanks ix
Preface xi
Introduction xix

Part I: Retribution 1
1 Into the Graveyard of Empires 3
2 "We were witnesses to history" 7
3 Ancient Roads to a New War 25
4 "You get nightmares from the things you had the option not to do" 29
5 Rearranging God's Furniture 47
6 "Holy shit, I just killed Afghanistan" 53
7 "Some of those lessons are learned in blood" 69

Part II: A New World War 83
8 The Pivot 85
9 The Battle of Debecka Pass 89
10 Type of Control and Method of Engagement 101
11 Shock and Awe 107
12 Chasing Saddam 119
13 Dragging a Nation out of a War 133
14 Rescuing Jessica Lynch 137

Part III: Evolving the Machine 151
15 Building a Global Architecture 153
16 "The insurgents turned that place into a meat grinder" 159
17 In Iraq's Shadow 167
18 "You can't politely ask permission to finish a war" 171
19 "Our targeting was incredibly deliberate" 189
20 The Birth of Digital Close Air Support 199

Afterword	215
Glossary	217
Endnotes	219
Selected Bibliography	225
Index	227

Author's Note and Thanks

As with any book, there are too many people to thank for this outcome. A few, in particular, were pivotal to this first entry into the history of the close air support community. First and foremost, my two boys, Aleksandr and Brayden. You are the reason I dedicated myself to finishing this work. The late nights, early mornings, and spare minutes in between every other thing we do together, it was because I wanted to leave behind a legacy you could be proud of. But as proud as I am for having written this story, it's nothing compared to how proud I am of you two. Thank you for inspiring me to do better every day. And my wife, Savanna, who saw me in my worst times, who knows me better than I know myself, thank you for keeping me out of the pit. My big brother, Jeremy, needs recognition for being the unwavering foundation upon which my writing ambitions rest. Your book is coming next, and it's going to be epic. Just keep writing.

The entire TACP community, to whom this first book is dedicated, is part of this endeavor. This community shaped who I am as a man and, other than being a dad, wearing the black beret is the thing in life of which I am the proudest. There are a few TACPs in particular who deserve explicit thanks. Robert Zackery III, for being the finest mentor, a sounding board throughout this writing, and a friend. Tommy Case, whose support never wavered, and whose unique positivity remains infectious. Kevin Laliberte, whose fiery motivation kicked me in the ass when I needed it most. Lance Maguire, whose feedback, mentorship, and utterly unparalleled wisdom helped me shape the first concepts of this book—thanks for being the first victim of my interview process. Andrew Richie, who uttered the words to me (and Lance) that "Someone's gotta start writing this shit down," well, I did just that, brother. No one else I'd rather have next to me in a gunfight.

To Matt and Carrie Harris, whose legal advice and expertise is second only to their esteemed friendship, thanks for keeping me level. Mike Kistler, I'm fortunate to call you a friend and to have had your mind as a sounding board; add this to the pile of books I've already given you to read.

All the XVII STS family, legacy and current. It's an exclusive club, and I'm still not sure why you let me in, but it was the high mark of my career to represent the unit to our Ranger brothers. And to those Rangers, for whom I was eminently humbled and proud to support, thank you for letting me be one of your JTACs,

100 percent, and then some. And a huge thanks to CSM Mike Hall (ret.) and the Three Rangers Foundation, for upholding the prestige, honor, and high esprit de corps. To the TACP Association and Foundation, no better VSO in the world.

To Joshua Huminski, who has had more involvement in my postmilitary career than anyone or anything else. Not enough space on paper to express my gratitude for being the man, mentor, friend, and colleague that you are.

And to the current and former teammates at the Center for the Study of the Presidency & Congress, thank you for helping me transition from the military to the civilian side. Without the platform and latitude to pursue all my crazy ideas, this book may not have been possible.

The biggest risk was assumed by Casemate Publishers, and there isn't another group better suited to this, and I will be forever grateful for the opportunity. To that team: Ruth, Tracey, Elke, Andy, my sincerest thanks for taking the very rough draft and making it a real book.

Preface

This is the story of how American warfighting fundamentally changed over the duration of the Global War on Terror. Further, as the content will show, the evolution of aerial-delivered fires in support of the ground force scheme of maneuver—doctrinally known as close air support—gave rise to the belief of continued American supremacy in warfighting by developing capabilities intended to solve unique problems in a new paradigm of combat. All the while, the global environment changed to circumvent those technological advantages enjoyed by the American war machine.

Close air support—the delivery of "aerial fires in close proximity to friendly forces, requiring detailed planning and integration"—is such a complex topic and one that dominates the all-consuming commitment of multiple career fields in the armed forces. How can one book—or even a trilogy—encapsulate what many have spent their entire lives trying to master? How can a small collection of narrowly focused stories from a handful of individuals in this community convey the complexity of this topic and still capture its human component—the most important aspect of any war? From the onset of this idea, I did not want this work to simply be a collection of verbal histories that regaled the reader with larger-than-life heroes or, as my former colleagues liked to denigrate, the "No shit, there I was" kind of stories. Although, the enclosed derring-do of these service members' harrowing missions will certainly meet those demands for engaging content. Rather, my hope was to critically analyze how uncontested domains and total battlespace supremacy fundamentally changed how the United States arrayed its fighting capabilities, a strategy that might have held the potential for defeating a scarcely understood threat to our national security (violent extremism), but one that has left the U.S. and allied partnerships facing a stark need to reorder themselves for the era of strategic competition.

Further, and perhaps most importantly, there is a public misconception that the use of air power in the War on Terror was an unbridled release of firepower, indifferent to the second- and third-order effects such weapons and capabilities would have on the environment—literal and human. Nothing could be further from the truth. While it is necessary to recognize and acknowledge when mistakes were made and tragic losses of innocent life occurred (these too are addressed in this work), the application of aerial fires from forward air controllers was one of—if not the most—careful, deliberate, and methodical uses of modern warfighting tools in a complex battlespace.

These stories took place during a time when a generation grew up playing video games that aggrandized the warfighter, where a certain number of kills in a multiplayer game mode would "unlock" some type of airstrike tool or bonus, and pressing a certain button would pull up a magical set of binoculars, resulting in a perfect strike on a graphic depiction of the enemy. Movies and TV shows would portray pithy one-liners like "bring the rain" while action heroes pointed unrealistically visible laser pointers at a target scant meters away, and the impact of a massive bombardment would produce some flying dirt and debris, where the good guys emerge unscathed, and the bad guys disappear in a cloud of smoke.

Those depictions are not close air support. They are a poorly understood manifestation of imagination and inaccurately reflect just how complex and dynamic the task of calling in fires truly is. This book aims to dispel the myth and notions of how the public perceives close air support.

The interviewees, who were gracious enough to share their recollections of the missions that defined pivotal episodes in their lives, recalled the details of those missions to the best of their abilities. Identities have been struck where necessary, and I have made every effort to corroborate the content with official Department of Defense records as much as declassification, Freedom of Information Act requests, and open-source material permits. It is these stories, beginning with the earliest phases of the War on Terror in October 2001, through its terminus in August 2021, that I intended to serve as the vehicle to arrive at the work's key point: that forward air controllers carried this war on their backs. There are occasional asides where I employ historical examples that relate to the evolution of doctrinal close air support, or reference geopolitical conditions, or reiterate actual U.S. military doctrine available from unclassified sources. These explanations are woven into the narrative accounts as necessary, all serving as critical context in understanding the complex relationships between human and machine in this lethal fusion.

Only in a Non-Contested Battlespace

Through two decades, the United States and its allies enjoyed uncontested domains in the battlefields of the War on Terror—supremacy in the air, space, cyber, ground, and logistics components of the battlefields in which they were engaged. At no point from the October 2001 invasion until the fateful withdrawal in August 2021 was the American military or its allies challenged for battlespace supremacy in Afghanistan, Iraq, or Syria. Due to the nature of the adversary—disaggregate, cell-structured extremist groups—the combat efficiency of American warfighting did not face a fundamental threat with the potential to overpower, weaken, or significantly degrade the vast capabilities arrayed in-theater. Rather, insurgency reared its ugly head in such a manner that could only be expected when the might of the American war machine was applied against a foe of such mean, yet pervasive ilk. This was not a war of attrition; this was a contest of wills. There is an old Pashtun proverb, often referenced and well-trodden by veterans of the Afghan war, which says to the international, modernized invaders "You have the watches, but we have the time."

It seemed counterintuitive that an underdeveloped nation like Afghanistan could withstand such technological supremacy, yet the "graveyard of empires" endured this form of disadvantage throughout the 19th and 20th centuries against overwhelmingly capable adversaries, with the occupation by Imperial British and Soviet forces long before the fateful events of September 11, 2001. So too did Iraq's fall in 2003 seem to portend another tally in the "win" column. The conditions of the battlefield allowed for early, swift gains by American and allied combat units, yet the failure to understand the operational environment led to a waterfall of strategy and policy decisions that resulted, perhaps inevitably, in the impasse of continued American operations in Afghanistan and the enduring security force assistance presence in Iraq and Syria (as of this writing). When the shock and awe of the 2001–02 campaigns successfully ousted the Taliban government, it appeared the modus operandi of overwhelming military might would once again ensure dominance in a truncated episode of American foreign-relations history.

But the protracted nature of an insurgency, coupled with the detour to Iraq that all but quelled the potential long-term success in Afghanistan, forced the American strategy apparatus to turn its considerable technological prowess towards a politically sensitive, highly publicized war of perception. Despite the incredible evolution of air capabilities and the innovation of the men on the ground who controlled and integrated these into the ground scheme of maneuver, a lack of strategic and policy comprehension, combined with misconceptions about close air support capabilities, would undermine two decades worth of heroic efforts to win a war that defied political outcomes.

The weapons became more sophisticated, the tactics, techniques, and procedures grew increasingly complex, and the rules of engagement became so inherently restrictive as to render those technological innovations less useful as the war moved into the shadow and confusion of an insurgency. The application of precision fires, namely, the development of "low-collateral damage" munitions—whose lethality is rooted in lethal effects while reducing the potential for proximal structural damage—was seen as a means for American and Coalition military capabilities to fight in these volatile and civilian-permeated battle spaces.

This technological refinement serves as a microcosm of the strategy for the War on Terror: by reducing the collateral effects of the munitions—delivered by the air-support experts whose livelihoods demanded technical mastery amid the most chaotic conditions of the human experience—the belief pinpoint effects could precisely eliminate violent extremism like a surgeon removes a cancerous growth. This mentality became indoctrinated into the strategists who were charged with winning a war that defied a projectable end state, against an enemy whose construct similarly defied the presumed response to attrition.

This is not to say that bigger weapons would have served as a successful alternative. President Donald Trump directed a statement offensive airstrike early in his presidency, opting for the "big guns" over a precision airstrike to decisively engage Islamic State–Khorasan forces. In April 2017, the president authorized the first and only employment of the GBU-43/B Massive Ordnance Air Blast weapon (the "MOAB," affectionately dubbed the "Mother of All Bombs" in military circles). The 21,000-lb munition, with an explosive force comparable to 11 tons of TNT, is the largest non-nuclear weapon ever detonated in combat. This munition was used to target a known underground complex housing Islamic State fighters in Nangahar Province, Afghanistan, to avoid U.S. and Afghan forces having to enter and clear the subterranean structure. A ground mission of that sort carried exponentially higher risk for casualties than an offensive airstrike. My former team commander, an Air Force air liaison officer named Dave, was the joint terminal attack controller (JTAC) who controlled the strike from the Joint Operations Center in Bagram. The MOAB's impact could reportedly be heard and felt by ground forces 20 miles away. Reports on the total enemy killed in action vary but I recall, from watching the strike remotely from my deployed location in real time, that the effectiveness of that weapon was negligible relative to the size of the munition. Further, confirmation of the battle-damage assessment could not be reliably verified due to the subterranean target.

The marked difference here is that the use of precision-guided aerial-delivered weapons, great and small, was perceived in the Afghan and Iraq wars as a game changer. Indeed, they were significant in the application of air power relative to a new warfighting paradigm, but the intended results were not reciprocal to the environmental demands or the strategic outlook. At no point in human history had such innovative, precise, exact, and lethal weapons been so effectively employed in close proximity to friendly forces, at least not to the same degree of success as in Iraq, Syria, and Afghanistan. The "Shock and Awe" campaign of the 1991 Gulf War manifested the potential of such precision-strike weapons, but such adaptive air power 10 years later would be wholly different.

On the topic of the 21st-century use of such air power, I called in thousands of airstrikes over the course of an 11-year career and I am proud to state none of my engagements resulted in fratricide or civilian casualties, even though many such engagements were often well within the "danger close" parameters defined by Joint Publications guidance for each weapon. The ability of American and Coalition forces to have such awesome firepower readily available to augment ground operations, provide timely intelligence, surveillance, and reconnaissance, and ensure extended communications across the tactical battlefield and beyond-line-of-sight, encapsulates how the American war machine was fundamentally altered in the two decades of the War on Terror. But this facet of the warfighting construct was not enough to successfully conclude the war to a desirable end state—one that saw Afghans and Iraqis self-determine their future without being propped up by the considerable technological supremacy of the U.S. military.

Creating an Artificial Supremacy

In December 2019, the eye-opening Special Inspector General for Afghanistan Reconstruction (SIGAR) Report outlined the total dysfunction of a long-term strategy and policy formulation to see Afghanistan to a successful, or at least tolerable, end. The report echoed what many of us who deployed to Afghanistan (in many cases, repeatedly) came to bitterly understand from an early iteration: there would never be a clean, simple solution to the problem of the American presence in Afghanistan. The infrastructure, the institutions, the very fabric of Afghan society, defied a Western, meritocratic approach to building the Afghan nation into a stable, liberal democracy. Corruption was rampant, oversight was either absent or in denial, and—as the Afghanistan Papers summarily defined—known by strategic leaders, and not reported. The collected lessons learned from tactical leaders reflected a failure of grand strategy in Afghanistan, and the inability to understand how the supremacy of the Coalition's warfighting prowess could not eliminate an enemy of non-state permanence. Iraq would forge its own version—the SIGIR Report—which would denote the impossibility of a multi-billion-dollar reconstruction project as the security situation became unstable amidst widespread fraud, waste, and abuse.

In congressional testimony to the Senate Armed Services Committee on September 28, 2021,[1] Defense Secretary Lloyd Austin defined the outcome: "We helped forge a state, but we could not forge a nation. That the Afghan Army [which] we and our partners trained simply melted away—in many cases without firing a shot—took us all by surprise." This was not an intelligence or logistical failure. As Chairman of the Joint Chiefs Gen. Mark Milley stated in the same hearing, "You can't measure the human heart with a machine, you have to be there." Being there, at the most basic level, meant a reality that the United States had created an insulated operational environment that predicated the entirety of the mission on total domain supremacy; that inherent dependence ultimately led to the collapse of the Afghan National Security Forces, which were wholly reliant on the air-power totality our presence achieved. The blame for this problem lay in the hands of the Afghan leaders who did not implement a functional governance as well. As Senator Jack Reed of Delaware stated the day after the Taliban seized Kabul on August 16, 2021, "This is not a Democratic or a Republican problem. These failures have been manifesting over four presidential administrations of both parties."[2]

This battlespace did not possess the same infrastructural, modernized factors as previous wars in the American "win" column—World War II, Korea, and *Desert Storm* for example. There was not a political will to break in Afghanistan, to use the Clausewitz definition for a war's role to a political end. The fight became engulfed by the delicate human arena, and the weapons were revolutionized to accommodate this sensitive reality. Further, the ability to forward stage logistical, intelligence, sustainment, and other mission-support components resulted in an inculcation of the "coverage" mentality—American and Coalition forces became accustomed to always having persistent air and intelligence support for combat and other operations. Missions were able to achieve extended timelines as resupply operations became more than a tertiary option; it became a common factor. Emergency medical evacuations easily achieved the "golden hour" principle, where a critically wounded casualty could be taken from the injury site to an appropriate surgical facility within 60 minutes, exponentially increasing the potential for life-saving interventions and saving thousands of service members' lives.

Every single one of these factors reflected the new battlespace paradigm, which is directly within the JTAC's responsibility—each mission component requires technical expertise to manage assets on both ground and air, kinetic and sustainment, collection, and dissemination. Close air support is the exclusive purview of the JTACs and their supported ground-force commanders, with close integration of higher echelons of authority to confirm or restrict the engagement of fires as deemed necessary in the tactical situation. The entire campaign in Afghanistan and Iraq—through the architectural web of capabilities, integration, and execution—lived and breathed through the radios at the fingertips of the close air support experts on the ground.

This book, and the volumes that follow, is my humble attempt to tell the stories of some of the many whose lives were devoted to the safe employment of this panoply of air-power capabilities. Their stories serve as the vehicle to tell the reader how the use of air power—in particular, close air support—fundamentally changed the U.S. military over two decades of combat in Afghanistan, Iraq, and Syria. Close air support defined the War on Terror, from the very first ground-coordinated airstrikes delivered against Taliban targets in Afghanistan by Special Forces and CIA paramilitary teams, to the fateful over-the-horizon engagement in August 2021 which killed ten civilians and drew harsh, rightful criticism of the use of American air power. It endured throughout the sustained air campaign against ISIS insurgents in Iraq and Syria.

I expect this work will draw its own criticism; it may be viewed as a harsh decry of American forces and their operational employment. Nothing could be further from the truth. I hope it will be understood this work intends to highlight the creativity, poise, and innovative capacity of American and Coalition personnel in the use of air power to protect and defend the world from a threat; the strategic critiques are a necessary lesson to be taken in tandem with the stories of these operators.

While serving as an Air Force Special Operations JTAC with Bravo Company, 3rd Battalion, 75th Ranger Regiment, I vividly recall how the then-battalion commander regularly reiterated a key point prior to training exercises: the most dangerous action U.S. service members undertook in combat was not a parachute jump, it was not an explosive demolition, nor was it a nighttime clearance of an enemy-held compound. The most dangerous action undertaken was "calling in close air support near friendly forces on a dynamic battlespace in the heat of combat."

This book is a celebration of the achievement of those service members who revolutionized how air support is integrated into the American battledress. The overarching narrative, however, seeks to dispel any misconceptions that may exist on the abuse of air power by the men who controlled it—a vastly different reality than the kinetic strikes controlled from afar which became the primary means of air-power employment in later years. This work will also look to address how reliance on this technical supremacy portends a risky endeavor if we assume future battlefields will allow the same level of battlespace dominance we enjoyed in the climes of Afghanistan and Iraq, and Syria. This book is both a celebration and a warning that American military innovation must be ready to revolutionize the battlespace employment of joint fires in future conflicts, ones which will be contested and, in many cases, denied by a peer adversary. This work is a critique of the vague, undefined, and ethereal strategic and political objectives for these wars' outcomes. What were the political objectives? What were the ways, means, and end state? No answer to those questions will emanate from this book. Rather, the collected stories will highlight how a small community of diverse and highly trained service members who spoke to the sky did everything in their power to bring the wars to an acceptable end, or at least did their professional best to safeguard friendly forces, prevent unnecessary suffering by civilians, and eliminate evil actors from the battlefield.

There is a key narrative that will be clear across these stories that drive us to the strategy and policy conclusions, a decidedly human element in a work of potentially stuffy policy research and recounted memories of what many of these men have called a "dark art." From the time of Napoleon Bonaparte's *Grande Armée*,[3] there has been a term for a kind of collective mentality, this shared suffering and hardship, which was called "élan"—the sense of specialization among an already exclusive cadre. Today, we use the term "esprit de corps," but that 19th-century word—élan—is far more concise and eloquent in its application, and proper when discussing the close air support tribes. The mentality that permeates the fires community, and the JTAC career field, is a unique animal in the warrior ethos. While all service members understand the inherent weight of their charter—that they might have to discharge their service weapon and take the life of an enemy combatant—JTACs wield the most advanced and lethal tactical weapons in human history at their fingertips. The extent of their influence over the battlefield at those lowest tactical levels is unlike any individual degree of lethality in previous eras of warfare.

Of course, this dynamic is extrapolated across the operational close air support team, which includes the ground-force commander (who determines if, when, and why an airstrike is to be conducted), the pilots/aircrew supporting the mission (who are experts in the capabilities and delivery profiles of the weapons being requested), and the command apparatus that presides over the mission, providing intelligence, sustainment authority, and strategic perspective. But the locus of all communications between ground, air and higher headquarters is the JTAC. That sole member must maintain situational awareness of all aspects of the battlefield: friendly positions in a dynamic order of battle, the "playtime" (fuel reserves) of the supporting aircraft, the proximate distances for safe employment of all munitions relative to those friendly positions (often relative to multiple scattered elements), numerous radio frequencies, priority of fires for disaggregate units and locations, and literally hundreds of other constantly changing data points throughout a mission. The JTAC is the conduit for all battlefield situational awareness. To paraphrase the iconic line from President Harry Truman's desk placard: the "buck" stops with the ground-force commander, but it is *spent* by the JTAC.

The individual who can successfully work in these conditions, particularly in the demanding and changing chaos of modern combat, is certain to embody a professional confidence bordering on (and many times, spilling over into) arrogance. While camaraderie is implicit in most military units and occupational specialties, the tribalism of the close air support community is in a league of its own.

This is the story of the forward air controllers in the War on Terror and how close air support changed the American war machine.

Introduction

The Most Dangerous Thing

It was a warning story, a tale of just how quickly something can go wrong, even when one presumed to have dotted every "i" and crossed every "t." It is a recounting that is branded into every forward air controller's (FAC) mind from the earliest phases of training—a lesson of when and how technology can betray even the most thorough of preparatory processes during the fog of war; Murphy and his damnable law trumps all assumptions and preparations.

I first heard the fateful story of the airstrike that nearly killed Afghan leader Hamid Karzai when I was in the pipeline to become a tactical air control party (TACP) specialist in 2009. Nearing the end of the swift campaign to oust the Taliban forces from their stronghold in southern Afghanistan, U.S. Special Forces (SF) teams fought alongside Pashtun fighters who were pressing southward through Shawali Kowt, near the infamous Arghandab River valley, north of the provincial capital of Kandahar—the seat of Taliban power in the south. Fierce, intense ground combat had been expertly augmented by a relatively new paradigm of integrating air power to support the ground maneuver—close air support (CAS).

During this phase of the campaign, Air Force TACP, combat control, and other government agency forward observers labored without rest throughout grueling gunfights and chaotic convoys over the rugged terrain, employing aerial-delivered fires against Taliban positions in close proximity to friendly forces without the benefit of pre-mission planning. The conditions on the ground demanded dynamic employment methods typically planned for in sterile rehearsal-of-concept drills. The story of the SF-teams' push to Kandahar has been told across several compelling mediums and popular print, all of which emphasize the exhaustion and demanding conditions faced by the best of America's elite fighting forces. Prominent among these exclusive units was Army Captain Jason Amerine's 5th Special Forces Group Operational Detachment–Alpha team 574, whose charge was to lead a disjointed force of Afghan partners hoping to change Afghanistan's future.

On December 5, 2001, Captain Amerine's A-team was regrouping ahead of a push into the village of Shawali Kowt in advance of the next phase offensive to decisively engage the Taliban in Kandahar. In the pre-assault interim, a U.S. Air Force FAC was conducting preparatory offensive airstrikes against Taliban forces across several ridgelines and defensive fighting positions. The weapon of choice was the newly minted Global Positioning System-guided 500-lb (GBU-38), 1,000-lb (GBU-32), and 2,000-lb (GBU-31) bombs, named the "Joint Direct Attack Munition." These munitions were never designed to be employed in a CAS paradigm. Rather, the GPS guidance system was crafted so aircrews on air-strike platforms could receive air-tasking orders with predetermined target locations—geospatial grids based on the military gridded reference system (MGRS), which aligns latitudinal and longitudinal lines over the global surface and provides the ability to calculate a multi-point grid—and release the preset ordnance with relative certainty of impacting within an accepted proximity to that grid. The precision of the grids was a significant factor in the weapons' effects; the MGRS system is a 15-digit coordinate, beginning with the "grid zone designator," a three-digit zone defining a six-degree-wide block aligned against lines of latitude, followed by a 100,000-meter-square identifier which channelized the geospatial area into a 100-square-kilometer zone. The final ten digits of easting and northing one-meter squares culminate in the final square meter of ground. Thus, a "ten-digit grid" is considered the most precise: to within one meter.

To employ the GPS-enabled weapons in a real-time capacity, an FAC would need to have some method of determining one's own location—a map or, preferably, a GPS system which accurately denotes the observer's ten-digit location in the world. Knowing this, by calculating the distance and magnetic azimuth to a target using a simple lensatic compass, and correcting for elevation change between the two points, an FAC may deduce the intended location of the target. Not only is the easting and northing grid to be briefed critical, but correctly determining the elevation of the impact point is pivotal for accuracy, as the weapon's flight path will correct for the target's elevation in its flight trajectory; an incorrect target elevation can cause a GPS munition to fall short or go long. Once calculated, the controller can relay the calculated grid to the aircraft releasing the munition, and the new target location could be programmed into the weapon's guidance system.

A critical point is distinguishing "precision" from "accuracy." Precision is when the weapon will impact within an acceptable proximity to the programmed aimpoint; thus, if a ten-digit grid is passed, all rules of physics and mechanical process will ensure with relative certainty the weapon will correct its flight path to arrive at that three-dimensional space. Accuracy, however, is inherent to the observer to ascertain to their utmost ability. Precision is the "specificity" of the grids passed because the GPS-guided weapon will in all probability travel to the grid programmed into the guidance system. But the real-world accuracy of the grids, the "correctness," is entirely dependent on how close to truth the projected aim point is.

On that day near Shawali Kowt, the FAC was correlating observable terrain against a topographic map based on his known location, provided by the AN/PSN-11 PLGR (Precision Lightweight GPS Receiver) in his possession, a standard-issue GPS device for ground units. The PLGR was a relatively modern GPS tool that could project a calculated waypoint relative to its tracking of at least three satellites in geosynchronous orbit for a coordinate fix, with at least four required for an elevation fix. In the relentlessly demanding combat scenario, the device's batteries inevitably died right in the middle of waypoint calculation. Replacing the batteries was a routine procedure, although, once repowered, the grid displayed on the screen was the fixed location of the actual device—not the projected waypoint derived from range and bearing calculus before the batteries died. This grid—the observer's—was then passed to the aircraft overhead, a Vietnam-era B-52 heavy bomber, comfortably loitering in a 10–20 nautical mile "racetrack" holding pattern more than 15,000 feet above ground level. Assuming the "accuracy" of that fateful grid, the weapon impacted within 50 meters of the A-team, the Afghan partner forces, and the delegation of Afghanistan's future leaders including Hamid Karzai, the soon-to-be president of the war-ravaged nation.

The 2000-lb weapon yielded devastating effects, those intended for the enemy and validated in a horrifying fashion to Americans and partners on the ground. The casualties, which included two American SF soldiers, prompted a heroic evacuation effort that demonstrated the best of what American resolve can achieve under duress. The remaining casualties and fallen remains were evacuated south to the hastily established Camp Rhino, seized by the Marines and U.S. Army Rangers at an austere airfield south of Kandahar. The mission to liberate Kandahar from Taliban control went on despite this terrible mishap.

This early fratricide incident highlighted the tenuous and dynamic nature of what CAS would eventually evolve into. The technology would change to prevent such mishaps in future missions because of the mistake. Later models of military GPS devices, notably the AN/PSN-13 DAGR (Defense Advanced GPS Receiver), would include software that presented a warning message indicating the initial grid shown on the screen was always the observer's position, and only a manual confirmation of the message would allow the user to continue with targeting procedures. Procedural steps, such as the development of the standardized "nine-line" CAS attack brief, would later become doctrinal mandates which double, and triple confirmed enemy and friendly locations relative to the observer and the intended target.

But the risks of employing CAS would remain implicit in the war and, as the complexity of the environment grew, so too did the risks. Nearly 15 years after the errant bomb near Shawali Kowt, American special-operations forces were in the far north of Afghanistan, near the provincial capital city of Kunduz. During the waning weeks of the fighting season, Taliban forces had mounted a massive assault on the city, home to a major component of the Afghan National Defense and Security Forces (ANDSF) and a critical hub to the northern region's infrastructure. On October 3, 2015, an AC-130 gunship struck a building in a dense portion of the city,[1] hitting a compound that had been misidentified by ground parties, further upended by technical problems within the aircraft's targeting systems. Based on reporting from partnered Afghan forces, the ground commander had directed the gunship to engage a compound based on description alone, without the proper target-location correlation or mensurated coordinate verification. That building was not a captured ANDSF intelligence center seized by Taliban fighters, as initial reporting indicated to the ground-force commander; it was a Médecins Sans Frontières (MSF, "Doctors Without Borders") field hospital, housing dozens of injured civilians and international medical volunteers.

All medical facilities in an active warzone—civilian and military alike—are placed on a "no-strike list" (NSL) that is widely distributed and regularly updated across commands. For ground-force commanders, FACs and aircrew, the NSL is one of the most important planning factors in pre-mission coordination and rehearsals. Further, it is highlighted on mission products and programmed as a redundancy coordinate in all targeting, GPS, and map/graphics systems before every single mission. Redundancies, however, are not guarantors of certainty under the kinds of overwhelming and chaotic conditions of a mass gunfight spanning entire cities.

The conditions under which American and allied service members must function in the fog of war simply cannot be described; it can only be understood by those who have experienced the overwhelming surge of adrenaline throughout, and the ruthless exhausting diffusion afterwards. Although many books, documentaries, and other media have tried to convey that experience over many years, it defies explanation when transcribed to written form.

The wars in Afghanistan, Iraq, and Syria changed that life or death experience of combat in such a way that even veterans of previous wars shake their heads at the stories told by veterans of the Global War on Terror. These locations took the most savage dynamic in the human experience and exponentially increased the complexity and difficulty of the act. The terrain, in many cases some of the worst and most difficult to navigate on Earth, made for nearly impossible mobility. The enemy was unlike any American forces had ever encountered, even if we consider the Vietnam War as the first manifestation of a guerilla-type insurgency that American military forces were to contend with. Compounding this complexity was the emergence of the CAS construct; this procedural employment of aerial-delivered weapons increased in complexity just like the war environment in which it was applied.

This raw, awesome firepower would become the lightning bolt that would characterize the war. Every facet of ground operations became interwoven with the ability to integrate air power into the ground scheme of maneuver. In later years, control of this capability would become the banner mission of the war; no operation would transpire without some form of immediate or on-call CAS coverage. Generations of aircraft, from the mid-20th century B-52s and gunships to cutting-edge fifth-generation stealth platforms, would become part of a diverse roster of flying systems that joined the CAS genealogy. This would eventually include remote-piloted aircraft, like the MQ-1 Predator and the MQ-9 Reaper, in later years largely supplanting the armed-platform mission demands of manned aircraft—like A-10s, F-16s, and other Coalition fighters and bombers—due to increased loiter times and high-resolution sensors.

Following President Joe Biden's April 2021 announcement that all American forces would withdraw from Afghanistan no later than September 11, 2021, the operation there became a waiting game for the Taliban. While American forces began the waterfall of missions and daily operations that led to one of the most impressive and heroic evacuations in modern history—an accomplishment tragically skimmed over in the broader drama—the use of air power began to manifest its futuristic, "remote" nature that exemplified one of the war strategy's greatest flaws. On August 26, an Islamic State of Khorasan (ISIS–K) suicide bomber successfully attacked a checkpoint at Kabul Airport, where 13 American service members were killed, along with more than 60 Afghans awaiting processing. The suicide attack was one of the single bloodiest days of the 20-year conflict. These 13 service members represented the very best of America: giving their lives while protecting and helping innocent civilians in a time of utter chaos. In a rushed effort to demonstrate resolve and achieve retribution for the attack, an over-the-horizon airstrike was conducted on August 29 after an armed MQ-9 Reaper had followed a reported vehicle-borne IED (improvised explosive device) through the city streets in Kabul. The vehicle under surveillance had been the result of extensive over-the-horizon collection efforts aimed to identify additional threats from ISIS–K attackers in the waning days of the American withdrawal. In the seconds leading up to the strike, analysts had reportedly warned strike-cell leaders against execution, which ultimately killed 10 civilians and a known U.S.-affiliated aid worker instead of the purported target, another ISIS suicide bomber.

The risks inherent to CAS—despite the advancements in signals-intelligence technology, increased mission coverage, and more refined lethal weapons—remained unchanged over two decades and multiple theaters. From the early mishap that nearly killed Hamid Karzai and claimed the lives of American and Afghan forces, to the MSF hospital airstrike, to the very end of the war with this new over-the-horizon targeting construct, CAS is still the most dangerous thing on the battlefield. When it is done properly, it can change the entire outcome of a battle; when something goes wrong, it can be catastrophic. As with any tragedy, these are the stories which often receive the most visibility; when the circumstances are due to human errors in judgment, rightly so. These tragic incidents highlight the unforgiving risk that is part and parcel to the employment of CAS in a dynamic battlespace. No other action in the military panoply compares to the difficulty and complexity of controlling and executing CAS.

The stories which follow, however, will attempt to convey what isn't as rigorously reported in the media—the successful airstrikes which eliminated enemy combatants, protected Coalition and partner forces, which took every reasonable step to safeguard civilians and infrastructure. Humans, a fragile species, made of bone and blood, muscle and flesh, fears, and ambitions, endure the rigors of battle and, in circumstances such as these, entrust a select few to employ devastating ordnance in close proximity to friendly forces for the sake of their country's national security interests. It is dangerous, it is exhilarating, it is terrifying, and the effects are always final. But CAS was not a clearly defined, doctrinal process before the war began. It evolved with the war, changing to accommodate the shifting environment in which it was applied. The complexities on the ground cannot be overstated, and select few appreciate the ruthless demands, the stress and rigors, and uncertainty in which the FAC must be decisive and as close to perfect as the most imperfect situations permit.

There are simply too many different stories to have effectively captured the depth and immensity of these career fields who share the "ETAC/JTAC/FAC" moniker. There were too many missions where air power and its integration by FACs into the ground scheme of maneuver made the difference in a gunfight. There were too many pivotal moments across the entire timeline of the war where a joint terminal attack controller (JTAC) was featured, from planning and coordination, to execution, to capturing lessons learned.

The endeavor to capture the impact of these CAS tribes into a single work which covers a 20-year-long war is a daunting ordeal. And, tragically, I had to leave many stories untold. In many understandable circumstances, key individuals declined to interview, and their wishes must be respected. Post-Traumatic Stress Disorder is the shadow which hangs over all of us who faced death in these battlespaces. And, for many of the men I reached out to for this work, that shadow remains a daily battle they continue to fight. By necessity, some accounts were omitted, despite my wishes to include them, due to the sensitive nature of the missions, classification levels, and other strategic implications. By more important necessity, many accounts were heavily redacted, "watered down," or streamlined on account of OPSEC (operational security). Many of the men who interviewed for this book were concerned their accounts would be aggrandized, oversold, or otherwise embellished for the sake of shock value and entertainment.

The truth, quite simply, is that not a single story in this project contains a single digit of polishing or exaggeration. Most required a great deal of simplification, as the technical and procedural widgets of what JTACs do are such a complicated endeavor as to seem fantastic no matter how watered down the transcription manifested. Therein lies the greatest challenge of this work: the labors and trials of these various tribes were often so far beyond the normal, relentlessly demanding obligations of deployed service members, that the stories seem better suited to a scripted movie rather than a recounting of historical events.

Many of the stories in this work do not feature any weapons being released from aircraft. The reasons vary, but all of these are critical accounts that aim to dispel the misconception that Coalition controllers were wantonly laying waste to battlefields. In many of these stories, munitions were not called in because the circumstances simply did not permit such actions—inability to definitively identify the intended target, risk to force or shifting front lines, or simply situations where organic weapons were more suitable than the high risk and complex integration of aerial-delivered munitions.

In other instances, however, even more critical for posterity, these men *chose* to not call in CAS. They did so because the risk of civilian casualties was too great. So, the decision was made by these individuals to hold fire, even though in some cases that decision would go on to dramatically impact the war. In other cases, the situational awareness of the controller is all that prevented a fratricide incident where Coalition soldiers would have certainly been killed by an airstrike based on misidentification and challenging communications mid-gunfight. That awareness of that sole member of the battlespace, the FAC, whose responsibility is to control such chaos, is often the one thing that prevented such travesties from happening far more often than what did occur.

Despite this tremendous demonstration of composure under fire, there were unavoidable effects on the broader war that resulted from the tactical successes of this new mode of air power. CAS changed the American self-assessment of its war-fighting efficiency. Because of the heroic and maestro-like ability of these FACs, consistently helping shape and evolve the mission of CAS in a changing battlefield paradigm, the strategists falsely attributed the battlefield successes against a strategic backdrop built on indecision. Twenty years of short-term continuations, absent either a clear end state—political, definite, and achievable—or a means to fit the tactical progress into the broader challenge of bringing a war-ravaged Afghanistan or Iraq into the cooperative embrace of the 21st century world order, means the incredible success of the CAS community is now a bitter pill for that fraternity to swallow after the conclusion. This unique paradigm firmly segregates the wars of Afghanistan and Iraq from any other war in history.

The Global War on Terror should serve as a repository for American and partner nation ingenuity, not a dark hole into which the United States, and the institutional professionals of arms, discard the tacit knowledge and innovative spirit that gave rise to a new era of American air power. Afghanistan, Iraq, Syria, and many other classified locations manifested the creative minds of the American military at its lowest, most tactical level of personnel, who continue to achieve incredible, uncommonly valorous feats as commonplace tasks. There are valuable lessons to be taken from the War on Terror, be it as a sobering defeat or a neutral disentanglement from a forever war. How we innovate our warfighting capabilities in the years and decades to come, built on the lessons we may take from the war, will ultimately determine the success or failure of America's longest conflict.

PART I

Retribution

Afghanistan: 2001–2002

If it is terrorism, if it is a war on terror, then the Afghan people will join you on terror.

HAMID KARZAI

CHAPTER I

Into the Graveyard of Empires

This had never been done before.

Afghanistan would serve as a staging ground for a future command-and-control architecture spanning multiple time zones, continents, and generations of service members. In late 2001, however, the arrayment of ground and air units would include a decidedly ad-hoc task organization, haphazard air-support requesting, degraded coordination, limited command and control, and significant lapses in air coverage, making the integration of effective air support a monumental challenge, and even more impressive for its successes.

The invasion of Afghanistan opened with a barrage of aerial-delivered fires from an unlikely platform, especially considering the operational target: an underdeveloped, isolated, and barely functional Afghan air-defense inventory. The first haymaker came from the bomb bays of the arrowhead-shaped B-2 Spirit stealth bombers of the 325th and 393rd Bomb Squadrons, 509th Bomb Wing, hailing from Whiteman Air Force Base (AFB), Missouri.[1] What made this maneuver so dramatic and incredible was that those first airstrike platforms flew out of the American heartland, executing a non-stop global transit to hit their assigned targets in Afghanistan. The total flight time was over 40 hours from start to finish, with only two aircrew per aircraft—a pilot and co-pilot—who shared flying responsibilities while alternating crew rest on a small cot at the back of the cockpit. While seemingly superhuman (though the aircrews were prescribed "go-pills" by Air Force flight physicians), the global circumnavigation was not a new tactic for the B-2 crews, whose doctrinal purpose is to deliver precision global-strike capabilities on such non-stop flights into denied or hostile airspace. The B-2s first validated such training by participation in Operation *Allied Force*, engaging Slavic combatants with airstrikes in 1999 via a non-stop 12,000-mile round-trip flight from Whiteman AFB.

The necessary route to facilitate the attack in Afghanistan was the longest possible navigation option, far greater than the route into former Yugoslavia. The shortest option—a direct northern flight over the North Pole and then south into Afghanistan—would have needed to overfly Russian airspace. Despite the Cold

War's end years before, notification to Moscow for route coordination worried air planners due to possible notification to the Taliban of the impending strike. The second shortest route, over European airspace, carried similar concerns for incidental notification and early warning of the attack. The selected flightpath, then, was a trans-Pacific route of more than 13,000 nautical miles one way. In every mission, from October 7–9, B-2 crews would depart Missouri, fly west over the American continent, and cross the Pacific and Indian Oceans, with multiple aerial-refueling missions along the way. They would service their assigned targets, then land at Diego Garcia Auxiliary Naval Air Station in the Indian Ocean to change crews. That first touchdown was only long enough for a ground refuel, minimal engine service, and crew swap. Landing back at Whiteman AFB, each B-2 had kept its engines running for more than 70 hours straight. It remains the longest-running bomber mission in history.

The purpose of a stealth bomber initiating this grand match was based on the marginal, but relevant, surface-to-air and fighter threat from the Taliban forces. The pre-planned targets included radar sites, surface-to-air missile launchers, and a geriatric fleet of former Russian fighter jets, mostly MiG-21 *Fishbed* single-engine interceptors, which posed a threat to the follow-on tactical bombing campaign planned by U.S. Central Command (CENTCOM), whose area of responsibility included Afghanistan. Those follow-on missions would consist of the bigger, heavier B-1s and B-52s, as well as U.S. Navy tactical fighter-bombers working from carrier battle groups in the Indian Ocean, and U.S. Air Force (USAF) and Coalition fighters operating out of air bases in the Middle East.

In most instances, the ordnance delivered was preset with coordinates matched against known enemy positions based on collected intelligence and satellite imagery, an inflection of previous wars, driven by the concept of fighting a peer-adversary. But, in these circumstances, the Joint Direct Attack Munitions (JDAMs) were employed to profound effect. The B-2 payloads alone were upwards of 40,000lbs worth of GPS-guided munitions, slung in the internal bomb bays for the multi-day flights. Programming each individual weapon required laborious typing of digits into the now-archaic weapons-control computer—the "Combat Track II." By 2001 standards, it was revolutionary. In one instance, on the second day of the bombing campaign, the aircrew serviced their initial targets in tandem with Tomahawk cruise missiles launched from the Indian Ocean, releasing 12 of their 16 weapons on pre-selected sites. After two hours in Afghanistan airspace, the aircraft turned for Diego Garcia when it was re-tasked by the Combined Air Operations Center (CAOC) at Qatar with additional targets for its remaining weapons. The follow-on task required re-programming the GPS weapons and, overall, added an extra 90 minutes of mission time to execute.

Of course, there was another component to the air war in Afghanistan that received less publicity but was no less influential in the opening act of this new war. Afghanistan saw the first combat employment of aerial-delivered fires from a remotely piloted aircraft (RPA), the RQ-1. Through the end of the 20th century, the introduction of the modern unmanned aerial vehicle made its way to areas of conflict in the European theater. Through the late 1990s, the RQ-1 was a DARPA (the Defense Advanced Research Projects Agency) program augmented by USAF pilots and exclusively reserved for low-impact reconnaissance by various components of the intelligence community architecture, primarily the Central Intelligence Agency (CIA). Initially designated the RQ-1 Predator from General Atomics, "R" denoted a "reconnaissance" role, whereas the "M" would designate an offensive firepower capability.

Rather than a comprehensive, technical-order-driven mission typical of USAF operations, the employment of the first fleet of Predators consisted of trial and error executed through a loosely configured and highly classified partnership of intelligence and military operators. The end of NATO's Operation *Allied Force* introduced considerations on the potential of this modern technology, resulting in the successful testing of armaments in mid-2000.[2] An AGM-114C (a low-smoke rocket-engine variant of the Hellfire laser-guided helicopter munition) was employed at a test range in Nevada on a stationary target complex; a new weapons system was born.

On October 7, 2001, one of the first airstrikes against the Taliban in response to the September 11 attacks was conducted by Predator 3034—the same tail number MQ-1 used to conduct the successful test of RPA-delivered fires in Nevada. There was no shortage of heartache and controversy involved with this first remote-piloted combat airstrike, however. Despite the progenitor DARPA–USAF partnership that developed the early operating standards for RPA employment in Bosnia, the program had been quickly usurped by the CIA, charged with the role of finding and eliminating high-ranking Taliban and Al Qaeda in support of the impending air war and subsequent invasion.

In that early night of the war, while strategic bombers were carrying out their assigned airstrikes against Taliban logistics and air-defense architecture, Predator 3034 was over the Taliban stronghold of Kandahar, flown by USAF crews, under operational control of CIA analysts searching for a high-value target: Mullah Mohammed Omar, the Taliban's supreme commander. Careful collection and monitoring of intelligence and real-time video surveillance on the new RPA platform pinpointed the Mullah's home in a compound outside the city. Fixed-wing aircraft were also on station, equipped with 1000-lb JDAMs, which would be better suited to a hard-structure target compared to the 100-lb Hellfire missile on the MQ-1.

Due to the unclear lines of command between the CIA-directed MQ-1s and the overarching CENTCOM authority with the air campaign, the CAOC cell—which was monitoring the Predator mission while managing the crewed aircraft—learned an airstrike had been approved, but not by whom. The MQ-1 employed the Hellfire on a vehicle outside one of the buildings in the Mullah's compound. The CENTCOM staff would have opted for the heavier, GPS-guided smart bombs to ensure totality of the effects and avoid the risk of losing such a high-value target. The Hellfire struck a presumed empty vehicle, allowing Mullah Omar and much of his key retinue to escape and flee into the Afghan environment, becoming a ghost that badgered the Coalition's efforts for years. There had been such a rush to initiate the air war that no attention had been paid as to who would be in overall control of the Predator drones, while waves of tactical aircraft began a two-decade-long persistent haunt of the skies over Afghanistan.

The RPAs offered increased loiter time, sensor modularity (thermal, electro-optical, and infrared), weapons variety, and reduced operation and maintenance costs compared to crewed aircraft. The employment of RPAs would steadily evolve from a strategic resource to a tactical asset across the full spectrum of the counter-terror domain. The RPA offered a platform that could execute the full sequence of battlefield engagement, from target development and intelligence collection to the final phase of engagement and post-strike reflections. But, as with all new assets, the command-and-control architecture was slow to adapt to the new paradigm.

It was in these early days that air power would change the American war machine forever. Thus, the first story vehicle to paint a ground picture of those early days will focus on the use of air power in the invasion, and the challenges of a new war which manifested on the ancient roads of an old battleground.

CHAPTER 2

"We were witnesses to history"

There are few men whose roles as forward air controllers were as pivotal, or underappreciated, as the actions taken by Steve Tomat from October 25 to December 15, 2001. The lack of awareness of his and other air controllers' actions are, unfortunately, the result of misattributed credit. The accounts of the first American military personnel into Afghanistan, portrayed in movies like "12 Strong," forgo mentioning the innovative use of air power, to usher in a new kind of war in this century, was unsuccessful by Army teams who were sent into Afghanistan without their Air Force counterparts. And once Tomat and other Air Force forward air controllers made it to the battlefield (thanks to the relentless and clairvoyant insistence of men like Tim Stamey and Air Force Brigadier General Michael Longoria, a combat controller at the Special Operations Task Force), the Taliban in the north were broken in a matter of days.

There was no manual for these kinds of operations, and limited command-and-control architecture to dictate operational sequences. The division between Army and Air Force was never greater than in those early days, and for good reason. With rare exceptions—cases such as Steve Tomat, who had already deployed three times around the world before invading Afghanistan with the 5th Special Forces Group—Air Force forward air controllers simply had not spent much time embedded at the team level, calling in close air support (CAS) in any significant manner. This dynamic was made worse by the limited number of Air Force controllers available to support the volume of ground forces going into Afghanistan in 2001 (and barely enough in the Iraq invasion two years later).

In 2001, the use of CAS was not an explicitly defined, elaborate process as it would become. Rather, it was deliberate procedural control methods intended for supporting a large combat force in the Eastern European Fulda Gap scenario:[1] with clear lines of demarcation between friendly and enemy forces, large swaths of heavily saturated airspace, and concentrated allocations of assets for ground areas based on a strategic snapshot of a major combat operation type of war. Afghanistan would undermine this paradigm and, as such, the ground forces who attempted to employ CAS without air-power experts like tactical air control parties and combat controllers would be ineffective in the first days.

It is chiefly thanks to the efforts of men like Mike Longoria ("LA" as he is fondly known across the JTAC community), who fought—in some cases almost literally—to get Air Force forward air controllers pushed out to the Special Forces teams operating alongside Northern Alliance and other Afghan militia forces, that CAS was able to make such an immediate—though not fully developed by doctrine—impact on this new war.

This is not to take away from the heroic and impossible task given to Task Force "Dagger"—the Army Special Forces teams who embedded with the Northern Alliance to topple the Taliban strength in the north. Those teams faced incredible risks and dangers and were the tip of the spear in leading American retribution for the attacks on September 11, 2001. However, what has gone critically unreported was the role of Air Force forward air controllers in the opening days of the War on Terror.

What follows is the true account of the first air support missions successfully controlled by Americans in Afghanistan.

On October 25, 2001, Steve Tomat, a tactical air control party (TACP) specialist, and Matt Leinhard, a combat controller, were headed into Afghanistan to call in airstrikes. They would be flying into the unknown, just the two of them, with the task and purpose of supporting Operational Detachment–Alpha (ODA) 595 from the 5th Special Forces Group, led by Captain Mark Nutsch. That A-team was charged by Colonel John Mulholland, commander of the Special Operations Task Force (SOTF), to secure the airfields near the northern provincial city of Mazar-i-sharif in Balkh Province, as well as the "land bridge" connecting Afghanistan and Uzbekistan, that being the overland route between the two landlocked countries which would be critical for allowing the insertion of follow-on forces, supplies, and military equipment necessary to pacify and stabilize Afghanistan after the Taliban had been overthrown.

The pressure on ODA595 and the other Special Forces (SF) teams entering Afghanistan was immense, driven by the highest levels of personnel in the United States Government, who were contending with pressure of their own on the domestic front for a perceived lack of action in achieving retribution for the attacks on September 11. The air war—pre-planned airstrikes conducted by stealth bombers, fighter jets, and the earliest drone deployments—were not suitably tangible results for an American public coming to grips with this new world of violent extremism.

But the team had been sent into Afghanistan without Air Force forward air controllers (FAC)—qualified personnel like Tomat and Leinhard—and were struggling to effectively employ aerial-delivered fires or enable the Northern Alliance forces, led by General Rashid Dostum, to seize key terrain, cities, and well-fortified Taliban strongholds.

When the "balloon went up" after 9/11, FACs—specifically TACPs, the preeminent specialists in close air support (CAS)—were in high demand. Based out of Fort Campbell, the 5th Special Forces Group had the highest concentration of SF-capable TACPs working in the special-operations contingent. The call went out across the community to bring up more FACs to support the mission. Despite the need for controllers out forward with the ground teams, the preponderance of qualified FACs were manning positions at the Combined Air Operations Center (CAOC) in Qatar and the SOTF—miles away from the teams sent into Afghanistan's hinterlands. Tomat would explain there was inexplicable consternation between the Army and Air Force as the haphazard joint special-operations component was contending with the task of invading such an austere country, noting that 5th Group's commander, Colonel Max Bowers, wanted this mission to be "Army pure," meaning those teams were deliberately sent in without the Air Force enablers that should have been there. It was an intense and vitriolic struggle to get Air Force controllers into the country. "An entire book could and should be written about the efforts of guys like Mike Longoria, Tim Stamey who went east to Kunduz during this timeline, Ed Schulman and Chris Griffin, who were working like crazy at the JSOTF (Joint Special Operations Task Force) level with Colonel Mulholland to get Air Force controllers pushed down to the teams who needed CAS."

Teams from 5th Group, and the Air Force's 23rd Special Tactics Squadron (STS), both arrived at K2 (Karshi–Khanabad) Airbase in Uzbekistan in the days immediately after September 11. The Army SF teams initially thought they would have the responsibility for Combat Search and Rescue (CSAR). But CSAR is a doctrinal Air Force Special Tactics mission so, with 23 STS establishing the airfield at K2 for that purpose, 5th Group was looking for a role in this new war. This is when the SOTF opted to send those teams into Afghanistan to link up with the local warlords in the north, east, and south. Fighting alongside indigenous forces is a traditional SF mission, "unconventional warfare" by doctrinal definition, and suited the Army teams far better than CSAR.

An unknown dynamic of those early days of the war in Afghanistan would shape the initial efforts to make any ground advance to the detriment of the operation. Those teams that opted to volunteer for this mission with embedded Air Force FACs were placed on standby for mission assignment. Colonel Bowers—who wanted an "Army pure" task organization for this sensitive operation—gave the teams a choice: go forward (without their Air Force enablers) or remain behind. The reasons for this were never made clear to the teams, but the impact of such a decision would soon become evident to those involved.

Those teams who opted to go into country without FACs were the ones given the first insertion into Afghanistan, and included ODA595. Of course, this is understandable; the United States was emotionally charged after the attacks on 9/11, and these teams were given the option to go into Afghanistan or be left back if they opted to retain their air-power experts. History cannot fault those team leaders and their soldiers who were keen to make landfall and begin a mission of retribution, but that made the job for men like Tomat and Leinhard much more challenging early on, and the story as it is known today is not accurate. As Tomat would recall: "I've kept this account close-hold for many years, as it is difficult to recount for the impact it may have on official narratives, but having stayed in close contact with many of the SF teammates I deployed with in those early days, I learned that many of the decision-makers—those who were resistant to TACPs and CCTs going in with the teams—are now persona non grata within the Special Forces community."[2]

The flight from K2 to the predesignated helicopter landing zone (HLZ) took four hours for Tomat and Leinhard, flying in an Army 160th Special Operations Air Regiment ("Nightstalkers") MH-47 Chinook, departing Uzbekistan at three in the morning to be on the ground before sunrise on October 25. The first attempt to land the helicopter would set the tone for the overall effort: the aircrew first set down at the wrong location due to a brown out.[3] After setting foot in Afghanistan for the first time, Leinhard quickly identified the mistake, as there were none of the expected contacts on the ground to meet them. The two airmen quickly retook positions on the aircraft, and the pilot reset the landing site another five hundred meters to the west, the correct location. This is where Capt. Mark Nutsch was waiting to meet them.

The first thing Nutsch said to Tomat was "I don't know what else to do here." The Air Force controllers acknowledged this was a demanding situation, but affirmed "Sir, no worries, this is the entire reason that we are here." By this point in his career, Tomat had been a TACP for 10 years, and was qualified as a FAC-instructor, giving him a fount of operational knowledge. Afghanistan would be his fourth deployment, having spent a sizable portion of his career supporting the SF teams. A few months prior to landing in northern Afghanistan, Tomat had been in Columbia with the 7th Special Forces Group as part of the counter-narcotics missions with Southern Command.

The first thing the Air Force controllers needed to know was the intended targets for CAS. "I told the captain to show me on the map, and we'll go from there." The group pored over the 1:250,000 Joint Operations Graphic (JOG) map, with Captain Nutsch showing Tomat and Leinhard where the Taliban positions and strengths were. The first issue to overcome was distance to these targets. With the terrain they would be fighting in, most of the positions selected for airstrikes were such that the controllers would have to be within approximately 1,000 meters of those sites, to establish positive identification and conduct the terminal control of aircraft.

The Taliban positions were between twelve and twenty kilometers away from the base camp and operations staging area set up by ODA595 and General Dostum's men. This was too far to make reasonable judgements and adjust fires on those targets, so the plan would have to evolve: they had to get closer. Captain Nutsch's argument—which was completely justifiable and reasonable—was that General Dostum did not want Americans getting that close to the enemy. "The general was willing to lose five hundred of his fighters so long as it meant not losing a single

American. I understood that, but Matt and I came here to do a mission, which we could not do effectively if we could not identify the targets we were requesting air support for. So, in short, I needed to ruck up and perform strategic reconnaissance. That was the first conversation between the captain and me on that HLZ."

With Air Force enablers now integrated, the team spent several days waiting in a small compound just south of a village called Day-e, before moving out on horseback towards the Taliban front lines. More days waiting passed, while Dostum was maneuvering through the area building his forces in preparation to push north towards Mazar-i-sharif. It was during this battlefield circulation that Captain Nutsch was able to link up with the general and explain to him "We have these two Air Force guys, who are experts in controlling airstrikes, but they need to get closer to the Taliban in order to do this correctly." Soon after this conference, the general accepted the need to work out a mission profile that would allow the Americans to move closer to the Taliban positions.

The Americans chose November 5 to begin engaging targets using CAS. Captain Nutsch had sent a three-man element to the west of the objective area, towards a town called Keshendeh-ye Bala, near the larger village of Keshendeh-ye Pa'in. That first team had been trying to call in airstrikes while on their special reconnaissance. The difficulties they faced during their extended overwatch were why Tomat and Leinhard were finally brought in to support the team, as they should have been from the onset.

While that recon team had been on overwatch, they did not understand the methodology and lexicon necessary to perform target talk-ons to the aircraft. "It is not as simple as giving directions to the nearest coffee shop. Vectoring aircraft above the ground onto a specific point with aerial-delivered weapons is an explicit and unique language, with specific brevity and verbiage which enables ground personnel—forward air controllers—to quickly and accurately correlate target information to the pilot who is ten thousand or more feet above the ground." Simply, the SF team members could not articulate what the ground targets were in a manner the aircrew could apply with reasonable certainty. Where many procedural components to the CAS process are set in stone by doctrine, the talk-on is an art form and takes years of experience and training to do correctly.

Additionally, these soldiers did not understand how to utilize their provided targeting equipment for CAS-guidance. They had taken an AN/PEQ-1B SOFLAM (Special Operations Forces Laser Acquisition/Marking Device) with them, a robust system designed to mark targets for aircraft-queuing sensor pods, as well as for guiding laser-guided munitions. The unclassified specifications denote the SOFLAM has a maximum effective marking range of about ten kilometers, and about half of that for providing terminal guidance for a laser-guided munition. The laser designator puts a pulsating-laser spot on the ground or target, which a laser-guidance nose kit is tuned or programmed to seek. It achieves this via the "pulse repetition frequency" or "PRF," which is the number of times the laser flashes per second. Thus, if the laser-weapon is programmed to queue to a PRF flashing 1,688 times per a specific amount of time, the ground controller will program the Laser Target Designator (LTD) to that same PRF code, and slew the designator to the target, where the sensor will usually pick up the termination point of the laser.

The challenge with a ground-LTD is that as the termination of the laser beam gets further from the designator, the beam expands; this is called beam divergence. For the SOFLAM, the beam divergence at five kilometers is a two-by-two-meter spot, still small enough for the sensor or bomb to acquire and track to that point, but, beyond five kilometers, the spillover of the laser energy becomes too widespread for the sensor or bomb to effectively acquire, let alone track, to the intended aim point. The SOFLAM is large, about the size of a desktop printer, and weighs 12 pounds. It is powered by five BA-5590 batteries, each weighing 2.2 pounds, and consistent designation will burn through those five batteries in 30 minutes, even less if temperatures are low or humidity is a factor. Other technicalities that impact the laser include reflective surfaces like water or glass which cause the laser energy to scatter. If the ground controller does not have the See-spot infrared (IR) optic attached to the device, the operator can only employ the 15-mm eye-relief sight, which has limited magnification. Shooting the laser beam without the See-spot IR optic is no different than sharp shooting with iron sights on a rifle; it can be done but it is ineffective for long-distance precision viewing. Attaching the optic itself requires a very specific and detailed connection and synchronization process to align to the laser lens.

The reconnaissance team tasked by Captain Nutsch prior to the airmen's arrival was trying to employ the SOFLAM on targets upwards of twenty kilometers away. Both Tomat and Leinhard brought in their own SOFLAMs, with the proper attachments, as well as the standard radios and FAC kits. But, more importantly, they were intimately familiar with the correct procedures for setting up and calibrating this specific equipment for effective use. Understanding the parameters of distances, spillover, and podium effect, and managing the battery life, is explicit technical knowledge that requires extensive training. The SF soldiers had no training on this very exacting equipment; they ultimately ended up stashing the SOFLAM in a cache near their hiding site because it was inoperable for them. "In addition, their talk-ons were infantile, to be candid, with regards to how precise and elaborate they needed to be to achieve the desired effects. The complexity of that environment, the battlefield itself, and the necessary skills to coordinate close fires required graduate-level expertise."

This difficulty resulted in consternation for both the SF teams and the aircrews, and many incendiary words passed back and forth. Both parties would end up addressing this issue in separate accounts, blaming the other, as one might expect. The truth is, this was an incredibly complicated task, it was the most stressful thing any of these men—both on the ground and in the skies above—had ever faced.

It takes a high degree of training to do CAS under sterile conditions, let alone the conditions these teams were operating in.

These capability deficiencies and lack of progress on mission objectives is what prompted General Mike Longoria to fight for TACPs to go forward, as Tomat would learn months later. "It came to the point where the CAOC advised Colonel Mulholland that if he didn't accept FACs getting pushed forward, those teams in Afghanistan would lose all air support." There was another issue at play which is also underreported in posterity: a message had been sent to Captain Nutsch via the JSOTF, originating from the Office of the Secretary of Defense. Donald Rumsfeld was frustrated at the lack of progress and wanted immediate results to brief to the president and the American people. There was a scathing response sent back up the chain from Captain Nutsch, saying the teams were trying to train General Dostum's men on 21st-century warfighting tactics while going into combat against tanks on horseback. It was disingenuous to downplay the fact the lack of progress had little to do with horses and militias, and entirely because they were not able to hit targets with airstrikes.

On November 1, the team took a few days to mount up—on horses—and perform the necessary reconnaissance and identify and confirm the targets being selected. Tomat suggested to Captain Nutsch and Chief Warrant Officer Bob Peddington (ODA595 team chief) that another three-man element—with Matt Leinhard attached—head to the eastern extent of the area of operations, near the village of Chapchal, while the first recon team remained in the west. Tomat would move through the valleys in the "center" zone with another small team as the three-pronged effort pushed north, in line with each other but separated by many miles. Tomat would provide primary command and control of aircraft, with both himself and Leinhard identifying and confirming targets. As aircraft were vectored into the airspace, Tomat would direct them where they needed to go—east or west—while simultaneously prosecuting targets in the central zone where the Taliban command and control was consolidated.

The objective was simple, but not easy: trying to cut off the head of the snake and clean up whatever functional parts remained at the flanks as necessary. Tomat's final recommendation to Captain Nutsch was that the captain and ODA595's 18E (communications sergeant) travel with General Dostum, having overall situational awareness of the three dispersed teams, while leaving the remaining SF soldiers at the mission-support site (MSS) to enable the ongoing operation.

The plan was well received by Captain Nutsch, but Chief Peddington was worried about splitting the team more than they already had, due to the security of the force. For this, the Air Force already had an answer: "I assured him that we would provide security—it would simply be flying at twenty thousand feet. But with our ability to communicate at distance based on our radio capabilities, we could do this effectively, while still protecting the Americans out forward."

The three elements would continue north from Dey-e, splitting to each sector and spending several days glassing targets—observing through telescopes and binoculars—with each team establishing recon sites and remaining under cover and concealment. This involved exhaustive communications between both FACs via the radio, ensuring both had accurate information which Tomat would use to fill out the DD Form 1972 JTAR (DD1972, Joint Tactical Air Request). This is the standard form used to request CAS. The JTAR template included all relevant data from the FAC, which the CAOC would receive to allocate aircraft sorties to the requested mission, based on callsigns for the controllers, grids for friendly locations and proposed target locations, desired effects, environmental information, and pre-planned nine-line attack briefs, if prepared.

The recon teams spent three days hidden on ridgelines developing targets. During this time, Tomat needed to do a cryptological key refill for his radio. Crypto keys allow for secure communications, as only radio sets with the same key fills can communicate. Even if both receivers are on the same frequency, without the same fill the operator whose radio is not properly loaded will only hear static. The crypto change would occur—as luck would have it—on November 5. On the night of the 4th, Tomat loaded the new crypto fill into his radio. However, he would discover that the KIK-13—an electronic fill-transfer device which the controllers carried for field use—had corrupted the crypto keys. The only option was to return to the MSS—a three-hour horse ride back down the mountain—to get to the communications sergeant who kept another crypto-fill device with him. It was pouring with rain, and miserably cold, but they arrived and reloaded cryptological keys, confirmed functional comms, and made their way back up the mountain in the dark morning hours of November 5.

The first sorties would be on station at 7:30 in the morning, based on the DD1972 mission data sent by the CAOC to Tomat, who would have priority of targets of the three sectors due to the Taliban's command-and-control bunker in the Central Zone. Tomat's team had identified this facility based on the volume of personnel traffic and the dense number of radio antennas mounted on top of the structure. Once that location had been neutralized, Tomat would turn the CAS aircraft onto anti-aircraft weapons, mostly old ZU-23/2s protecting the site. These were stationary anti-air cannons, the Russian twin-barreled 23-mm variety, which the Taliban had posted around the village. There were also several old Russian tanks being used as mobile support-by-fire positions.

Upon the return to the Central Zone hide site, Tomat's group would miss the first "time on target," as the SF soldiers he was with stopped to have chai with some of Dostum's local men. When Tomat argued they had a rigid schedule to keep, the SF soldiers countered that their mission was to build rapport with the indigenous forces. Fortunately, Leinhard was monitoring the radios from the east recon site and, with the first set of aircraft checked in on the control frequency, he began engaging targets in the east. "Good on Matt, but this created an issue which nearly caused a catastrophic mission shift. As I stated, the plan was for us to hit the Central Zone targets first, where the Taliban had their command center set up, and by doing so up-end their ability to react to our assault. The problem with us missing the first vul (aircraft mission time) and Matt initiating the assault was that the Taliban command center in our sector was fully operational, and the east team's hide site was quickly compromised. Those Taliban forces in the east were able to organize and began a counterassault. The hide site Matt and his group had chosen was closer to their targets than we were to ours, so it did not take long for the enemy to close in and move to overrun them."

As more aircraft checked in, Tomat decided to forego any strikes on the Central Zone targets, and began funneling everything in the sky towards Leinhard, ensuring enough overwhelming firepower overhead to defend themselves and avoid being overrun. This irked the team to the west, who relayed to Tomat they were also being engaged—reportedly by a tank—but they remained far away from their targets and were not in the same dire straits as the eastern team. "Quite simply, the tank was errantly firing into the high ground, and with the slant angle and upward trajectory of the main cannon, it wasn't effective fire, based on their known location and reported grid of the tank maneuvering through their valley." Tomat was able to deduce this information by map plotting the known friendly hide site against the reported location of the Taliban tank—all while controlling the airspace and vectoring aircraft toward Leinhard's beleaguered recon team.

"Matt did some great work that day against overwhelming forces maneuvering against his three-man team. As he began to turn the tide of this battle, I started retaining some of the inbound aircraft to target the Taliban [who] were organizing forces in our sector, who were moving en masse to the east to reinforce the enemy which Matt was putting to the sword with CAS. This was our chance to cut the head off the snake as originally planned."

As Leinhard was finishing a strike with F-14s, Tomat broke into the net, notifying Leinhard of the grid for one of the reinforcement bunkers where the Taliban had gathered an immediate reaction force. The F-14s were already out of bombs, and only had their 20-mm cannon remaining. The issue with employing the gun in this scenario was that all American aircraft were restricted above 5,000 feet relative to the ground, but the situation dictated immediate action. Tomat directed the pilots to call the CAOC and request approval to break their hard deck, which was quickly approved. Tomat quickly passed an attack brief to the F-14s, with a final attack direction of southeast to northwest. This would have their gun run splitting the central and east elements equixially, and two strafes from the fighter jets would neutralize this large group effectively, ensuring Leinhard's team could break contact and get some relief from the counterattack. By now, they had a B-52 on station as well, which Leinhard utilized on the remaining forces in the east sector.

This would leave the two command-and-control bunkers in the Central Zone, which Tomat would engage with bombs. The remaining airstrikes would eliminate tanks and anti-air weapons. In total, both FACs' BDA (battle-damage assessment) from those initial strikes was over 150 enemy killed, which included several senior Taliban Defense Ministry personnel, with many more being captured by General Dostum's forces as the Northern Alliance pushed into the village.

While the recon elements were working through this first day's assault, the battalion command element, or Operational Detachment–Bravo (ODB), functioning as the Special Operations Command and Control Element (SOCCE), had inserted into the MSS in the early morning hours; this included Colonel Bowers and his entourage. They arrived not long after Tomat had reloaded his radios and returned to his overwatch position. Several Air Force personnel came with them, including another combat controller—Master Sergeant Bart Decker. Decker is famous for being in the foreground of a picture associated with the "Horse Soldiers" story of this time, riding a white horse surrounded by militia forces after they had broken through the Kuh-e Al Borz Gap, sometimes referred to as Tiangi, just south of Mazar-i-Sharif a few days after this initial contact.

Tomat's first encounter with a member of Bowers's command element was not a cordial one. "As I am at the OP [observation post] engaging targets, the battalion executive officer rode up to our site, telling me that the colonel had some targets he wanted me to engage. I would later apologize to this individual at the Pentagon years later, but my response was 'Tell Colonel Bowers to fuck off, I have already plotted targets and we are in the middle of dealing with the enemy.' It was frustrating for the ODB to have inserted themselves into this dynamic when we already had the mission planned and well in hand, not excepting the inevitable changes we were dealing with. To be completely candid, after being out there for a week and more, the SOCCE showed up just to take pictures of the targets we had engaged, and to be seen where ODA595 had just spent days living under incredibly austere conditions."

Captain Nutsch was several kilometers east of the staging area and Tomat's recon site, ready to push through the Central Zone along with General Dostum's massed forces. These groups were waiting for the CAS engagements to end so they could begin

Tim Stamey, another Air Force TACP, calling in airstrikes with ODA585 near Kunduz December 2001. (Photo provided by Steve Tomat)

clearing the villages which had just been overwhelmed by airstrikes. Due to the timeline changes and shifting of all fires east first with Leinhard's team, this meant the timing of the clearance operation was skewed. As Tomat was finishing the final engagements, the front line of the Afghan militias was closing with the last few targets. There was no means of controlling them or coordinating with them, as this was not a cohesive fighting unit like an American military platoon. None of the Afghan militia had radios, meaning only the Americans and a select few key leaders under the warlord's direction had any semblance of command and control. These were a constant challenge faced by the team working with the Northern Alliance. Communication and friendly battle tracking—two of the fundamental capabilities provided by trained and qualified FACs—would be the source of repeating challenges in these early days. "There was an incident where one aircraft engaged Afghan forces as a result of an errant talk-on from one of the ODA members and bombs being dropped without receiving clearance from me." Tomat was off the radio temporarily as the teams began to adjust positions and prepare for the clearance, resulting in a ground-force member trying to vector the aircraft overhead.

As nightfall approached, the entire force, including the east team and the MSS, moved west through the valley to collect the western recon team, all on horseback. Tomat would learn then the reasons why the team out west had been unable to successfully eliminate any targets with CAS up to this point. Their hide site was a full 10 kilometers from the intended targets, meaning their SOFLAM was entirely ineffective in trying to vector aircraft onto any aimpoints in that sector. To circumvent this, the western recon team tried to simply carpet bomb the entire town of Keshindih-ye Bala, just to take out the one tank that was seen maneuvering throughout. Tomat took this opportunity to give them some brief instruction and feedback on the SOFLAM capabilities.

The operation's opening shots began many miles south of Mazar-i-Sharif, the ultimate goal for the Northern Alliance. It took several days to get there, to the point where the terrain was so rugged that, in many stretches, the force dismounted their horses and led them while rucking on foot. By the time the team and their partners were descending from the worst terrain, the animals were exhausted. "We walked two nights, all through the night, moving about sixty kilometers, which brought us to our rendezvous point with the remainder of General Dostum's forces, at a place called the Kuh-e Al Borz Pass, or Tiangi. The Tiangi is the dominating terrain feature just south and southwest of Mazar-i-Sharif, and the road through the Kuh-e Al Borz is the only route through the ridge. This made it a key piece of terrain and critical for us to seize from Taliban control before entering the city."

On the night of November 7, the team prepared to hit the gap. This first required calling in an aerial resupply, allowing the Americans to refresh kits and prepare for the push out of the mountains. They were planning to move through the gap when the force was engaged by Taliban positions occupying the south face of the ridge, as well as groups inside the gap. Initially, they thought it was artillery, due to a tremendous volume of intense, high-explosive fire that decimated Dostum's forces advancing into the gap ahead of the Americans. "We saw men and horses literally fileted, cut in half, amputations, just brutal devastation. It was not artillery as we initially thought, it was a multiple-launch rocket system which the Taliban had kept in working order, what appeared to be an old Russian BM-21."

Amid this initial volley, Captain Nutsch found Tomat, telling the airman to engage the rocket launcher. "I told him that I would need to get eyes on to give aircraft a proper target talk-on to ensure we hit it on the first strike." The initial reports indicated this vehicle was on the north side of the gap, firing its rockets through the pass, meaning Tomat would need to mount the ridgeline to see the target. Tomat and another of the team members, William Smith, had pushed into the initial impact area, trying to perform combat triage on the Northern Alliance fighters who could be saved. There were not many who survived the first salvo, but the Americans were applying tourniquets and dragging the wounded off the "X" into some kind of cover. After Nutsch found Tomat, they rode back to the trucks where Tomat's ruck and radio were; having secured those, they passed through the carnage to begin climbing the ridgeline.

The Northern Alliance force continued to receive rockets and assorted small-arms and machine-gun fire throughout the remainder of the afternoon, as the captain and Tomat were climbing the ridge. It was getting later in the day on November 8, nearing dusk. "We left our horses behind and low-crawled the last few hundred meters to get to the crest, while Captain Nutsch sent another overwatch team to the west for the same purpose. That other team began firing down into the enemy forces, into multiple vehicles and several bunkers built into the north side of the ridge. Due to the slant angle, their organic weapons systems were ineffective, and they were unable to see the BM-21. "Once the captain and I crested, we were able to quickly identify that armored rocket launch system and many other Taliban forces besides."

To maximize the sortie time with the aircraft overhead, Tomat established a "bombing box," a free-fire area into which all effects would be permitted for the aircraft, so long as their munitions landed inside the area briefed to the aircraft in the nine-line. For most CAS strikes, the controller provides one attack brief for one target, occasionally multiple targets if they are near one another, and provides clearance for those targets as required. In this case, there were so many targets to be struck, starting with the BM-21, that it would be most effective to open the target area and allow the aircraft to turn in as much as needed, where Tomat would provide re-attack clearance as necessary.

With a B-52 on station, Tomat passed all relevant grids and brought them into the target. Right before the bomber rolled in on the first pass, the captain decided to stand up for one quick glance; Tomat hurriedly pulled him back down. "It is hard to imagine now, twenty-plus years later, but there was a decided lack of combat experience across the force back then, something where common sense tells you *don't stand up in a gunfight*. And only a handful of people—folks like me who had the rare occasion to be in gunfights immediately prior to the War on Terror—knew what it felt like to be in those moments." The bomber came in, putting one bomb directly on the rocket-system, then neutralizing the bulk of the remaining targets. After multiple successful attacks, General Dostum's men were able to move through the Tiangi gap, into the assortment of villages just north of the Tiangi. The path to Mazar-i-Sharif was now wide open before them.

It was a surreal experience for the Americans on the trek through those villages. "The villagers came out of their homes and were cheering us as we rode through, overjoyed to be freed from years of Taliban repression. It was like the scene from an old Western movie, down to the minutiae of a bunch of Westerners riding horses, the irony of which was not lost on us." The team quickly secured the airfields near the city on November 10, having first circled wide to the west and taking the prison at Qala-i-Jangi, whose name translates into "House of War." This prison would become infamous a few weeks later when Mike Spann, one of the CIA paramilitary officers who first went into Afghanistan after 9/11, was killed during the prison uprising. Qala-i-Jangi, an imposing fortress and distinct terrain feature with commanding views out to several kilometers, would become General Dostum's temporary base camp as his forces continued to pacify and clear the Taliban from the city.

While holding at Qala-i-Jangi, a CIA paramilitary team—one of the *Jawbreaker* units who prepared the way for American SF teams—informed Captain Nutsch about a holdout of several hundred Taliban in an abandoned girls' school near the center of the city. The abandoned school was just to the east of the Shrine of Hazrat Ali—a beautiful and magnificent blue mosque and one of Mazar-i-Sharif's most distinct features. Leading this hold out of Taliban forces were foreign fighters from Pakistan, as Tomat's team would learn from their agency partners. These foreign fighters had been recruited to take up Jihad and support Al Qaeda against the West. "These guys were the real hardliners, unwilling to surrender, even though the Taliban had been crushed and swept from the rest of the city around them. Several local mullahs had attempted to intercede, begging these fighters and their Taliban cohorts to surrender to General Dostum's forces." In the negotiation process, several of those mullahs had been killed trying to broker a peaceful surrender. Additionally, multiple civilians who happened to be nearby during one of the negotiations were killed. "I remember the agency guys telling us that a father and daughter were among the civilians killed in the crossfire, which struck me deeply."

Two of the CIA officers, including Mike Spann, asked if Nutsch's team would be able to engage this building. After discussing the options, the team reorganized and set out to get eyes on the building with a small contingent of Northern Alliance personnel. They drove a pickup truck taken from the Taliban stockpile. Using directions given by the CIA paramilitary officers to the remaining mullahs of the city, the team stopped to get the most recent situation update for the school. The mullahs asked the Americans to give them another chance to negotiate with the fighters holed up in the school. "We told them that, in no uncertain terms, this enemy had run out of chances. We spoke on behalf of our Commander-in-Chief, President George Bush: none of these men have the chance to surrender now, for having betrayed the trust of the local leaders and the civilians they have murdered."

Looking towards the center of the city, Tomat and his team determined which buildings nearby would give the best vantage to observe the target and potentially enable Tomat to set up a SOFLAM to guide the bombs in on the target. "I had been relying on a 1:250k-scale JOG map for this entire operation, which serves well for plotting latitude–longitude coordinates, and it covers a wide area. But was not helpful inside a city, especially not one as sprawling and widespread as Mazar-i-Sharif. I procured a far more detailed map from our Agency partners, a street map imagery with grid lines overlaid in a crude fashion, but it worked. This would enable the talk-on process. Collaborating with Mike and Dave—another paramilitary officer—we identified a tall apartment building approximately three-hundred eighty meters away from the multi-story school, one which would offer us an elevation and line-of-sight advantage."

They drove to the backside of the apartment and cleared their way up the stairwell to reach the rooftop. Tomat asked his Army counterparts to set up the SOFLAM as he plotted targeting information. This airstrike was no longer a CAS-mission, but a very deliberate, procedural strike inside a civilian-dominated area. It would portend the difficulty and complexity which would underwrite the remainder of this war: having to bring devastating force in close proximity to friendlies, civilians, and infrastructure. Tomat and Leinhard had swiftly mastered engaging the Taliban forces in wide-open country. This in-city attack brief had to be both precise and accurate, with no room for human error. Collateral-damage mitigation was not a doctrinal standard in this early chapter of the war, but these FACs were already thinking through this complex dynamic as a matter of course.

Steve observing the target building through the SOFLAM (center), with Dave (CIA) standing left, and two ODA595 members plotting map data. (Photo provided by Steve Tomat)

The first attack plan was to lase the target and guide the bombs using the SOFLAM. Tomat had Navy F/A-18s on station, and when he brought them in for the target mark, neither aircraft was able to get eyes on the target prior to engaging. This was attempted twice with "Dash-1," the element leader, and once with "Dash-2," but they simply could not acquire the target. "That's alright, I've planned for this, now is the time to break out the graduate-level CAS expertise. Laser guidance was the 'easy mode,' now I would have to do this the hard way." The most likely explanation for the laser failing to work was podium effect: the beam was obfuscated by the building and surrounding urban canyons, and it may very well have been glancing off windows on the school, scattering the laser energy to untraceable dispersal. "And that was a knock on me, I didn't check the SOFLAM after it had been set up to ensure it wasn't pointing into a window."

The next iteration of the attack started with the talk-on, using the doctrinal method "FIDO." Starting with the blue mosque—the only significant and obvious terrain feature in the middle of the city—Tomat moved to a nearby sports stadium with a running track, whose length was established as a unit of measure. Then, referencing the unit of measure, he estimated the distance to the building itself, with an exchange of multiple confirmatory remarks about the target: compass orientation, the American-occupied building nearby in the proper offset direction, and everything they could think of until Tomat was confident the pilots were looking at the correct building. This took 15 minutes, but there was no room for error or misunderstanding. This is inherent to what FACs do: identifying common or uncommon objects that are recognizable to someone at 15,000 feet, and translating that into a level of certainty to call in a bomb.

"I brought in the lead aircraft, who called "In" and I passed clearance, but he was unable to line up his shot for this strike on the first pass. Dash-2 was able to acquire the building on his in-call, clearance passed, and his bomb smacked the dead-center of the target building. He could not have placed it any better if he drew an X with a piece of chalk by his own hand. But this is a large building, so the 1,000-pound bomb doesn't reduce the structure. Now we are being engaged from enemy personnel nearby. Dash-1 was, of course, able to find the target from the first strike, so I brought him in on an immediate pass, gave him clearance, and he got a hung bomb, meaning the release bolts on the weapon seized, and he was unable to release the munition. I approved him to depart the airspace to try and release the weapon in a safe area away from the city, in accordance with guidance from the CAOC. I brought Dash-2 in for a reattack and, with subsequent strikes, we reduced the entire building, effectively ending the Taliban in Mazar-i-Sharif."

After this strike had successfully concluded, one of Tomat's Army counterparts made a comment about the airman's demeanor: "I had been with this soldier since leaving the base camp on Day One, so he had gotten used to my mannerisms by now. He told me 'This is the first time I've seen you smile since you got into Afghanistan.'" Tomat's response reflected the emotionally charged nature of this strike. "We were in an urban environment, with the escalated risks of collateral damage and friendly proximity, at the time this strike was considered Danger Close [within

1,000 meters was standard for all free-fall munitions in 2001]; this was my chance to do something inarguably dangerous, but as noble and challenging as anything I had done in my career. The inherent need to do a perfect target talk-on was critical. And I did it about as well as possible, even with a few hiccups throughout. That was an incredibly rewarding feeling, knowing we had eliminated the bad guys while keeping everyone else safe."

A few hours later, local militia conducted a BDA, confirming the airstrike killed all but about one hundred of the insurgents holed up there, who were captured by General Dostum's forces. The team retired from the city, back to Qala-i-Jangi, where they would spend the remainder of the rotation in Afghanistan. Mission success, commander's intent was met: they had seized the airfields and land bridge into Uzbekistan, liberated Mazar-i-Sharif, and broken the Taliban in the north. Over the next few weeks, they would occupy themselves by bringing in resupply missions to the airfield, weapons, and equipment, as well as a large collection of old Russian uniforms for their Northern Alliance partners. "That was probably a surreal vision for a local, seeing Russian uniforms worn by Afghans a few years after Russians had occupied this place. We were witnesses of history, being in Afghanistan at that time."

***

"This opening episode of the war in Afghanistan highlights why it was so critical to have qualified forward air controllers on the ground to make this mission happen. It is not something you can hand off to a soldier who is an expert at being a soldier. It requires someone who is FAC-qualified, and it is still the most difficult job anyone has ever undertaken in combat. And wouldn't you know it, that is the main reason that TACPs were created—to ensure bombs were put on target, minimizing collateral damage, and mitigating the risk of friendly fire from the air."

"I think that reality was lost among these teams, and across the JSOTF, they assumed that their casual, referential training—maybe they had done an emergency-CAS event at a bombing range back in the States—would suffice for their needs. That does not make you a qualified controller, there is a reason we have a process, why we have a community-wide standards and evaluations program, why we have things like "currency controls," where we have to be on the radio with live aircraft multiple times a year at a minimum, just to be current."

"Mark Nutsch even addressed this skill gap in his book *Swords of Lightning*, where he articulates the difficulty in having those conversations on the radio with the pilots. The CAS dialogue is its own language, and even though it's English, it is almost impossible to understand if you don't learn to speak it fluently, and it comes with its own dialects and idioms and lexicon that evolve quickly."

"It is no different than a general physician, who may detect something wrong with your heart. But they cannot perform surgery, they refer you to a cardiologist, who further determines the precise problem, and recommends treatment. And then you are referred again to the cardiovascular surgeon who does the actual procedure, but only if they are board certified to do so based on rigorous standards and specific qualifications. Qualified forward air controllers are cardiovascular surgeons when it comes to employing precision aerial fires on the battlefield. Others might be able to do a small sliver of the requirements, but not at the level of ability which we can."

"When we passed through Qala-i-Jangi, we met up with the CIA personnel there, including Mike Spann, who went on to advise Afghans clearing Mazar-i-Sharif once we arrived, and one individual named 'JR.' This paramilitary officer would remain with us for the majority of our time clearing through Mazar, helping coordinate the clearance of the city and providing us with timely and critical intelligence from the ground units. As we were driving from the prison into the city, I asked JR what he thought about this new war so far, and his response was 'I don't think we could have done this without air power.' That is a sobering thing to hear, and even more so to think about years later, how critical our role was in this early fight. It was telling that in the span of five days, from the 5th to the 10th of November, we crossed several hundred kilometers of enemy-held territory and broke their ability to fight—a push that many strategists thought would take between several months to a year to uproot the Taliban and Al Qaeda across Afghanistan. And we did it in days."

"There were challenges, notably the Qala-i-Jangi uprising a few weeks later, when we lost Mike Spann—the first American life lost in Afghanistan—and we took retribution for that as well. The story has it that General Dostum called in artillery to take back the prison, but that is not true either; just like the rest of this story, the uprising has not been recounted accurately. We were there, calling in airstrikes on the prison, as were a team of British SAS [Special Air Service Regiment] controllers. It is another instance of forward air controllers being present and active in every major event of this war on terror. After the dust settled, I was in the truck that drove John Walker Lynn to the airfield at Mazar-i-Sharif to be collected by the FBI. I did the same thing for David Hicks, the Australian citizen fighting for Al Qaeda. We, the forward air controller community, were there for all of it from the beginning to the end."

"If we don't consider the next twenty years of senior leadership failures, and a lack of strategic vision, but only look at those first few weeks of the war, it took small units of American forces mere days to defeat an enemy state on

Steve (middle) with members of ODA595 at the gates of Qala-I Jangi ("Place of War"). (Photo provided by Steve Tomat)

its own turf in the north. A few more weeks to clear as far east as Kunduz, and a few weeks more for our teams in the south to break the Taliban stronghold in Kandahar, and the capital city of Kabul. That would not have been possible without air power from the Coalition being effectively integrated into the ground scheme of maneuver by experts who were specially trained to perform that job."

"I worry over the fact that many other career fields began to immerse themselves in the CAS enterprise, but without training to the same near-exclusive focus as we did. And when anyone attempts to treat joint fires as a part-time training standard, they can cause those fratricide incidents. Even experts can have mishaps, even when they train to that high standard. It happened with the PLGR [Precision Lightweight GPS Receiver] incident—the bomb which nearly killed Hamid Karzai in those early days while I was in the north—but that story was misunderstood, misreported, and taken out of context. But those mishaps can still happen, even to the best of them."

CHAPTER 3

Ancient Roads to a New War

The Battlespace Was Defiance

The early phases of the Afghanistan campaign reflect the challenges which the United States military could very well face in future conflicts. Across the diverse environmental and ecological locales that constitute Afghanistan's provinces, quality maps with accurate datums, up-to-date imagery, and accurate, navigable infrastructure were utterly absent except in a select few circumstances. Even those resources of navigation relative to the existing infrastructure were limited early on, where special-operations units were performing the initial insertion and organization of Afghan warlords and tribal fighters to overthrow the Taliban. Afghanistan at a sociological level, the "human domain" of military operations, further complicated the deployment of military forces into the austere state, whose national identity was fractured at best, owing to the proliferation of the tribal identities of diverse ethnic groups. The human domain posed a challenge that would badger and stymie international efforts to develop a democratized nation in the years to come.

The complexity of the literal geographic and infrastructural environment, combined with the labyrinthine human domain and the 20th-century American military inventory, would challenge the strategy and policy apparatus from the campaign's onset, as the war machine and its operators were in no way prepared to function in the environment they faced. The demands that make Afghanistan a unique battlespace would forge the American and Coalition militaries into adopting wholesale changes to equipment, task organization, and personnel management in ways previously unseen in a cross-oceanic campaign.

Afghanistan is a landlocked state, requiring the forward staging of combat, sustainment, and intelligence forces utilize surrounding sovereignties to establish logistical-support hubs before entry into the battlespace. Even the relative proximity of the Indian Ocean for carrier battle groups creates a sustainment constraint due to distance and elevation change from sea level. It is not unlike the potential scenario where U.S. and Coalition forces may be forced to rely on partner nations at vast distances in contending with aggression from Chinese, Russian, North Korean, or Iranian forces in a future escalation of hostilities.

The ecology and climate of Afghanistan poses a particular challenge to external forces. In the south, wide swaths of open sand and rock in the Registan Desert recall images of Frank Herbert's science-fiction masterpiece *Dune*. In the west, jagged ridgelines shape the terminus of the Hindu Kush's Central Highlands, segregating a diverse scattering of tribes and villages across immense valleys and redoubts. In the north, broad plains abut the rising steppe over wide distances that appear barren and devoid of life, but are teeming with ethnic groups. In the far east, near-tropical jungles and terraces are home to sweltering humidity, vegetation, and vertical-walled valleys that provide entrance to the Federally Administered Tribal Areas over the Pakistan border. The Hindu Kush themselves, in the heart of Afghanistan, form the most rugged and daunting terrain on earth and, indeed, some of the most renowned names of the war call this unforgiving region home: The Khost–Ghazni Pass, Takur Ghar, Tora Bora, Kamdesh, and the Pech Valley. It is into this impossibly diverse environment American and Coalition forces were charged with creating a breach and seizing terrain en route to confronting Taliban and Al Qaeda forces sprawled across the country.

The American architecture, of course, changed dramatically in the two decades of the war, specifically the density and coverage capabilities of the space apparatus that enable long-distance communications, transmission of critical battlefield data, imagery and intelligence collection, and other command-and-control necessities. But, at the time of the Afghanistan invasion following the September 11 attacks, the hyper-connectivity of today remained a theoretical exercise, imagined in movies and science fiction, and certainly not an array of capabilities disseminated to the lowest echelon of war fighters.

Battlefield imagery, a feature second nature to mission preparation in the latter phases of the war, was impossible to acquire save for incredibly myopic circumstances. Long-distance communications in later years were built on the architecture of satellite burst communications, not always clear and loud, but functional so long as the ground receiver and transmitter had clear skies above. In 2001, long-distance communications relied upon line-of-sight antenna theory, where high-frequency signals could achieve adequate range, but only on radio suites built for vehicles and requiring upwards of 150 watts of power. The man-portable radios, which utilize very high frequency and ultra-high frequency, were only reliable if the radio operator had literal unimpeded line-of-sight to the aircraft or another ground station and were subject to interference by any terrain, structure, or the ionosphere that refracted sky wave antenna signals. Such "man-pack" radios were limited to 20 watts of power at best, while individual team channel radios operated at a passive 1 watt to receive signals, and only transmitted at 5 watts.

The very dynamic of Afghanistan, circa October 2001, defied the "limited" capabilities of the American arsenal of the era. Previous combat operations of significance for the Defense Department in the decade before the Afghanistan invasion were air-power-centric operations against relatively modernized state militaries, or at least in marginally developed infrastructural locales. The first was the transitional Operation *Provide Comfort* and *Northern Watch* missions—the former being an air campaign to extricate Kurdish victims of Iraqi leader Saddam Hussein's genocidal operations, and the latter being an enforcement of the "no-fly zone" between the 33rd and 36th Parallels, ensuring Iraqi compliance with United Nations (UN) resolutions on preventing further ethnic cleansing. Further, the American military was a critical component in the UN peacekeeping mission Operation *Allied Force*, performing targeted airstrikes against aggressor Yugoslav forces following the nationalist cessation of Bosnia–Herzegovina, Croatia, and Slovenia. Notably, former Air Force Chief of Staff David Goldfein, then an F-16 fighter pilot, was shot down and later rescued by members of U.S. Air Force Special Operations. In *Allied Force*, airstrikes were intended to deter continued violent repression by the Belgrade-based Serbian forces who were engaged in mortal terror campaigns against the assorted ethnic groups attempting self-determination from Yugoslav leader Slobodan Milosevic.[1]

While the 1990s air mission over Iraq was considered a success, as Iraqi ethnic aggression before 2003 was stymied by persistent American and Coalition air sorties, the targeted airstrikes were limited, oft-times, to reactive fires against Iraqi ground forces employing surface-to-air weapons, although occasional offensive engagements against Iraqi radar and communications sites occurred.[2] The effects of the air campaign in Bosnia and Kosovo, however, were much more difficult to ascertain for effectiveness, due to the limited involvement of forward air controllers providing terminal guidance and targeting nomination from the ground. Most airstrikes were pre-determined sorties based on collected intelligence sources and advanced-force operations by special-operations components. Further, the lack of battle-damage assessments, owing to the limited role of forward air coordinators and controllers on the battlefield, made for a laborious and ineffectual application of kinetic effects on the battlespace.

The approach used in these air missions of the 1990s still echoed the strategic, albeit precision, employment of aerial munitions against assumed fixed or limited-mobility targets—shades of previous large-scale combat operations that had not been observed in the American arena of combat operations since the First Gulf War, Panama, and Grenada. Despite these doctrinal and fundamental mission missteps, and a resistant paradigm shift, the end of the 20th century of American air power did give rise to a new staple in the air power panoply: permanent forward deployment of air controllers. It would be evident almost immediately just how critical this capability would be from the war's earliest hours.

CHAPTER 4

"You get nightmares from the things you had the option not to do"

Chief Master Sergeant Robert "Zack" Zackery (ret.) spent 26 years in the United States Air Force (USAF) as a tactical air control party specialist. His first operation was as a radio operator, maintainer, and driver during the Balkans conflict, providing tactical command and control as an air-power apprentice. From there, Zack enjoyed one of the most prolific and accomplished careers in the USAF, rising to the position of Command Chief Master Sergeant at Laughlin Air Force Base, Texas, before ending his career on staff at United States Special Operations Command, directing the Operational Health of Special Operations Forces initiative.

Zack's story was important to write for multiple reasons. First, he has served as a mentor, professionally and personally, for more than two decades to countless men and women across dozens of partner nations and has been a critical figure in the efforts to write this greater story on close air support in the Global War on Terror. Second, Zack's story of success and his unique role as one of the first Americans into Afghanistan in late 2001 are noteworthy not only for his part in history but, as a Black American, his rise to the loftiest perches of the Defense Department's most exclusive clubs are impressive by any standard, doubly so for a man who has faced racism and discrimination his entire life. Not only does Zack help open the story of close air support, because he was there at the beginning, but his resilience and determination are reflective of the very best of America when merit and performance meet dedication and commitment to the highest ideals.

"My story begins on September 11th, 2001 … 'Where were you on 9/11?', right?"[1] Zackery had just returned from Kuwait, his second conventional tactical air control party (TACP) deployment, right around his four-year mark in the Air Force. His first deployment was a peacekeeping mission in Bosnia with an armor unit, having only been in uniform for 15 months. Zackery, and close friend Abel Martens, were stationed together with the 14th ASOS (Air Support Operations Squadron) at Fort Bragg (now Fort Liberty), North Carolina. Neither was satisfied with the career field as a whole and were looking at how they could distinguish themselves at a time with no conflict. "At that time there was nothing going on. We were both young ignorant guys, and we convinced each other to go to Ranger School; then, let's go to try out for SOF [special-operations force] TACP and work with the Rangers."

Both men would assess for the Army's elite units and were invited back. Upon successful conclusion of this ordeal, both had planned to transition from active-duty Air Force to the Army to join their new units. It was in the months before this—early 2001, that Martens was going to go to Ranger School, and Zackery would deploy to Kuwait City.

Zackery's Kuwait rotation would last from Spring 2001 to September 5. He was on post-deployment block leave on that fateful day that changed American history. "I don't remember anything about those days before the 11th; I'm on leave, relaxing, had just spent several months overseas, training, calling in airstrikes on live ranges in a way you can't really do stateside." It was just prior to Zackery's deployment to Kuwait that Jason Faley (a fellow TACP from the 19th ASOS, Fort Campbell, Kentucky) had been killed during a training accident at Udairi Range in Kuwait (see Chapter 10). Zackery's team was the first to re-open that range and the OP (observation point) of the incident following the investigation and its closeout. "I still have a piece of the bomb fragment and part of the HMMWV^2 from that accident in my office to commemorate Jason and the other lives lost that day."

Back home at Fort Bragg, Zackery was at the Post Exchange (PX) on the morning of September 11, 2001. This was the only PX on base at that time, with Fort Bragg far less robust than it is today. "I'm walking through the mini-mall corridor and pass by the barber shop, but no one is cutting hair, everyone is staring at the TVs. It was weird, no one is upset that their hair isn't being cut right? I look at the screen and see smoke coming out of the World Trade Center. And me being the young, immature type that I was, my first thought was 'There it is, we're going to war,' as if my unit was shipping out in the next fifteen minutes." Of course, no one was leaving then and there, there was too much confusion and uncertainty. Zackery would eventually arrive at his unit, amid the chaos and new security measures, to find the more experienced TACPs already preparing their gear.

Within a week, the 14th ASOS commander would pull Zackery into his office, saying, "Sergeant Zackery, I know you've qualified for SOF TACP, and that you have your orders to report. But you've just come back from your second deployment, you have shown your maturity and reliability, so would you like to go to Afghanistan?" Zackery, like many Americans, didn't even know where Afghanistan was, but "Damn right I wanted to go to Afghanistan."

He was supposed to leave on October 5, but the opportunity to exact revenge on Al Qaeda and their Taliban hosts was too compelling to pass up. "I can always go to selection, but how many chances will I get to go to Afghanistan?" Zackery and Martens went into country together, but it was neither a smooth process nor simple endeavor. "I don't remember anything about the trip over there, how I got from North Carolina to the war. I don't remember any of the stops, but I do remember we landed in a C-17 in Uzbekistan, and we are the only two passengers being dropped off. This turned out to be Karshi–Khanabad Airbase (K2), I didn't know if it was late at night or early in the morning." It was the darkest kind of night Zack had ever seen. The crew chiefs got the two airmen and equipment crates pushed off the ramp, and then the aircraft immediately taxied back onto the runway. There were no lights, nothing distinguishable in the absolute darkness, just two men with an absurd amount of gear standing just off the edge of the runway in a foreign country.

After their eyes adjusted, at the edge of vision they could see a dim light in a hut. It was no more than just a crack in the door jamb, so they walked to it. This faint light was further than the two men initially thought, requiring several minutes of walking through the wide-open airfield to get to this isolated structure. The building turned out to be something straight out of old Soviet occupation. "We walked to the door and there was one guy sitting in the middle of this room—one desk, one chair, a dim swaying lightbulb overhead—totally tropey austere war scenario. Abel and I start with the pointy-talky 'Hey, man, where the fuck are we supposed to go?' and this dude's response was 'Who the hell are you two?'"

A few minutes later, they heard all-terrain quads and pickup trucks rolling up, operated by support personnel from the ISOFAC (Isolation Facility) coming to collect the two confused forward air controllers (FAC). "We did not go into ISOFAC stateside, I know a lot of the stories told about those early weeks before the invasion had people isolating before leaving the continental U.S. But not us, we did our isolation in Uzbekistan. So there we are, in isolation, getting linked up with a Fort Campbell Special Forces team." The two airmen were escorted to the isolation compound, sleeping in an Army standard-issue Alaska tent. The drag of the international flight weighed heavily on both men, who slept late into the morning since arriving so late.

Zackery had initially been assigned to a team preparing to head over the border into country, but another FAC (a TACP), who had already been waiting at the ISOFAC for several weeks, said in no uncertain terms that Zackery wasn't about to roll in and out with a ready team. "Wait your turn is what he told me. Roger that, so then I got paired with ODA542,[3] we linked up and the support troop LNO [liaison officer] introduced me as their new ETAC.[4]

The first encounter between Army and Air Force was acrimonious. The team sergeant took one look at Zackery and said, "I don't need a fucking ETAC, I've been calling in airstrikes since before you've been in the Air Force."

"That's my welcome to the team—'Fuck you, Air Force'—and back then, I was still young, cocky, more confident than maybe I should have been. I responded with 'Look, man, whether you like it or not I'm your ETAC, whether or not we get along … nobody gives two shits.' One of the other team guys told me to put my gear up along the side of the tent and chill out for a while."

The TACP community had assignments within the Army Special Forces (SF) groups, but these were limited in number. Zackery, having been stationed at Bragg, was generally familiar with the Operation Detachment Alphas, and had trained alongside SF teams while deployed to Kuwait. "I spent time supporting Armor, and then I went to Fort Bragg, which was an Airborne unit. Then I had started selection but had done nothing formal to prepare for being on a SOF team, I had no clue what was what or who was who."

The challenge was only just the beginning for Zackery and Martens, among the other FACs adjusting to a whole new side of the military. Zackery was issued a PRC-117F manpack radio, a multiband system which was brand new. "I've never seen this piece of equipment before. Back at the ASOS, we were still using the PRC-113 multiband radio for UHF/VHF, the PRC-113 for VHF/FM, and the PRC-104 to talk long-range HF. The 117F was a 15-pound, multiband portable radio that was the size of three reams of printer paper stacked together. It could conduct VHF (FM), VHF/UHF (AM), and SATCOM communication and had all the new software bells and whistles. They also gave me a device called a Viper, which was the generation before the Mk-VII hand-held laser range finder. Again, never touched one or seen one. They gave me a Suunto watch (the original one with the little bubble in the watch face) and an eTREX Garmin GPS."

TACPs locate targets, mark them, and communicate that information to the aircraft. Everything Zack needed to do the core tasks of his job was handed to him, but it was equipment wholly unknown to him, and for a team that had immediately discounted what he could do to enable their mission. "No stress, right? And it's not like I'm a super experienced guy either, I've been in the Air Force four and a half years at this point. I spent the next few days teaching myself the new equipment, especially the radio. Self-taught by reading the technical manual and just scrolling through the different menu options. I taught myself the GPS, the laser range finder, self-made in the 'fuck things up' category."

Zackery would maximize time training with his new ODA out of simple necessity. The most valuable training, by his assessment, was live-tissue training. Additionally, weapons proficiency and long-distance marksmanship, and demolition training—something which most TACPs, let alone Air Force personnel, never do—rounded out his expanded repertoire. Zackery would use this as an opportunity to teach the team close air support (CAS) basics. The opportunity to demonstrate knowledge of CAS was the beginning of credibility within the team for Zackery. "We also did rehearsals on riding quads (all-terrain vehicles) which would come in handy later. None of this stuff was core competencies for Air Force, right? None of it was on the METL [mission essential task list]. I learned how to do chest tubes and decompressions, cricothyrotomy, the first time I've ever tried a tourniquet on something that is bleeding out and I have to do it right or risk losing the patient."

These intermediary weeks were spent trying to learn all of these "basic" skills upon which one's life and the lives of every American around them—a very small cohort in a foreign country—depended on everyone's ability to do well. And it must be noted that the hierarchical infrastructure for requesting CAS in the later years of the war—the request formats, the Air Support Operations Center doing the allocation process—these things didn't exist. The next problem would be figuring out how they would get CAS when needed. "We had four different methods of requesting CAS, and none of them were reliable, it was all a crapshoot of getting on the radio at the right time and talking to the right body. We had SAT channels, but there simply was not anything like the architecture that cropped up over the next few years."

"One some occasions, such as the times when we were doing the SR [special reconnaissance] detail, we might call back to the team headquarters element itself and ask for CAS, who would then pass it along to the Operational Detachment–Bravo [ODB] or the battalion. Sometimes I would simply push up the request to one of the airborne C2 [command and control] birds who would serve as relay, JSTARs or AWACs, but that wasn't a formal procedure, it was all trial and error while the rest of the defense enterprise was slowly getting its ass into theater. We were already there, trying to make this up on the fly." Whatever structure or architecture that would define the Afghanistan air war for the next 20 years was being conjured up by those men leading the charge into country. This first wave of enlisted terminal attack controllers (ETAC) hadn't been briefed on what it was and were just figuring it out day by day.

After a few days of training, rehearsing, and building cohesion on the team, Zackery and ODA542 finally learned where they were headed: Orgun-E, Paktika Province, right on the Afghan–Pakistan border.

Their task and purpose was to assist the preparation of the indigenous forces for an assault on Taliban strongholds in the eastern province of Khost, bastion of the Haqqani cohort of Al Qaeda. For the infil, they flew on two MH-53 Pave Low helicopters carrying two pickup trucks, courtesy of Toyota of Nashville; Zackery had a B-1 bomber overhead. Additionally, the team had two quads, and an impressive amount of sustainment materiel. The trucks weren't Hiluxes—the iconic small pickup truck that would become synonymous with the climes of Afghanistan over two decades—but regular Tacomas straight from a dealer. Zackery was listening to the B-1 scanning the drop zone as the team was releasing equipment ties-downs in preparation to disembark. They would link up with some other government agency (OGA) teams—CIA paramilitary officers working under the *Jawbreaker* banner—who were already on the ground developing local militia support forces. Standing in for every hot-blooded young American male in 2001, Zackery saw a seeming once-in-a-lifetime opportunity: "I turned to the team sergeant and said 'Look man, I'm only going to get to do this once, let me drive the quad off the ramp into Afghanistan'; it just seemed like a cool thing to do."

The behemoth helicopters set down at an austere patch of dirt more than 150 kilometers south of Bagram, a flight taking nearly five hours. Bagram Airfield was the location for the closest American QRF (quick-reaction force) to ODA542. Nearby in Gardez, other ODAs were establishing similar outposts, but only Bagram had a functional airfield and the logistics necessary to support large ground forces. The distance, and the dominating peaks of the Hindu Kush in between, meant there was no QRF. ODA542 and their Air Force FAC were completely on their own in the most austere and isolated place on the planet, tasked to integrate with ground forces waiting for them at this lonely site on the blackest of nights in southeastern Afghanistan. "No big deal, 'Hold what you got airborne,' so off I went riding this quad, big-ass ruck on my back, talking to B-1s overhead with a big-ass boner."

The team offloaded all the vehicles and equipment, and the Pave Lows quickly pulled collective power on the rotors to leave. The OGA paramilitary officers were indeed there, making light of the scarcely believable scene unfolding—two groups of Americans finding each other in the dead of night. "They took us to some old dude's house, which I'm sure he had been offered cash that was eight times as much as it was worth, just so we would have a bed-down location and initial operations center." ODA542's new home was a small compound with a wall around it, typical of so many Afghan compounds which Coalition forces would clear time and time again. "It was barely big enough for us to cram all of our shit into."

The indigenous militia, or "G-force," that ODA542 was tasked to organize and enable was led by a warlord named Zakim Khan.[5] Working with the agency in this new cooperative effort brought with it some capabilities which, once again, the team had scarcely prepared for. "We had a couple helicopters that were on the level—DoD birds with issued callsigns and all that. And then we had helicopters who were not on a formal tasking list, whose callsign was merely the nomenclature and tail number.[6] For example, "Orgun-E, this is Mi-6 arriving with personnel, equipment, etc., etc." Clandestine aircraft under sterile callsigns is a common paramilitary tactic to avoid compromise of the force in restricted operational zones.

As the Air Force controller, if it flew, it was Zack's responsibility, whether he had trained for it or not. Having attended the Army's Pathfinder School and being certified as a drop zone safety officer, he was prepared for most of these responsibilities. "I would clear their approach and we did business that way—using legit and clandestine air power. The birds would come in, I would run up to the LZ [landing zone] with my quad with one or two of the team guys, mark the touchdown points for each aircraft, and then I'd 'rope'[7] them in using my infrared pointer. Imagine a giant lightsaber beam that reaches out to a kilometer that can only be seen under night-vision goggles, that's how we brought in the birds at night."

The Soviet-built Mi-6 helicopter and the Mi-8/Mi-17 variants are ubiquitous with Afghanistan and, in those early days, Americans were flying these endlessly in the Afghan darkness. These, as well as U.S. military helicopters, brought in goods and

Zackery (left) and a Special Forces soldier training Afghan militia on weapons handling. (Photo provided by Robert Zackery)

materiel, weapons and ammunition, water, and other critical sustainment. Zackery or an SF soldier would high-five the aircrew, bring all the kit back to Orgun-E on the quads, and then immediately return to training the warlord's forces.

Lacking conventional or Western means of identification, vetting the indigenous force soldiers would consist of matching each G-force member with their assigned, American-issued weapons. "We would issue AKs that had been *acquired* for distribution, and the serial number on each weapon would be assigned to each member of the warlord's fighters by name. So, for example, '*Bill*, your AK number is XX-1234, this weapon is your ID card.' And if they didn't come back with the AK that matched the name we had registered for that weapon, well, then we had a problem. That was our entire vetting process."

"And people have spent decades talking shit about how the Afghans didn't want to fight, but we had guys who knew that teaming up with the Americans meant danger to their lives and their families' lives, but they chose to come to us anyway, they chose to fight for their country. We had all manner of people coming in, farmers, regular villagers, old-school Mujahadeen from back in the day, guys who had pushed the Russians out twenty years before. We told them 'Give us your weapons and we'll issue new ones.' It would be necessary to issue new weapons, as many of the warlord's fighters were showing up with their own personal weapons to fight the Taliban. "They came and found us with their Lee Enfield bolt rifles that the Brits left behind. We gave them an AK-47 with a stamped number and told them 'Come back with your gun if you want to get your daily pay.'"

Orgun-E now consisted of four distinct groups working together: the two Agency paramilitary officers, both of whom went by "Mike," the SF team ODA which was piecemeal, the warlord with his entourage—henchmen from a mafia in reality—who were American "protection," and the locally recruited G-force. The locals did not like the warlord's henchmen, the latter achieved local power and influence through violence and intimidation. Meanwhile, the locals recruited into the G-force were emboldened by the fact they were now working for the Americans. There was sometimes tremendous friction between the two groups of Afghans under ODA542's purview.

"One day, one of the team guys and I are packaging gear or some other busy work inside the compound, and the warlord's guys walked up and start running their mouths to the local militias. We didn't speak much Pashtu, but you could understand body language—arms waving, 'Fuck you,' 'No, fuck you'—one of the warlord's guys then went and butt-stroked the G-force guy in the chest with his AK. They both backed away from each other and racked the bolts on their rifles. A breath later, two hundred dudes are all racking their AK-47s and we're stuck right in the middle."

Like many facing the challenge of invading a scarcely known nation on the other side of the world, Zackery had almost no cultural training or knowledge about Afghanistan, its tribes and their rivalries, or the stern dynamic that would confound scholars and experts alike for two decades. "That Special Forces foreign internal defense or irregular-warfare training kind of goes out the window when you're stuck in the middle of a pack of a couple hundred dudes who are about to mow themselves and everyone around them down in a wave of AK fire. The only thing we could do in that moment was vacate the compound. We hauled ass outside of that mounting catastrophe, straight over the compound wall. Word was relayed to Zakim. A few minutes later, he goes into the compound and starts yelling at everyone. It came down to the most rudimentary things of all: 'You guys are costing me money.' So he sorts out the two guys who had gotten in each other's faces, who would be tied together, back to back, hands and feet bound. Then one of Zakim's enforcers just beat the soles of these dudes' feet with a stick, hard enough to break bones. This public humiliation went on for at least two hours. We never saw those dudes again."

The tension boiling under the surface meant the team always kept an American awake. They continued recruiting, building up the G-force, and started preparing for an upcoming operation called Task Force *Hammer* and *Anvil*. The ODAs in Khost and Gardez were *Hammer*. ODA542 would be *Anvil*, setting up shop in the Naqa Valley, just south of the Khost–Ghazni Pass. The plans for this operation were exceptionally complicated, an item of note for Zackery and the ODA team. The proposed timeline for this operation was late January or early February. "The OGA guy who was attached to us smirked at me when I mentioned the insanity of this plan's complexity, and he tells me that this plan was 'created by experts,' and me being the smart-ass from Tennessee I said, 'So was the *Titanic* but look what happened to that.'"

The other SF team at Gardez had faced similar incidents, including a dust-up with those local warlords' forces. Several Afghans had died and several more had been evacuated with significant wounds. As a result of this infighting between militias, the whole plan was delayed until March. *Hammer* and *Anvil* would set conditions for, and ultimately evolve into, Operation *Anaconda*.

The delays would portend a strategic challenge that would hang over Afghanistan for the next two decades: graft. "We spent so much time validating our G-forces after what happened to the team up in Gardez, that the warlords started milking the opportunity: 'If you pay us more money this kind of thing (green on blue) won't happen.' So we did it, we played the game and paid them more. But after we finished *Anaconda*, that warlord up in Gardez disappeared. It wasn't done by Americans, SOF or paramilitary or otherwise, they don't do assassinations. So, something happened to that Gardez warlord that was outside of American purview."

Zackery and ODA542 moved from Orgun-E to a place called Zaraq, where they would experience their first troops in contact. Entering one of the valleys accessing the dominating mountains leading into the Hindu Kush, the G-force was ahead of the Americans. Gunfire began cracking off, and half of the G-force started running back downhill towards the team, the members of which were yelling at them to go back up the mountain. It was a small skirmish, likely not even the Taliban and in all probability just mistaken identity. "Local villagers seeing a huge force coming in didn't care about who's who, bullets are impartial." After this first encounter, no incidents ensued, and the team took over an abandoned school in the village. This compound would serve ODA542 as the mission-support site for *Anvil*. After refining the order of battle to prepare for the push into the mountain passes, they started looking at where and when to employ the special-reconnaissance detail. Being the only air controller in this part of Afghanistan meant Zackery had to go out with those recon elements to prepare the battlespace.

The team had been taking prescribed drugs, including mefloquine for malaria, limited multivitamins, and other prescription medicines to offset sleep deprivation. "We're at the edge of civilization out here, no one has taken a shower in weeks. We're eating local food—goat meat and rice, the naan bread that they stamp flat with bare feet and leave it in the sun to bake on rocks—none of it was clean but it tasted good. The cook who prepared our food didn't wash his hands and probably had dirt under his nails from 1978. But he made some bad-ass rice and beans and we had to eat because we were burning so many calories. I remember an Afghan who we called 'Little John' who brought us bread every day, he was the biggest Afghan I had ever seen, even taller than me at six-foot-four."

Cultural competence would appear from strange places in this strange time too. Zackery, a Black American, has fought the stigma of racism and humble beginnings, but in the military had already enjoyed professional and personal success on account of his initiative and drive. But he remained a Westerner and, at this point in his life, had a Western view of the world. "One day, a couple of the Afghans came to me and said, 'You're not an American,' and I countered, 'Yeah, man, I am American, I'm from Tennessee, bro.'" But the Afghans held firm: "No, you're not American, you are my brother, you see this?" The Afghan man then pointed to his dark skin, and then to Zackery's, "You see this, we are brothers. This Middle East you talk about? There is no such thing.[8] That is something the white conquerors call these places. They have no recollection of history, or respect for people's boundaries. You are either African, Asian, or European. This is Afghanistan, this is part of Africa. That makes us both African, which makes us brothers."

To Zackery, this perspective was profound and stirring. "So, these 'dumb' villagers as the West thinks of them so often, they aren't stupid or ignorant. And it wasn't an anti-white sentiment; they were just stating the facts as they saw it from their cultural perspective."

Zaraq is surrounded by the oppressive Hindu Kush mountains, 10–17,000-foot peaks rimming the valleys, easily some of the most daunting terrain on Earth. Having previously been stationed at Fort Lewis in Washington State, Zackery knew mountains. Mount Rainier is visible from hundreds of miles away at 14,000 feet. In Afghanistan, and particularly where ODA542 would lead a local militia into combat, Mount Rainier would have just been a ridgeline, completely lost among the dominating peaks, many of which exceed 20,000 feet. Those mountains would be occupied too, to the bafflement of the Americans observing them. "At one point, we observed an overt light on a ridgeline. I couldn't tell you the exact location because we couldn't get to it ourselves, but several thousand feet above us, and there is no way a goat herder is that high up. I had tried to get aircraft to go check it out, but they couldn't pick the spot out of these mountain passes. I had even tried requesting a strike just to get more aircraft into the area to look, but all requests were denied." This game of cat and barely seen mouse went on for hours, never resolved. Zackery would learn months later there had been another SOF team, nationality and unit unknown, up there looking into ODA542's valley, trying to call in airstrikes on their location. Without any established command and control inside Afghanistan, everyone looked like the bad guys.

A large force of locals would also occupy the valley, taking over a school, vehicles, weapons, settling in and expanding those forces aligned with the Americans. There was no SOLE (Special Operations Liaison Element) at this time, ensuring coordination between the different SOF teams throughout Afghanistan. Cross talk was entirely absent, and communications proved to be a challenge every day when it came to talking with aircraft. "Not everyone is talking on the same cryptological fills for their secure radios. The Navy F-18s, when we'd get them from the aircraft carriers in the Indian Ocean, were usually workable, but F-15s coming from the bases in the Middle East were almost impossible to communicate with in the green (secured)."

Zackery and the other FACs would work out all these bugs and hitches in real time, not knowing if it was the aircraft, the outstations, the limited C2 from higher headquarters, or the brand-new multiband radio they had acquired a few weeks before being the source of poor comms. "I'm supposed to do my charter mission set—call in close air support, control medevacs, manage airspace—with a Suunto watch, a Garmin eTREX from REI[9] in Tacoma, Washington, a Viper laser range finder that only ranges three kilometers, and a radio I hadn't seen before deploying." The maps available—the most critical piece of equipment for targeting purposes—were hardly usable. Air controllers normally used 1:50,000-scale maps for plotting and reading MGRS (military gridded reference system), but all that was available for Afghanistan were 1:100,000-scale maps written in Russian, meaning topography was much less detailed for correlating terrain features, and it was all written in unreadable lexicon. The datum was not WGS 84 (World Geodetic System globally surveyed in 1984), the most recent global survey, nor was it the alternative NAD 27 (North American datum from 1927). The maps were Russian attempts at staking out elevations and grid lines on incredibly rugged terrain. The teams had been issued WGS 84 overlays that were supposed to correct the grid line and elevation discrepancies, but these were just blurry lines making the maps even more unusable. "Every map we had looked like double vision, and guaranteed every lat/long or MGRS grid read off of those maps was off by hundreds of meters, even if you tried to correlate using the GPS."

The team also began to assimilate local garb and tack to be less obviously identifiable to the suspect Taliban and Al Qaeda informants living in the area. "We wore DCUs in order to adhere to Geneva conventions—military personnel in war have to wear a uniform item—but everything else was local garb, head scarfs, the like." At Zackery's retirement in February 2023, Abel Martens would regale the crowd with a story of meeting Zackery back in K2 post-deployment, describing the latter as having returned with a burly moustache and a "massive Afro … dude was already tall, but with that hair he didn't cut, he was over seven feet tall."

The Shah-i-kowt Valley was the location for the fateful Operation *Anaconda*. Just south of that valley is a funnel through the mountains which opens to the Naqa Valley, which belonged to ODA542 and would serve as *Anvil* for this operation. The plan was for the ODAs in Gardez (Task Force *Hammer*) to push into Shai-i-kowt from the north and demolish the Taliban and Al Qaeda strongholds, pushing whatever forces remained through that funnel where Zackery would go kinetic with airstrikes. During that two-day battle in the valley, on a ridgeline overlooking the funnel, Zackery could hear all the comms from the aircraft preparing Shah-i-kwot Valley for the offensive, but not the forward air controllers on the ground. The immense ridgeline that separated the two spaces impeded any chance for ground-to-ground comms. "I can see the B-52s dropping rows of bombs, the massive array they were releasing from over twenty thousand feet up. When the sun is behind them, they look just like Tic Tacs being poured out of a canister. From sun-up to sun-down and all through the night, non-stop kinetic strikes by the forward air controllers with *Hammer*." Zackery and his ODA teammates had a near-front-row view. Admittedly, Zack wanted to be part of that barrage against the Taliban and Al Qaeda redoubts, but their purpose was to pinch the remaining terrorists in place as they attempted to egress into Pakistan. They could see the explosions which would light up the ridgeline, whose shockwaves would course through the hardest granite on earth beneath their feet.

Zackery, along with two ODA542 team members, had to climb the mountain out of Zaraq to reconnoiter the Naqa Valley. Because air controllers must be entirely self-sufficient, he carried all the equipment thought necessary on his person—batteries, the AN/PEQ-1B SOFLAM (Special Operations Forces Laser Acquisition/ Marking Device) laser target designator with tripod, the five-bay battery pack with five BA-5590s—using a heavy BlackHawk X-1 rucksack with the SOFLAM tripod strapped to the side. All the batteries were stowed in the external dump pouch that came with the kit, 30 pounds in all, slung as a front pack to counterweight the ruck on his back. The ruck weighed 90 pounds alone and with weapon, ammunition, weather gear and all else, his load was more than one hundred fifty pounds of gear. He wore Matterhorn leather boots purchased from REI in Tacoma.

It was freezing cold, snow on the ground, and whatever wasn't covered with snow was frozen as hard as the rocks they were climbing over. "At least our diet was good, and we were getting adequate sleep, right? We called it the Afghan cardio plan. Back then my 'fighting weight' was around 240—I'm a big dude to begin with, big barrel-chested freedom fighter—so with all this equipment, climbing a frozen mountain at almost 400lbs, that's a hell of a workout. I'm from Tennessee; now it ain't Alabama, but I'm hauling this Tennessee Black Snake around too, and that motherfucker is heavy all by itself." The two ODA members weren't nearly as loaded down as Zackery, as they didn't need to bring all the targeting gear, huge radio, extra batteries, but they too were bearing heavy rucks and equipment.

The Zaraq base camp was at 8,200 feet, 2,000 feet higher than Colorado Springs. It takes weeks for the human body to acclimate to major changes in elevation, and the entire team came from Fort Bragg or Fort Campbell, barely above sea level. Though they had been in Uzbekistan for weeks prior to arriving at Orgun-E, setting forth at this elevation was an endeavor none of them were prepared for. "We didn't have strength coaches back then, or dieticians and conditioning programs like there are today. Health and wellness was a different animal back then—we had physical training as simple as 'You have to move twenty miles for this objective, just get there as fast as you can.' So we get to walking, and about ten minutes in I thought to myself 'I'm not going to fucking make it.' I wasn't going to quit, I was ready to keep pushing until my legs fell off, but my body was in such a state that I didn't think it had the literal capability to keep going. So now I am going to be the fucking Air Force guy that let down his ODA, but I just kept going." Another 10 minutes went by, and legs are turning to jelly, and air is coming in ragged gasps from the three men. Thirty minutes into the movement, one of the SF guys said aloud, "Dude, I ain't gonna fucking make it!", much to Zackery's relief. Misery loves company, and sharing the struggle gave each man the motivation to continue. That was a moment where Zackery, still the Air Force outsider with a group of hard-ass Army dudes, truly began to become part of the team.

"There are many events where human beings bond, but three stand out, and I believe that these are critical aspects of this human experience. Those instances are when you *break bread*, when you *break a sweat*, and when you *break skin*. And when you do all three, like when you're eating parasite-ridden goat with these guys, when you're climbing a mountain with them carrying one hundred percent of your body weight, and when you're in a gunfight and spilling blood with them, those are the things that make bonds tighter than anything else in the human experience."

Each man brought water, Zackery opting for a Camelbak bladder, which froze solid within the first hour of the movement, even though he was sweating. The boots, brand new, had not been properly broken in before this climb—hikers will shower in leather boots and wear them all day to speed up the soles conforming to the shape of the wearer's foot and arch. No such luck with these, as no one had showered in weeks. The cold staved off the pain of blisters and foot cramps because their feet had gone numb.

Morale manifests in strange ways in these extreme circumstances. "We had limited entertainment obviously, but someone had brought a portable movie player and one of the movies we had watched dozens of times was *Joe Dirt*. So, as we're walking up this mountain, every crest would end up being a false peak, and the real ridgeline never seemed to get closer. There is a scene in the movie where Joe Dirt is covered in shit, and we paraphrased that scene, continually asking each other 'How much mountain is up there, is it done yet?' just like that scene. We keep walking and wondering how much mountain is up there, how much mountain is on me? You have to laugh to keep from losing your shit, man; it's not gallows humor per se, but if you don't find a way to cope with how miserable you are, then that overwhelming suck will break you."

One ridgeline on the movement was plated shale—the type of rock that cracks when stepped on, that gives way and slides out from under the climber. The team was trying to make a timeline and once committed to this finger of terrain, there was no turning back. Three men shimmying along this sheer face made of brittle, slippery rock, and 300 feet straight down is certain death. The weight of their rucks was pulling each man backwards, who were kissing the wall with faces and hips, leaning in as hard as they could. Each one voiced aloud "What the fuck am I doing here?" More gallows humor, as each would joke to the others, "You know what, the fall wouldn't be that bad, it'd be over quickly on those rocks." They didn't expect to return from this operation—there were too many Al Qaeda flooding into the valley, and the terrain was treacherous in the extreme. "The irony was that this wasn't even the mission, only the movement to get to the place for the mission."

Several hours into the climb, they determined they could not sustain the pace and make it to the OP (observation point) in time. They looked down into the valley from a 9,000-foot perch. Ahead, the terrain became steeper, where a short movement can take hours just to cover a couple hundred meters and, after another hour, the intended ridgeline has gotten no closer. The false peaks were endless, and with every treacherous step Zackery felt as if "all you're ever doing is looking up." The terrain became so treacherous that a 20-foot movement required a five-minute break, because the incline and loose rock was more technical climbing than hiking, each man needing to move on hands and knees, grabbing rock clefts to pull themselves up. They made a tactical decision and called back to the base camp to have several G-force fighters join them to cross-load equipment.

They had given the G-force walkie-talkies to communicate internally. As the Afghans approached, Zackery and the soldiers could hear them long before they arrived, yelling—not whispering or being tactical—into hand radios turned to full volume. By the time they got to the exhausted Americans, the batteries had died from non-stop transmitting. After another brief respite, the Afghan militia helped carry the gear to the top of the mountain where Zackery could see down into the valley. The Afghans put new batteries in and left, talking all the way.

On the first night, Zackery got a call from the command post stating there was a high-value individual who was supposed to be entering the valley. The name of this individual meant nothing to the Americans at that time, but carries the weight of history now. "The intel sergeant stated that an individual going by the name Abu Musab al-Zarqawi was going to be in our line-of-sight; he traveled with a certain number of people, in a particular type and number of vehicles and would be arriving at a specific place in one of the village redoubts in the valley." This was allegedly the same al-Zarqawi the Americans would spend years chasing in Iraq. On this cold night, there was 90-percent confidence in the reporting that he would be moving into the Naqa Valley amid the carnage happening in Shah-i-kowt.

The OP was at 10,400 feet; the three men had never been so cold. They took turns "sleeping" in two-hour increments, with clothes on because at any moment they could get ambushed or compromised. "You're not really sleeping; you're just sitting there with your eyes open. On my first shift during daylight hours, I took out my map, GPS and rangefinder and made a terrain sketch of the valley. I made target reference points and started doing patterns of life. We found the target compound, it had over a dozen children running around, half a dozen women, and we watched them wash clothes, watched the kids play with a soccer ball, just doing human things and being human. We watched this village for two days, waiting for this al-Zarqawi dude to show up."

On the third night, one of the other Americans roused Zackery from dozing to look through the spotting scope as a convoy pulled into the village. An individual in the center of the commotion matched the description for al-Zarqawi, entourage and all. In a war that would be defined by collateral damage, and both real and alleged civilian casualties, Zackery made a decision that would affect the war on a strategic scale.

"I mentioned the pattern of life, watching the women and kids playing because it is a critical point in our mindset on this mission. My uncle was in Vietnam, a mortarman, two rotations with the cavalry and a Purple Heart recipient, his name was Charles Ford. He talked to me about the military a little bit, but not much, like a lot of Vietnam vets. My father-in-law, Manuel Cooper, was also a Vietnam veteran, a Marine infantryman who had been at Khe Sanh, also didn't really talk about his experience. They both told me—separately and unbeknownst to each other—about things to do to stay alive, about not getting attached to people because it makes you think emotionally, irrationally. You can't save your buddy's life if you're dead, you have to sometimes finish the mission and kill the enemy, and then you can do something about your buddy. You have to kill the enemy first. If you get too close to people, you forget to kill the enemy. That was one of the lessons they took from Vietnam."

"They also told me that, in war, in combat, you don't get nightmares from the things that you had to do, you get nightmares from the things that you had the option not to do."

The team was in overwatch on this village, below them a high-value target. Zackery called back to the base camp to confer with the team commander, announcing positive ID on the target, and they received approval yet again to go kinetic at their discretion. "I had an AC-130 and F-15s overhead. I passed nine-lines and had call-for-fire missions prepared, sorted, and passed to the aircraft, all of whom were chomping at the bit to be the ones to go live on this target. I had to assess and make a determination on whether to drop. The team commander stated plainly and clearly 'Zack, it's your call.'"

"But we had kids out there, women and children scattershot throughout the entire complex of buildings. I remember the aircraft reiterating over and over 'ETAC, attack profile is ready.' But in the words of those wise old Vietnam veterans who came before me, you get nightmares about the things that you had the option not to do. And I asked myself, was that one bad guy worth the lives of those women and kids?"

"Hindsight being 20/20, people can judge the decision however they would like. And knowing now who al-Zarqawi turned out to be in the future and the American lives lost because he was still alive is certainly a factor. The fact is, I can't say with certainty that it was in fact al-Zarqawi, we were out there alone and receiving injects from higher headquarters. But I chose not to get an early combat drop, and I called off the airstrike. The target was there, everything was lined up, all I had to do was say 'cleared hot' and that entire village would have been gone, but I chose not to. And I'm ok with that decision to this day. Our job is to take life, it's that simple, but we also have the power in most cases to choose not to. Now, of course, I will never know if that was in fact Zarqawi, all I can go from is the intel from higher on telling us as much. But I could have wiped that village off the map like a dry erase marker from a white board, I had the power and the approval."

They remained at the OP for two more nights, continuing to pinch the fatal funnel in the valley. Radio chatter picked up from Taliban comms portending multiple groups of Al Qaeda who knew the Americans were somewhere up in the high ground, and were climbing out of the valley to find the source of the strikes that had continued killing terrorists fleeing the carnage at Shai-i-kowt. By now, FACs had already become notorious to Al Qaeda, who had put two and two together about heaven's wrath falling to earth 500 pounds at a time. The recon team, with a distinctive operator adorned with antennas and a larger-than-normal rucksack was an unmistakable target, and now they were compromised. "This was long before the *Lone Survivor* incident, but enough teams had been compromised in the days prior, and now we had to make a hasty exfil before being outnumbered by the Taliban and Al Qaeda after a major operation."

As they broke down the OP in preparation to egress on the final day, a random villager walked right up to their hide site. "He had to have known there were Americans up there, and was looking for us, because he had no business being up there otherwise. But then, we had no business being up there either right? This man had a small kid with him, who couldn't have been more than five years old too. So, me and the two team guys have a conversation about what to do now. We still had our mission; do we kill them? Do we kill just the adult? Is the kid going to grow up and be a terrorist if we do? We did not understand that, in Afghanistan or Iraq, just being Afghan or Iraqi didn't mean you were the enemy. We couldn't kill the kid of course, and the adult … who knows right? But we didn't have the benefit of a lengthy philosophical discourse, we can't sleep on it and see how we feel in the morning, we're on a mountain top surrounded by enemy forces and now we are compromised in our hide-sight." They decided to have the Afghans walk with them off the mountain. There was a chance the Afghan male could have walked them into an ambush, prompting Zackery to call back to base camp, let them know of the OP compromise and egress with civilians in lead, and that they might need immediate support.

The team made it off the mountain and linked up with the rest of the ODA at Zaraq. Within fifteen or twenty minutes of dropping kit and trying to regain warmth in their feet, they heard explosions on the side of the mountain ridge, seemingly not far from where their OP had been—the men who had been looking for the

Americans were now firing mortar rounds into the high ground. Yet it was not the gunfights or overwhelming terrain that would stick in Zackery's memory.

"In my office when I was a command chief, I had a little display of one of those jelly slippers that were popular in the 1980s, and it was signed by one of the militia commanders, who has the mate from this pair. His point in giving me this simple piece of foot gear was to always keep things in perspective. In my mind, at least back then, I was a total badass leading an invasion, on a special team with a beard and a baseball cap—all the cliche branding shit; 'tacti-cool.' We started walking off the mountain and I'm the last guy in line. Even today, I wouldn't let a five-year-old child walk across the street back in the U.S. unless I was holding his hand. This Afghan child was walking on cliffs with two-, three-hundred-foot drops, footpaths fifteen inches wide, covered in snow and ice. Places a goat would not traverse. And this kid is behind the adult, so that if he did slip, the older male could not even reach back to catch him, wearing those jelly slippers. And this kid is carrying on like 'This is just a Tuesday.' And I thought to myself, who is the special operator here? Who is the badass? Me with all my cool-guy shit, or this kid walking in the snow at ten thousand feet in loafers like it was nothing? It is all about perspective."

***

"These Afghans had been spilling their blood into Afghan soil for twenty years, hoping, not for themselves, but for two or three generations hence to have some kind of stable democracy. Maybe not some Jeffersonian democracy, but something that legitimized the Afghan state and saw some kind of human rights emerge. There is a human element here, and this is not a political statement, nor an indictment on one party or another. It is meant about everyone involved in the political machine that made the decisions—a lack of integrity. We have people in our government who will not make tough decisions because they're afraid they might lose their job. Or choose to not do the right thing because they may lose clout, their parking space, their title, or prefix, you know, 'the honorable' so and so. They won't make the right decision, and then have the audacity to talk shit about the people who were spending their lives doing the right thing. Over there, because there is no trust, you do not know if the corrupt dude you're dealing with is double-crossing everything that the good guys are doing and working with the Taliban."

"So, of course, the whole thing collapsed in 2021, everyone was making side deals in preparation for when the Americans left. That is all they've ever known, and there were key leaders in D.C. who gave the good Afghans no reason to have any faith in American surety. What else did we expect would happen in that extreme kind of environment? Some dudes bleeding for a better Afghanistan tomorrow, some of them playing both sides of the war, and no constancy coming from Washington or anywhere else."

"How could we be surprised that the ANDSF [Afghan National Defense and Security Forces] fell apart as soon as we started to leave? We gave them high-tech weapons that required complex maintenance, reading technical orders, to people who do not know how to read. That is just one problem that arose in Afghanistan and Iraq, but when you point out one flaw in the strategy, a thousand more problems stem out of it. But it is important to understand, the military complex is not made to build culture and education for a foreign nation, especially not somewhere like Afghanistan where the typical education level for most adults does not exceed primary school, and we expect them to understand detailed technical manuals for maintaining aircraft, radar systems, logistics supply chains? And guess what, the Afghan government, GIRoA [Government of the Islamic Republic of Afghanistan], never went beyond the walls of Kabul."

CHAPTER 5

Rearranging God's Furniture

Air-to-ground Coordination before the War on Terror

Close air support (CAS), at its most basic conceptual level, is the ability to fuse an extraordinarily lethal capability into an otherwise fair fight between two opposing forces. All firepower beyond the soldier's rifle is inherently a force-multiplying capability—with the objective of creating an advantage over the combat power of an individual or opposing group of human fighters. Most importantly, the use of CAS to augment or enable the ground scheme of maneuver is a relatively novel approach to one of the oldest principles of combat: finding and turning an enemy's flank. Air power creates a new flank within a three-dimensional battlefield, whereas traditional warfare may be thought of as a geometric plane between two opposing forces; lethal air power delivered in close proximity and adjustable to changing circumstances creates that third dimension of zones an adversary must defend.

Of course, air power is not a new paradigm in combat; the experimental use of air power for combat augmentation predates even the 20th century. In 1862, the Union Army employed hot-air balloons to aid in the adjustment of artillery fires in the American Civil War. The use of aircraft for aerial-delivered munitions dates to World War I, where dirigibles, biplanes, and other air platforms employed small hand-held projectiles, flechettes, and relatively small bombs on enemy trenches. World War II was the first true iteration of mass air power, when the skies over the European and Pacific theaters were darkened by millions of sorties that employed munitions across the battlefields of history. Air support for ground forces would be qualified first in *Army Field Manual 31–35*[1] in April 1942, identifying "Air Support Officers," "Air Support Party," and "Air Support Missions" as enablers operating on the ground to request, coordinate, and control aerial-delivered munitions to enable the maneuver of ground forces against objectives.

In the Pacific, the integration of air power into a once-exclusive maritime theater of operations fundamentally changed warfare forever, evidenced by the rise of the great floating airstrips known as aircraft carriers. This revolutionary paradigm shift replaced a century worth of instructed and practiced war theory that naval power rested in the titanic ships of the line. Great battleships with ever-increasing artillery were once the standard against which naval power was measured. All other vessels in this doctrine were thought to merely be accessory set pieces to vector the battling fleets to a final, conclusive slugfest. Whoever employed the artillery of the flagships to greater effect would prove decisive. Before World War II, navies had no significant use of air power beyond observation and reconnaissance.

Japan employed ship-borne aircraft to incredible effect, forward-staging offensive aerial firepower to increase the ranges of the fleet and overwhelming the minimal air coverage in adversary ports across the Pacific Rim. The most audacious thrust was the surprise air raid on Pearl Harbor on December 7, 1941. The idea of crossing the widest body of desolation far from logistical support and permanent infrastructure was so anathema to established paradigms of warfighting that the possibility was dismissed on account of its extreme unlikeliness, leading to the United States being unprepared for the attack. While the Imperial Japanese Navy's evolution of the use of ship-borne aircraft initially steamrolled across the Pacific, the industrial titan of the United States would ultimately win the Pacific War, thanks to better logistics and, most importantly, a rapid build-up and development of naval aviation.

In small sample sizes, a version of CAS occurred in different theaters of World War II. This era's use of air power was strategic bombing against industrial epicenters and cities, which led to countless military and civilian deaths. Yet coordinated air support was exercised in the battlefields of the Pacific, in Burma, and when Allied forces crossed the Rhine. In the Korean War, rockets and gun runs from fixed-wing aircraft were requested and coordinated in a limited capacity as United Nations (UN) and Republic of Korea forces fought desperately to dislodge the North Korean communist forces from their sprint across the peninsula.[2] It is notable that, as General Douglas MacArthur's task forces surged north across the 38th Parallel, North Korean leader Kim Il-Sung unsuccessfully lobbied Joseph Stalin for more aircraft to deter UN forces advancing to the Yalu River. Only overwhelming numbers of Chinese communist forces were able to slow the advancing Western liberators. Air power had already proven to be a decisive tool in modern combat.

CAS, by its modern doctrinal definition, first made its appearance in the Vietnam War. This is where the progenitors of the modern joint terminal attack controller (JTAC) make their first marks on the battlefield. Further, it is in this conflict where the coordination of multiple fires platforms—air, artillery, naval surface, and organic weapons—became the foundation for the application of a battlefield multiplier requiring detailed planning and integration. Vietnam showed similar concepts to previous wars' use of air power—carpet bombing with strategically organized mass sorties, and the pre-planned targets with limited adaptability for changing battlefield circumstances. But for the first time in American military task organization, an entire career path was established for air-power experts to be fully integrated into the ground scheme of maneuver with direct influence over the battlespace.

These early air-power experts were known as forward air controllers (FAC). Typically, these were rated officer pilots who were administratively reassigned from their aircraft cockpits to a ground unit. These early cadre were selected as the de facto air-to-ground coordinators, and it was due to the level of comfort (the lack thereof) which air planners associated with the ability of ground forces to "speak aircraft." Simply, entrusting an infantry soldier with three-dimensional integration and comprehension of aircraft capabilities and limitations was untenable for senior Air Force planners. Thus, responsibility for understanding the relation between ground units and air power became an air officer's charge; to do so, such an officer needed to embed with the ground units.

FACs hailed from every flying component of the Defense enterprise—Air Force, Navy, Marine, and Army. They often came from the supersonic fighter community, while plenty hailed from bombers, and the transition to their FAC role was a decided culture shock. The preponderance of air controllers in the Vietnam War often operated as solo pilots in small Cessna O-1A Bird Dogs, a single-engine aircraft, or the twin-engine Cessna O-2A Skymasters. The aircraft were not typically armed with offensive weaponry. Rather, they were outfitted with a salvo of white phosphorous (WP) 2.75-inch rockets, dubbed "Willie Pete," and a communications suite comprising three radios requiring manual switching between the handset and the transceiver for communications between High-Frequency for long-distance, Very High-Frequency (VHF) for air-to-ground communications, and Ultra High-Frequency for air-to-air coordination between the FAC and supporting aircraft. While few dramatizations in media recognize the feats of superhuman proficiency achieved by the FACs, 1988's *BAT21* with Gene Hackman and Danny Glover admirably depicts these airborne air controllers with aplomb.

To control CAS in the jungles of southeast Asia, the FAC would first have to perform basic mission coordination with the ground force before the mission—timelines, locations, scheme of maneuver, ground commander's desired effects, radio frequencies, and an intelligence picture of the enemy and expected responses as a result of the mission. Further, the FAC would have to research and understand the broader air picture—available sorties with appropriate munitions, locations and flight times of those sorties, air frequencies, request parameters, and gaps in air coverage. Additionally, the FAC would still be required to perform pilot duties and responsibilities—confirming proper maintenance and airworthiness, fuel and load out, properly configured radios and cryptological radio fill keys, maps and air-transit restrictions, and airspace coordination.

These responsibilities repeated every mission, even the on-call, patrol sorties as part of the air-coverage plan which did not always coincide with supporting a specific ground force. Once prepared to support the aligned ground unit, the FAC left the staging base at the allotted time block and proceeded to the mission area. Once the FAC navigated through the congested Vietnamese airspace, they would patrol overhead to assess the battlespace for possible enemy activity. If identified, the FAC would switch to the VHF radio and contact nearby ground units, attempting workable comms with the friendly party. At this point, the FAC and the ground unit would coordinate locations of friendly and enemy positions and establish priority of fires if appropriate.

When combatant forces converged, the FAC's job was to maintain situational awareness of the friendly ground forces maneuvering through the dense vegetation of the Vietnam jungle, while proactively scouting and relaying updates on enemy scheme of maneuver, assessed strength and arrangement, and serve as the conduit for all information between the ground force, himself, and sortied fast-mover aircraft providing aerial fires. In many circumstances, communications with the ground unit were barely functional, leaving air coordination to depend on inference and guesswork, achieved only by the extreme low-altitude operability of the FAC in a vulnerable aircraft.

Delivery of fires would seldom be executed using map plots and coordinates, but rather via "talk-ons," where the observer (the FAC) would identify notable terrain features presumably visible to the attack aircraft above and, using cardinal directions, measurement references, and other ad-hoc terminology, attempt to put the other pilot's eyes on the intended target. Occasional use of "Willie Pete" rockets for a direct target mark offered some advantage, but the coordination between the ground and the air in this era still left much to chance—especially when entire salvos of direct-fire high-explosive rockets, machine-gun engagements, and 250-lb-plus free-fall bombs were landing near friendly forces engaging the adversary.

Fratricide was all-too common in this era of air power. The weapons, integration, and square-peg-to-round-hole alignment between FACs and ground units were the influencing factor, as was the lack of formal, doctrinal methodology between the air and the ground.

After the latter years of Vietnam, and entering the 1980s, enlisted terminal attack controllers began to assume the final control duties once assigned to those fighter and bomber pilots. These officers were originally accompanied by an enlisted assistant—a radio operator, maintainer and driver—who drove the ground vehicle outfitted with the high-powered radio pallet which enabled long-distance communications between the ground and the aircraft. What this organizational shift enabled, to the benefit of the entire CAS community, was the early generation of dedicated, permanent air-to-ground integration.

The establishment of enlisted air controllers into the task organization of the command-and-control enterprise is the ancestry to the modern JTAC. The term would become a doctrinal certification that was not beholden to Air Force personnel or pilots. Members from every one of the services—soldiers, sailors, and Marines—would send occasional personnel from their special-operations components to complete the requisite standardized training to perform CAS.

The preponderance of JTACs would remain the Air Force's main contribution to the air–ground tribes, however, even as the demanding training and requirements would limit the available airmen to integrate across the Department of Defense's request for forces to perform the duty.

An important dynamic to explore is the relationship between the Air Force FACs and their aligned Army unit. In most circumstances, due to the limited availability of FACs, these would often be the sole Air Force member on the ground assault force. While FACs typically serve as the lynchpin of situational awareness and the conduit of communications between air and land, they do not fit into any broader military community. To their Army counterparts, they will always be "the Air Force guy," although, once established, become folded into the small ecosystem that is the ground assault force, appreciated and respected for their abilities, so long as they prove themselves dependable and competent every single day. Their Army team trusts them but understands the potential for disaster which the FAC wields at their fingertips.

To the Air Force writ large, JTACs are always viewed through a cautious, if not overly distrusted, manner—being a scarcely understood weapons system within the Air Force architecture—by their fellow airmen. Typically, the Air Force enjoys a different standard of living and conduct, the likes of which often stands in stark contrast to the field conditions for which the Army has a particular predilection. For a member of the Air Force to willingly subject themselves to the Army lifestyle, it makes the FAC anathema to expected Air Force norms. Further, many Air Force personnel are unlikely to see combat—their purpose is to enable the tremendous air-power capabilities of their service: maintenance of aircraft, weapons loading, intelligence, cyber, and logistics. CAS does not happen without those countless other Air Force occupational specialties performing their assigned duties, but only a handful of airmen are directly involved in combat—predominantly the JTACs who wear the camouflage garb of their Army partners.

The dynamic is much deeper than simply wearing the uniform of another service's colors. In nearly every instance, Air Force tactical air control party (TACP) units are located on Army bases, serving as geographically separated units from their Air Force higher headquarters at air bases. By colocation, TACPs become fully embedded in the day-to-day operations, training, and sustainment of their aligned Army units. On the conventional side, TACPs will participate in most, if not all, major training exercises put on by their counterparts, and a daily routine involves TACP inside the walls of their partner units' battalions and line companies. In the special-operations realm, TACP spend more time in the company walls of their Ranger and Special Forces teams than in their own squadron. No major training exercise or special training occurs without JTACs integrated into the preparation and execution of these mission-essential development events. Combat control units (special tactics squadrons) are often geographically distanced from Army partner force units, yet those airmen spend as much time as possible integrated with their counterparts.

In many instances, the TACP may be older and have more experience than his supported ground-force commander (GFC)—often, a 1st lieutenant in command of their first platoon. Because the JTAC has already experienced working with platoon and company leadership, that repository of the JTAC–GFC dynamic is a critical aspect in developing the young Army leader, who now faces the potential authority to authorize the use of the most devastating weapons on the modern battlefield. The platoon sergeant serves as the most important member of the Army maneuver team—ultimately responsible for ensuring the team functions, meets readiness standards, and holds the distinction of being the most experienced member of the platoon. Thus, trust between the JTAC and the senior enlisted member of the platoon is every bit as critical as the dynamic with the GFC. Any FAC worth their salt takes great pains to learn the names and backgrounds of as many members of the platoon and company as possible. These lives are likely to be in the air controller's hands at some point in the future; the close-knit familial nature of these small ground forces directly contribute to how the JTAC is received and integrated into their tribe.

The young GFC who, in later years of the war, was usually a captain-grade company commander (though in earlier years was just as likely to be a young platoon leader/lieutenant), is expected to understand the basic components of wielding CAS, but the doctrinal-level expertise rests with the JTAC. The exchange between the two is a fluid conversation—the GFC receives battlefield updates from the aircraft via the JTAC, while conducting their own battle tracking through the inter-team command net. With this picture in mind, the GFC begins to nominate targets and problems, the JTAC provides air-power options for resolving those problems. Enemy personnel in the open far away from friendlies—while still posing a threat—may not require an entire bomb bay worth of munitions from a heavy bomber. The JTAC is the expert who understands a gun run from attack helicopters may pose the most effective answer to the problem, which must be expressed to the GFC quickly under the duress of combat.

As the relationship and trust deepens, the ground commander relies on the insights of the air controller. Ultimately, the commander defines intent, the desired effects, and the controller has to figure out how to achieve it or provide alternatives if the available air power cannot resolve the issue. Restraint, then, is the hallmark of a good air controller. There are, on occasion, instances where the JTAC must advise "no," especially in circumstances where a younger and less-experienced GFC may wish to employ fires in situations which call for limited interdiction. Because the controller occupies a unique position outside of the Army chain of command, but is responsible for providing the overwhelming capabilities the Air Force possesses, they operate as an objective voice. The trust between the controller and the Army team and its leaders is what permits the "no" in those most challenging of moments.

CHAPTER 6

"Holy shit, I just killed Afghanistan"

The following interview with Matt Achey, a retired TACP, highlights a variety of critical contextual points in this broader anthology on the role of air power in the War on Terror. Specifically, Achey's story emphasizes the sheer lack of coordination and architecture in the early stages of the war. Plenty of official narrative has been established related to the order and execution of Operation "Anaconda," the mission to fully uproot the Taliban and Al Qaeda forces dug into the Shah-i-kowt Valley in eastern Afghanistan, and former CENTCOM commander General Tommy Franks qualified the operation as "an unparalleled success, but one where the plan did not survive first contact with the enemy." The reality is that the operation was far less effectively planned than memoirs and novels would have it seem.

Notably, the command-and-control infrastructure, both for the ground forces and the air components assigned to support the effort, were a convoluted matrix where the battlespace commander and senior-most ranking American officer, Major General Frank Hagenbeck of the 10th Mountain Division, did not have total operational control of all maneuver and air forces assigned to the clearance of the valley. As noted by Richard Kugler in a comprehensive National Defense University case study of the operation:

> Considerably less attention, however, was devoted to preparing for tactical air support of Operation Anaconda in the event that large numbers of air strikes became necessary. This was the case largely because the operation was viewed by Task Force Mountain and CFLCC [Coalition Forces Land Component Command] as being mainly a ground assault in which air forces would play only a minor supporting role. Thus, the ground and air components did not enter the battle with an accurate common operational picture of how events actually would transpire, and of the critical role that the air forces would be compelled to play. CFACC [Combined Forces Air Component Command] and CAOC [Combined Air Operations Center] were not involved in the initial planning and officially became aware of the impending operation only when General Hagenbeck's operations order was issued February 20. Air Force liaison officers assigned to Task Force Mountain were more involved, but did not exert a great deal of influence over the plan. Initially they proposed heavy saturation bombing of the valley for two days before ground forces entered it, but although this idea was supported by CFACC/CAOC, it was rejected by Army officers because it would compromise surprise, thus enabling enemy fighters to flee before the ground assault began.[1]

Achey's story, told with no shortage of hard-earned contention for the lack of joint force preparation and planning, demonstrates the tremendous and dynamic requirements made of forward air controllers from the earliest phases of the war during one of its most chaotic and disorganized sequences of the 20-year campaign.

Achey was a senior airman (E-4) with Charlie Company, 1/87 Infantry Regiment, 10th Mountain Division, at Fort Drum in New York State. When the company learned of their role in Operation *Anaconda*, it was assumed the "shooting war" was over, all the hard parts were done, and the special-operations (SOF) teams had done most of the heavy lifting. *Anaconda* was supposed to be 10th Mountain's chance to acquire some operational experience, and all assumed it was for publicity. "I hate to say that there was complacency, but it is the truth, and there was plenty of that. We were supposed to have gone in there, brought some humanitarian component with us and a bunch of signs in Pashto that said, 'U.S. forces here, if you cross this line we will use lethal force.' We would do some stability ops, enable the signals intelligence [SIGINT] teams, but no one thought we would be the pivot in a major offensive operation."[2] They went into the valley on March 2, 2002, anticipating a quiet venture in an austere valley.

At the turn of the century, tactical air control parties (TACP) doctrinally consisted of a two-man team: an enlisted terminal attack controller (ETAC), the senior-ranking and more experienced airman, and a ROMAD (radio operator, maintainer, and driver), primarily the radio operator and not qualified to perform terminal attack control, i.e., "final clearance." The ROMAD was ordinarily embedded with a company or platoon maneuver element, while the ETAC would remain with the ground-force commander for coordination and overall control. Having a ROMAD out "forward" would provide the ETAC with someone who could speak the close air support (CAS) language and provide more accurate front-line-trace information and target data for the controller.

Achey's battalion only deployed ETACs in support of *Anaconda*, meaning he and another ETAC, who would serve as the battalion air liaison officer, went in with Charlie Company. *Anaconda* was supposed to be the convergence of two major movements, previously named Task Force *Hammer* and Task Force *Anvil*. The 1/87th was intended to be part of the *Anvil* effort as blocking positions, while the various the SOF teams were to be the *Hammer*, pushing Taliban and Al Qaeda forces out of the valley while the blocking positions sealed the southern edge.

Charlie Company was supposed to land early in the morning under cover of darkness, but the difficulty and inexperience moving that many people via helicopters meant the force didn't infil until well after sunrise. The first indicator something was wrong became immediately evident after departing Bagram and on initial approach into the target area. Unexpectedly, all the door gunners started shooting; these weren't test fires—the aircrew were actively engaging targets. None of the ground force shivering in the cargo bays knew what was happening, and nothing had been briefed in advance, leaving no expectations for enemy contact this early. Across the war, helicopters seldom flew without being shot at, even errantly, but this was a new experience for Achey and the men of the 1/87th. "You had guys in the belly of the helo looking at each other and yelling 'What the hell is that?' I looked out the window and saw the AH-64 attack helicopters break off suddenly and had no idea why. I don't want to say that we were out of it, or nonchalant about the ordeal, but we had no idea what to expect."

Achey was seated in the far back of the bird, by the ramp, templated to be the first to step off the Chinook. As near as he could tell, the only reason the Army bothered to bring him along was because of his radios. "They did not really comprehend or understand what this Air Force guy was doing with us, other than my ability to do communications. All we expected is that we would encounter maybe a couple hundred villagers with families in tow, everyone would surrender and that would be that. That would be about as inaccurate of an assumption as possible."

The helicopters set down on the LZ (landing zone) at 9,000-feet elevation. Having barely rehearsed helicopter off-loads, the force rushed to get off the birds, overburdened with equipment. "The Chinooks manage to offload everyone in piles and take off, and we are all facing south. At the crest of a small terrain change, well outside of small-arms range, we see a random male just standing there waving his arms. One of our personnel started waving a signal panel in response—we have no idea who this cat is, so taking the chance that he might be friendly, we opted to try and communicate with him at first." At that moment, reality set in; a burst of gunfire from the high ground, and the scenario immediately devolved into the anarchy of an ambush.

"I did not even start shooting back right away. I've never heard what gunfire aimed at me sounded like, so I'm still absorbing this change in the environment. Some of the more senior Army NCOs [non-commissioned officers] in the company had been in Somalia before this, and at least knew what those buzzing sounds meant. Those few started getting everyone down, behind cover, get the company on-line and shooting back at wherever we were being engaged from. And here I am, the clueless dipshit airman, trying to remember where in the fire team wedge I was expected to be, what I'm supposed to do for immediate action drills. I'm lugging around all my equipment in this fiasco." Eventually everyone managed to take cover, resulting in a short lull in the gunfire.

The American infantry company had two Canadian liaison officers with them, who started yelling that the first individual they had seen was a friendly. Unseen to Achey, that individual had also been waving a signal panel in response but, when first contact occurred, everything went haywire, and that first individual didn't weigh heavily on the scale of issues they needed to address in the immediate interim.

"That should frame the dynamic for this entire mission—we barely managed to land the assault force, had almost no situational awareness of who was near us, and we're trying like hell to orient ourselves." Eventually, the command team got the company moving south towards their assigned blocking positions: BPs *Heather* and *Ginger*. These were at the very southern end of the valley, facing north with eyes on Marzak Village. Takur Ghar dominated the scene to the ground force's right side (east). They had barely begun moving as a cohesive formation when mortar rounds began landing near and in between elements, as well as rocket-propelled grenades (RPG) streaking down from the high ground.

"In my fire team wedge, I was on the far left—that's where the squad leader wanted me to be so that's where I went. But this meant that I'm closest to the people shooting at us from high ground. I hate to keep reiterating the point, but the sounds and sensations of being shot at for the first time were such novelties to all of us, and especially me, that I didn't know how to react. At some point it clicks in my head, when we have turned towards the high ground to our east, and I took cover behind my ruck like we were trained to do." The force was looking through optics, but in that terrain were unable to make out anything but muzzle flashes. "For a moment I hesitated—the reality that I'm engaging in combat is slapping me in the face now. Do I need to get someone's permission before I pull this trigger? But in that instant it all came together, I started shooting back, aiming for the muzzle flashes. The novelty wore off."

Few on the ground force could pick out a solid target. Achey would regularly look behind his prone body to see how everyone else was oriented. These first few glances showed the company on-line and still stationary under fire. "My element was at the back of the formation, the northernmost part of the company as it had pushed south to seal off the valley. I can finally make out one insurgent clearly, a moment where he exposed himself to engage our formation. He is shooting and I'm shooting back, and I got the guy ... eventually. Took more than a couple of shots but I am still proud of making the shot at that distance with my standard-issue M4." After a few more minutes of intermittent gunfire, the sound of mortars began again. The thuds and thumps were faint at first, further south, but it soon became obvious that those rounds were impacting closer and closer. "At one point I thought I could even hear the 'whump' of the round leaving the tube, which made me think 'Damn, I must be close to that tube.'"

The mortar rounds came from multiple positions all along the ridgeline and, finally, one of them landed right on Achey. "I had the cogency to think to myself 'Well, this is it,' this is the end; it was loud, and it hurt like hell. One minute I was in the prone behind my rucksack, and the next I'm sprawled over it looking backwards at the world upside down. After a brief haze passes, I can see Army dudes running—away from me—and that hit me in a way that even the mortar round did not." His seeming final thought then was "If dudes are running away from me, then that mortar round did enough damage that I'm not worth saving." "I told myself that I would die quietly, I'm not going to be some screaming nightmare for somebody else, I'll just go quietly into the dark."

"And I was a little pissed off in what I thought were my final moments on this earth. None of us wanted to go into battle without making a difference, and I was going to be the guy who got killed in the first few minutes." Achey's thoughts would turn macabre in the bizarre situation; even though only a few minutes would pass, it seemed like an eternity. "I knew for certain that I didn't want some fat senior NCO going to my mom's house and telling her what happened, yet I still visualized that entire scenario unfolding. I had all kinds of stupid regrets about my short life, not many regrets, but there were some."

It was basic body functions that would break Achey's inner monologue. "I had to pee so bad. On the flight in, I drank a huge bottle of water and really had to piss, but as soon as we landed everything went crazy. I didn't want to look down, because I was afraid that if I saw my injuries, then the pain would arrive. I was in shock and wanted to stay that way, I was going to just bleed out and let it be over." Waiting in silence, he could hear the firefight continuing apace, increasing in intensity. "I'm at peace with what is about to happen, because what else am I going to do at this point?"

"I finally relaxed enough to relieve myself, I wasn't sure where or how it was going to come out, but I started taking a piss right then and there because why not? It happens after you expire anyway, right? Then I could feel my pant legs getting wet, which means I could feel my legs, so maybe my legs weren't injured that bad. So my next thought was 'Fuck, I just pissed myself for nothing.'" He slowly lifted the tips of his boots up to inspect them, and realized feet were still attached to legs, and the legs still worked. He had somehow, miraculously, survived a near-direct impact from a mortar explosion and, barring a few scrapes and cuts, could still fight.

The rucksack and the radio took the brunt of the blast, as well as small-arms rounds. Even more miraculously, the radio—a PRC-117F—still worked. His next step was to get on the radio, using the assigned strike net, and get hold of the AH-64s overhead, whose call sign was *Killer Spades*. Achey could hear them on his headset, but they could not hear him. "I was able to get comms with the other TACP on the ground with 1/87. He was pissed off, asking where I was, and I told him that I was still on the LZ and hadn't moved very far. Of course, that wasn't the time to tell the story about riding a mortar round onto my rucksack, and his next comms was telling me to move to where he was. I have no idea where he is because I just spent the last few minutes pondering what I thought were my last moments and have no idea where everyone has gone. I have an assumption that the company has moved 'behind' me someplace."

By now, the sky overhead was saturated with aircraft and, looking north, Achey could see helicopters moving south, the door gunner clearly visible with his crew-served weapon. "So I'm waving my arms and hoping that he doesn't decide to just open up on me. Those helicopters immediately broke off, headed west, and started razing the ridgeline where we had been taking small-arms fire. I took that as an opportunity to get up, grab my stuff, sprint south, and try to find the rest of the company."

Charlie Company consolidated in a large bowl a few hundred meters south of the LZ, and Achey stumbled through the uneven terrain, eventually finding the headquarters element for Charlie Company. Those in the bowl were all wondering where he has been this whole time, and Achey opted to keep those details vague, "Pinned and couldn't move until now." With the ground force consolidated, none of the radios seemed to be working. Company command had been trying to communicate via SATCOM using the 117F, but the radio key-switch had been set to "Plain Text" instead of "Cypher-Text." Even though they were loaded with cryptological fill keys and could be heard by anyone on that channel, they couldn't hear everyone else talking through their crypto-fills. The PRC-117F was new to everyone. Neither the soldiers nor the older forward air controllers (FAC) had taken the time to learn how this new radio worked; few had even seen them before. Fewer still had spent time learning this equipment before hitting the ground in Afghanistan. "Back in those days, radios were the ROMAD's job. Us younger dudes who were new ETACs still treated the equipment as if we were ROMADs and knew it more intimately."

After several minutes of hasty troubleshooting, Achey managed to sort the radios and establish comms. The other TACP asked for a GPS, but all of Achey's FAC-equipment was in the ruck that had taken a direct mortar impact, including the GPS stowed in a side-pouch, which had been shredded by small-arms fire. They needed a GPS to start calculating impact points for CAS attacks on the ridgeline, but the only other GPS, a PSN-11 PLGR (Precision Lightweight GPS Receiver), had been given to the company fire support officer (FSO). As soon as the gunfight started after unloading the helicopters, an RPG landed right next to the FSO, who had dropped the navigation device. When inquired, the officer told Achey he had seen it lying on the ground next to a signal panel, a bright pinkish-orange overt marking device carried by all Coalition personnel.

"Well, someone had to run back up to the LZ and go retrieve it, and guess who that person ended up being? I run up to the lip of the bowl where everyone is still shooting back, and I find a young soldier laying on his SAW machine gun. I tapped him on the shoulder and told him that I needed to sprint back to the LZ and find this missing piece of equipment. He responded with a 'Roger, Sergeant'—because I guess my senior airman stripes made him think I was an NCO—and asked what I needed. I needed covering fire for this thunder run back to the LZ, so I can try to find this signal panel and hope to hell the PSN-11 is sitting there next to it. 'On the count of three, we go,' and I started running. He didn't fire at all."

Halfway down the terrain towards the LZ, the enemy fire increased dramatically. At this point Achey had become intimately familiar with what near misses sound like, so it certainly seemed like the lion's share of attention from the insurgents on the ridgeline focused on his rush back to the LZ. Zigzagging across the open space, he managed to retrace his steps without getting shot. As luck would have it, the GPS was indeed on the ground right next to the discarded signal panel. Wasting no time, he circled back on the other side of the small terrain to get back to the bowl where everyone else was.

"Here is what pissed me off about that whole episode: I ran out there to grab this military GPS, but I had one of those brand-new Garmin eTREX civilian GPSs, those blue ones you'd get from the outdoor store, and it was strapped to my wrist. It was the coolest thing ever back then; all of the SOF guys were rocking them, and our squadron commander had approved purchasing several for those of us who supported this operation. Before I chased down the PSN-11, I suggested using that eTREX to project waypoints for targeting grids, but that was shut down immediately." Once returned to the C2 (command and control) element, Achey began working on range-calculations for the ridgeline, preparing airstrike briefs to regain fire superiority.

Even though Achey had the radios adjusted properly, none of the air nets were functioning. But some implicit knowledge beaten into all FACs are the emergency Guard frequencies,[3] which aircraft are required to always monitor, even downrange. "I had heard over and over through tech-school that all aircraft monitor this frequency. You are not supposed to transmit on it, so on and so forth, unless it's an emergency. But I think I'm going to be slick here and pretend to be an aircraft, declare an in-flight emergency using my ETAC callsign (*White Lightning*) and just get someone to respond to me." The first aircraft to respond was a Navy P-3 Orion, a four-engine turboprop surveillance and anti-submarine aircraft, orbiting overhead and collecting SIGINT. But the ground force finally had an aircraft they could talk to on the strike net. "I didn't wait for him to give me any kind of aircraft check-in, I started diving into who I was and what I needed assets to do for me—'This is *White Lightning*, my position is at this grid, I have targeting solutions for enemy locations along "The Whale," request aircraft type and ordnance available'—the pilot came back to me saying 'I'm a P-3 Orion, I have four Beretta 9-mm pistols aboard with 60 rounds apiece—not sure what effects we are able to provide but we will do what we can.'"

Amid all that chaos, the new sensations and experiences, and having just walked through an ambush, a mortar impact, and everything else, one smart-ass pilot making a little joke got Achey out of the mental lurch he was stuck in. Of all the things to happen in a new war, this small comedic slight broke the tension and he was able to refocus. "I relayed that joke to everyone else standing in our makeshift TOC [tactical operations center], but no one else thought it was funny."

The P-3 relayed their situation update back to the command-and-control platform nearby, (callsign *Bossman*), who relayed to the CAOC (callsign *Kmart*) back in Qatar. After multiple actions to confirm Achey was indeed *White Lightning*, the hodge-podge of aircraft relays notified the FAC he was getting a B-52 (*Tremor62*) routed for support. Ten minutes before the bomber arrived, Achey scrambled around the bowl trying to find the battalion commander, a lieutenant colonel, to notify him of CAS inbound. "The Army guys were dealing with quite a few casualties from the ongoing mortar fire, by then at least a dozen wounded soldiers. I told the commander that we were going to bomb the ridgeline, but all I really got from him was a shrug and dismissive 'okay.' It wasn't really a yes or no, so when I got back to the company element, as far as any of us could tell we were good to send it."

Tremor62 checked in on the strike frequency with 27 unguided 500-lb bombs, and twelve 2,000-lb GPS-guided GBU-31 JDAMs. Achey and his fellow FAC passed all the targeting information and notified the aircrew of their estimated position, west of the line of targets and about four hundred meters away. Their maps were old Russian-made surveys using geodetic datums from 1927, meaning none of the grids were particularly precise or accurate. "I grabbed one of the M240 gunners, who had some kind of optic on his machine gun with drop-compensator reticles, and asked for his best distance estimate based on where his shots impacted. For that volume of munitions, we briefed it as "Danger Close." It was wonky the way we executed that strike—I did all the map and GPS work to calculate the target grids, the other air controller passed all of that information, but I ended up being the one saying "Cleared hot" on the mic. There was a weird stigma hanging over the battlefield within the TACP community, because it was just a few months prior to this mission that the PLGR incident occurred down south (see Introduction, "The Most Dangerous Thing"), and we were about to rip dozens of these bombs on targets I had calculated with that very same piece of equipment."

The approach of a B-52 in the clear Afghan sky is like seeing a freight-train coming down the tracks. The huge aircraft's contrails appear to rip a seam in the atmosphere. Once all final details for the strike were briefed and clearance provided, *Tremor62* came in south-to-north, the only time a Coalition aircraft used that attack direction on the day. Time of flight for the bombs was over three minutes, longer than normal attacks for these weapons on account of the high altitude. "I was nervous because we were going to drop all twenty-seven of those 500-lb bombs on the first pass—thirteen thousand, five hundred pounds of ordnance landing within a one-kilometer stretch. I don't think anyone who hasn't experienced that kind of firepower can truly imagine or appreciate what that felt like, it was wild to say the least." The targets were close and higher in elevation than Charlie Company. The unguided bombs used point-detonation, meaning no extraneous shockwave going upwards, the fragmentation did that. The force of the explosion went straight down, right into the granite-hard rock of eastern Afghanistan's most daunting mountains.

"It felt like we were riding an earthquake. I thought to myself 'Holy shit, I just killed Afghanistan.'"

The ground force could still hear fragmentation and rock falling a minute after impact, but the incoming fire had stopped. Company command assumed this would be the chance to move all the wounded personnel to the center of the bowl. No sooner had the teams started maneuvering in and around the bowl than enemy fire began again. Achey requested an immediate reattack from *Tremor*, this time putting all 12 of the 2,000-lb JDAMs on the backside of the ridgeline. It would become apparent here, and soon after the battle, just how many fighting positions and tunnels had been carved into that piece of terrain. "Even with the devastation we had just unleashed, there was no chance we would get a completely clean sweep of the enemy with that first pass, but it was worth trying to get fire superiority."

Charlie Company had brought one mortar tube with them, a 120mm, but as soon as the force made initial contact, the mortar and crew took a near-direct impact from incoming fire which fractured the baseplate and injured the entire mortar crew. Achey turned control over to the other ETAC and started grabbing ammo cans and carrying them to the gun positions around the lip of the bowl. Once the gunners had been resupplied with ammunition, he started collecting casualty information alongside the medics so he could prepare a medical-evacuation brief.

At the direction of the CAOC, all parties transitioned from the Guard frequency back to the allocated strike net, in order to keep everyone on one net for situational awareness. This would be another manifestation of old doctrine, one where CAS was used against Soviet tank hordes and asset allocation was based on priority of fires. In Afghanistan, gun fights, even those as complicated as *Anaconda*, would dictate that different controllers needed their own fires nets and a coordination net to deconflict airspace. The CAOC made this change to keep track of who was doing what. After *Tremor62* was off-station, Achey retook the fires net just as a set of F-15s rolled in, callsign *Habu*, which was another source of confusion. "The name is from a venomous Japanese snake. I had never heard that word before, and I kept calling them all kinds of weird names in confusion, things like 'Have you,' eventually I just started calling them 'Dash-1' and 'Dash-2.'"

Habu had been assigned to another mission but, having heard the previous strikes with the B-52, re-rolled to support Charlie Company. They would prove to be better than *Tremor* in terms of helping the controllers ascertain targets, flying with Low-Altitude Navigation and Targeting Infrared for Night/Advanced Targeting pods. "They could look at the ridgeline with a sensor. They also had a full loadout of laser-guided bombs (LGB), so we could pick targets and have a relatively decent chance of putting their bombs on a specific target instead of Vietnam-style carpet bombing."

Achey gave vectors based on where the B-52 bombs had hit, which had left huge scorch marks in the snow—a useful target reference point. From those "stakes,"

Habu would scan until they found occupied enemy fighting positions, which the controllers would confirm using both talk-ons and map correlation. Once the pilots were confident of each target, Achey brought them in north-to-south and hit each with a single GBU-12, a 500-lb LGB.

Some Cold War training would pay off in this battle. "One thing we trained on religiously at Fort Drum was the 'Smoky Sam' drill: where aircraft would do a CAS engagement, and the range would simulate the launch of a surface-to-air missile [SAM]. The brevity term ETACs are trained to say immediately is "Smoky Sam!" with a direction from a known point on the battlefield. They do this so the pilots have an idea of where it came from and where to break off to. After one pass, I saw a bright-white smoke trail, which I thought was weird … it looked just like those Smoky Sam simulators back on the range. 'Oh, shit, SAM launch, SAM launch, 6 o'clock low from your target!'" *Habu* immediately kicked afterburners and tore straight up into the sky, throwing out flares in a brilliant display. "I don't want to piss on the *Top Gun* movies, but what most people don't realize is that flares aren't going to defeat a lot of the SAM threats out there. I asked to Dash-2 if he had seen where the smoke trail originated from and, if so, then he was approved to engage." *Habu-2* did indeed see the launch site and rolled in on an immediate strike, but the ground force was not able to determine if the strike killed the insurgent who fired the SAM.

Soon enough, they were out of bombs, and gave a battle-damage assessment and check out to Achey. "I asked them if they had loaded their M61A1 20-mm cannon—a six-barreled gatling gun that fires about 6,000 rounds per minute—and, after a brief pause, they confirmed. So we got a few more attacks off, using an air-to-air weapon for a ground attack. I cannot confirm this, but I'm certain this was one of, if not the first time an F-15 had pointed its nose at the ground and used that 20mm to engage a ground target in Afghanistan." The M61A1, found on the F-15, F-16, and F/A-18, is mounted inside the aircraft on a 6-degree upward cant. It is an air-to-air weapon, thus, when firing at an enemy aircraft, the projectiles drop off due to the distance. The upward-cant design compensates for the drop while dogfighting at hundreds of miles per hour. For a ground attack, this maneuver is extremely difficult as the pilot must perform an even-steeper dive due to the shells leaving the barrels at an incline. It also means the pilots have less time to recover from the dive and get back to altitude.

Gun runs complete, the ground force began to assess effects. Many of the aircraft assigned to *Anaconda* had been flying with tactical datalink, an aerial network used by airborne command-and-control systems to track and identify aircraft in a certain airspace. But no nodes or control systems were present on the ground, which would cause repeated confusion for controllers in the battle. "As soon as the first flight of *Habu* departed, another set of F-15s checked on, with the same callsign and exact same loadout. I paused in confusion as to why this callsign—which just told me they had

Soldiers from the 10th Mountain Division (Light Infantry), participating in Operation *Anaconda*, prepare to dig into fighting positions after a day of reacting to enemy fire. Operation *Anaconda* was part of Operation *Enduring Freedom*. (U.S. Army photo/Spc. David Marck Jr., sourced from Wikimedia Commons)

checked off—was on-station and ready for targets. If I had been plugged into a data-link system, I would not have lost precious seconds, but that just explains how much we either did not know about our systems or how to utilize the tools we had available."

The second set of *Habu* went right to work once the confusion over comms was clarified, Achey continued to suppress the ridgeline using the same laser weapon tactics as before. "Even though we were hitting targets and pressing the fight to the enemy, the incoming fire never really stopped. The small arms trailed off a little bit around this time, and we're still trying to get all the wounded collected while mortars continue to drop around us."

A small element from Charlie Company had positioned itself just outside the lip of the bowl, observing the ridgeline since the ground force initially set in. One squad leader was regularly contacting command via the company net with updates on visible mortar firing positions, as well as insurgents moving in groups on the ridgeline. Among those groups, weapons systems were easily identified using optics on marksman rifles and binoculars. These locations were relayed to Achey as six-digit coordinates accurate to within 100 meters. For engagement with GPS-guided JDAMs, targeting grids needed to be ten digits, or accurate to within one meter. Some of the previous strikes had been based on target references passed to Achey from the soldiers who could see these fighting positions, but the continued incoming fire clearly indicated these weren't always effective. "This is the first time we've employed these weapons in proximity to a large American force, so it's all an incredibly steep learning curve. A lot of trial and error."

Later in the day, F/A-18s checked in, coming from the carrier strike group in the Gulf. Charlie Company's observers had line-of-sight into Marzak village, which was a priority reference point and known to house insurgent groups the operation was intended to flush out. Those F/A-18s engaged a group of enemies who left Marzak, once again dropping LGBs as part of a pre-planned package. These intermittent pre-planned strikes occurred throughout the day, in addition to reactive airstrikes on visible enemy. "It was constant, myself and the other ETAC would take turns, and if one of us wasn't on the radio, we were relocating ammunition, water, helping with the wounded, digging fighting positions of our own, and all the while we are exchanging small-arms fire and machine-gun fire with the positions in the high ground. And no matter how many we engaged, there always seemed to be more."

As the sun began to disappear in the west, Company leadership discussed whether they might get a gunship tasked to support. AC-130 gunships are limited to flying exclusively at night, but only if the moon illumination was low. Any lunar illumination would constrain that possibility, and this night was a full moon. "Despite my doubts, we did get an AC-130 coming our way, and I was very much looking forward to that. I had trained with gunships extensively back at Fort Drum and while stationed in Germany, and had trained with a specific crew right before 9/11, and as luck would have it, that same crew who would be supporting me that night."

The immediate issue was extracting the wounded, which at this point in the operation had reached 26. The Army helicopters that infilled Charlie Company would not return to the valley due to the presence of SAMs and the small-arms threat. "I got on the radio with *Bossman* [AWACs], trying to coordinate something so we can get our injured personnel out before their injuries compounded or risk losing them to exposure in that frigid valley. The same threat to medevac aircraft also prevented us from getting reinforced and resupplied. But the Air Force rescue birds were willing to grab our wounded, we just needed to set up a new LZ." Seizing the initiative, Achey left the bowl to find flat terrain nearby. "I went around asking everyone if they had spare IR [infrared] devices to mark a covert landing zone for the rescue helos. I eventually managed to acquire enough strobes and IR chem sticks to draw a giant box on this flat piece of ground. I've never worked with helicopters or made an HLZ. Future forward air controllers would do this without a second thought, it just became a standard task. But in 2002, I had no idea what the hell I'm doing or if I'm doing it correctly. We didn't have TTPs [tactics, techniques, and procedures] or training manuals, it just wasn't something TACPs formally trained to."

As soon as Achey and his Army security team finished setting up the LZ, they ran back to the bowl, under fire the entire time. There were tracer rounds dusting all around, with several coming from a point of similar elevation, the rounds passing by on a flat trajectory. "I stopped running and watched a couple of them go past me. The sight of that tracer illuminating the snow was, for lack of a better word, really pretty to look at. I vividly remember it, and it was such an odd thing to be captivated by." The next tracer skipped off the ground in front of Achey and hit the chest plate of his body armor, cracking the plate and knocking him to the ground.

"So fucking stupid, I got distracted by how 'pretty' these flying bullets looked and one of them got me. I was fine, it wasn't nearly as bad as the mortar round landing next to me, but I had the wind knocked out of me and a lost a chunk of my front plate. I was so out of it from sleep loss and adrenaline that this barely registered. I stood up, made sure not to piss myself again, checked all my gear—minus a couple busted M4 magazines—and ran back to the cover of the bowl."

By now, it was dark, and they could hear the gunship circling overhead. "There was an issue with the C2 network with all the controllers out there. Some random ETAC came up on the net claiming priority of fires, trying to pull the gunship from me. The pilot asked this other *White Lightning* callsign if he was currently in a firefight. He wasn't, and that pretty much squashed the issue. It's unfortunate that this conversation had to occur on the mass channel, but God bless those AC-130 guys for sticking to it and not getting sucked into the command-and-control fiasco we fought for that entire operation." Once established in their holding pattern, Achey tasked the gunship crew with offensive scans, looking for firing positions. Despite the force continuing to receive enemy fire, the aircraft could not discern any sources of the gunfire.

The medevac helicopters came in, two Air Force HH-60 Black Hawks with PJs (pararescue jumpers, Air Force search and rescue), and the ground force moved to load the wounded on the angel birds. "I was carrying one wounded guy, an absolute bear of a human being, all the while we can see more tracer rounds passing over the tops of the helos. Before I started carrying the wounded to the LZ, I left my rucksack with the radio stashed, having already told the AC-130 that if the rescue birds took any fire, the gunship was approved on any targets of opportunity." The gunship acted on Achey's instructions immediately, targeting muzzle flashes firing towards the helicopters. The aircrew still couldn't see insurgents anywhere, until a 40mm struck a cave opening. This was akin to kicking an anthill, with insurgents pouring out of spider holes and trenchworks and into the surrounding terrain. Charlie Company continued to load wounded as waves of insurgents emanated from this cave, and finally the medevac helicopters lifted off with the wounded.

Once returned to the relative safety of the bowl, a B-1 bomber checked in, call sign *Bone*.[4] The bomber notified Achey they were executing a pre-planned kinetic engagement for the entire village of Marzak. "What do I do with this information? I am 22 years old, I've been an ETAC for about six months, I'm not approving this because this is well above my pay grade. I pulled up SATCOM and called the ASOC [Air Support Operations Center] at Bagram, asking if this was kosher. They confirmed it was a pre-planned mission, and I was the only one who was able to provide final clearance. So I did, I don't know what the intent for that strike package was, but that was just one tiny segment in this chaotic tapestry of firepower being laid against the Taliban and Al Qaeda forces in the valley." At multiple points throughout the day and night, there had been MQ-1s owned by the CIA that arrived during various CAS engagements as well. These remote-piloted vehicles utilized the *Wildfire* and *Prairiefire* callsigns, asking Achey and other FACs the same thing—clearance on targets that had never been briefed to the ground forces. "The AC-130 asked me to kick those UAVs from the airspace because it was slowing down or directly inhibiting their ability to engage the insurgents directly firing at us."

There was no formal airspace deconfliction in the sky above Afghanistan in 2002. Ideally, a restricted operating zone should have been established, where aircraft needed ground controller permission to enter and leave, as well as remaining in assigned altitude blocks. Instead, aircraft avoided one another using airspace coordination measures that had not been briefed to ground controllers, making deconfliction a slow, laborious affair. "At that point in my career, the only airspace deconfliction I had done was for artillery, offsetting the aircraft from the gun-to-target line. The skies of Shah-i-kowt Valley were as congested and disaggregate as any engagement in the war in Afghanistan. There was no 'stack,' just aircraft cycling in and out. I'm not sure how those pilots made it work but they did it."

A wide variety of other fixed-wing fighters would arrive on station, including Marine AV-8B Harrier jump-jets, from amphibious carrier groups in the Indian Ocean, carrying GBU-12s. Achey then ordered the gunship to continue engaging the personnel maneuvering towards the bowl, tasking the AV-8Bs to engage a large bunker using their LGBs. While successful, there was no formal or doctrinal routing and safety of flight, the aircraft just avoided each other and did their sequencing as Achey and the other controllers were simply trying to get targeting briefs out as quickly as targets presented. The next dawn was approaching, with first light arriving around four in the morning. By now, most of the action trailed off. Strategic bombing missions were ongoing, with more B-52s and B-1s hitting Zurki Khel, Marzak and other smaller locations. Those pre-planned missions took the pressure off Charlie Company holding their shifted blocking positions as the fight continued beyond the valley. "We had intermittent comms with some of the SOF ETACs out there, some of whom I talked to because they could either see the enemy but didn't have comms with aircraft, or some other reason, so it was really the worst game of 'Telephone' humans have ever played."

Dawn would yield a complete and anti-climactic lull for Charlie Company, 1/87. They made ready to reload birds—now comfortable re-entering the valley for the return to Bagram. "We started policing our equipment, which was scattered in and around the bowl. It seems like I recovered more equipment than anyone else, I'd be out wandering around trying to collect gear, talking to the AC-130, who would tell me that there were insurgents really close to me, asking if I wanted them to engage; fuck, yes I want you to engage, I'm trying to haul this shit to the LZ so we can get out of here. At that point, the rush of controlling air strikes had worn off."

Once the force was back on the Chinooks, the battalion commander asked the TACPs to call in a strike on the LZ, as the ground force still left a significant amount of gear behind. In the hectic ordeal of the ground force moving to exfil, Achey was unable to strike the LZ, and the fate of those sleeping bags, rucksacks, and other paraphernalia remains a mystery. The force landed back at Bagram, exhausted, strung out, carrying mismatched gear and equipment. Achey was the last one off the bird, loaded with extra equipment he had secured on his way to the exfil. "After a while, I just took a seat right on the tarmac and looked up at the sky. I was tired, and that adrenaline crash was overwhelming. And of all the things, some Canadian soldier walks up to me and asks me if I need some help. I said yes, so he goes off and grabs this weird little tank, like an M113 Bradley with the top cut off and a bunch of benches in the back. We chatted on the way back to the tents; I told him nobody died so that must be a win."

"When I got back to the staging area with all these weapons and extra equipment, the Army perked up immediately. Something in that dynamic had changed, like 'That's him, that's the TACP, he's the one who got us out of there,' and that was a cool feeling. There would be no going to sleep for us though because Roberts Ridge [see Chapter 7] had just happened. I had to get new body armor, refit my gear, and we were all spun up to go back out. We only knew that a helicopter had been shot down, but I cannot plan anything off that information. We didn't do the rescue, of course, but we did end up returning to the area of Shah-i-kowt Valley to continue whatever the next phase of *Anaconda* by a different operational name. Nothing as exciting as those first 24 hours."

***

"There were some negative and detracting mindsets in the community before the War on Terror began, a lot of 'If it's not my job, I'm not going to do it' personalities. I remember plenty of senior NCOs telling me that I'd never control a B-52 or a gunship. They told me that I'd never shoot my rifle, and they never thought a TACP would plan or establish an HLZ. I did every one of those things in the first 12 hours of my combat career on my very first mission. My biggest gripe with the career field in those days was the mindset about a TACP shooting his gun—if you're shooting a rifle, then something has gone wrong, and you aren't doing your job. Well, no shit, if I'm shooting my gun something is wrong, but I can still do my job while engaging the immediate threat."

"There is a significant part of the story of *Anaconda* that isn't told, though it has been captured in case studies—at least glanced over—and that is the tension between the Air Force and the Army. It was a major factor in all the things that went wrong. TACPs as a community hadn't really validated ourselves to this new Army of the 21st century yet. The lack of true command-and-control architecture was a major factor. The fact that the TACP career field didn't make noise about its needs—resources, training, integration—before 9/11 forced us to make do without training and equipment. We spent twenty years not being effectively equipped to be truly efficient to do our jobs and support the Army. But we always managed to find a way to get the job done. Hopefully, this posterity shines a light on how the career field has never gotten the credit it deserves, but still fought an entire war for two decades. Nothing else like it has ever happened, and it never will happen again."

CHAPTER 7

"Some of those lessons are learned in blood"

The following interview concludes the U.S. opening engagement during the pivotal battle known as Operation Anaconda. While Coalition forces were consolidating lines of effort to stabilize the further reaches of Afghanistan, Special Forces teams continued to pursue Al Qaeda and Taliban targets into the hinterlands and border with Pakistan. Carnage and turmoil surrounded the crash site of "Razor03," a special operations MH-74E Chinook, whose SEAL team and its casualties remained a sobering reality for Americans grappling with a new, post-Cold War form of conflict—one that no longer favored the overwhelming firepower of American military might and would instead require new heights of integration, communications, command and control, and high degrees of situational awareness.

Master Sergeant Peyton Knippel (ret.) was one of many whose military career as a TACP endured nearly all the war's duration. His first deployment came weeks after the attacks on September 11 and would continue until his retirement in 2020. The story that follows highlights several critical contextual components of the opening months of the War on Terror, notably, the lack of coordination between Coalition units forward staged to the war zone, the congestion of communications, and the sobering burden that chance and coincidence could, and often did, place in the hands of young air-power experts from a career field still developing its identity as joint-force multipliers.

Knippel was 20 years old, stationed at Fort Drum, New York, with the 20th Air Support Operations Squadron (ASOS), when he learned he was going to Afghanistan. As an airman 1st class, a radio operator, maintainer, and driver (ROMAD), he had only completed the basic TACP (tactical air control party) course months prior to arriving at his first duty station. "Thinking back on the community at that time, we were still very much in a Cold War, Fulda Gap mindset—everything was VISRECCE,[1] big airspace procedural control, all about smacking enemy armor columns—nothing remotely similar to what we were going to have to do in Afghanistan."[2] Immediately after 9/11, once all the Special Forces elements had arrived in country and begun engaging the Taliban and preparing the battlespace, there were two conventional units just behind: the 101st Airborne Division (Fort Campbell, Kentucky) and the 10th Mountain Division.

"I know most people think of 9/11 and probably have some stark, clear recollection of where they were, what they were doing, for me it was largely a blur, or at least my story on that day wasn't much different than anyone else's." The order to prepare for invading another country was made, and 10th Mountain would answer. This started with preparation of the UTC (unit type code) by battalion: "Humvees," radios, and anything related to supporting the Army with close air support (CAS); soon after, all checks complete, they loaded it in C-5s on Fort Drum's flightline. For many, seeing the gargantuan cargo planes for the first time was a shock. They left on December 3; not only was it Knippel's first time leaving the United States, "It was my first time going anywhere of note outside of basic training and my move to Fort Drum." They would stop in Germany, and then immediately proceeded to K2 (Karshi–Khanabad Air Base), in Uzbekistan. No one within this task group understood at the time why they went to Uzbekistan instead of straight into Bagram, Afghanistan. "But then, of course, I was a twenty-year-old E-3 [airman 1st class], I knew literally nothing that was going on around me and not important enough to be briefed on those things."

Information flow was limited all around, but one thing stuck out: no one among them had any combat experience. A lone senior non-commissioned officer from Knippel's unit had been in *Desert Storm* a decade prior. Very few TACPs had done anything resembling air support in combat throughout the 1990s, and none of the forward air controllers (FAC) in Knippel's group had any combat experience. "When the time came, we had nothing left but to fall back on but the muscle memory from our training, which is pretty much all the TACP community did back then—train, train, and train some more."

The approach into K2 was more exciting than any anticipated. With the landing strip being unlit, it was, by necessity, a combat approach—high level into the initial traffic pattern, and then a series of rapid, descending circles until the nose is lined up on the approach vector and then a swift air brake onto the ground. Such maneuvers are matters-of-course for smaller cargo planes like C-130s, much less something bigger than a 747 commercial airliner. They landed and a great deal of confusion emanated with whatever ground support was allegedly there. "We didn't even have fuel for the HMMWVs, if I recall correctly, we had to wave down a random fuel truck that was just simply meandering around the airfield at random points just to get our trucks fueled and staged." Even now, months after the initial seizure of K2, and weeks after the successful overthrow of the main Taliban forces in the north and south, the logistics and infrastructure had not caught up with the combat forces.

Military life is infamous for "hurry up and wait," and Knippel would experience this firsthand in the journey from K2 to Bagram—a lot of hurrying from one site to another, only to wait for further instructions. Operation *Anaconda* had concluded a few days prior to his arrival in Afghanistan in March 2002. "Technically my very first mission was during the very end of *Anaconda*, but in reality we closed it out. We were going back into Shah-i-Kowt, and our designation was something called Operation *Polar Harpoon*. That mission's task and purpose was to defeat the Taliban remaining and achieve stability, which pretty much covered the time from *Anaconda* through … the year 2021?"

Though the intensity of *Anaconda* had died down, returning to Shah-i-kowt would not be peaceful or calm, and they were finally briefed on the details of the operation with the weight of a downed MH-47 helicopter hanging over the American force. "Our first objective was to re-secure Roberts Ridge. We even infilled to the same, or nearly the same, HLZ [helicopter landing zone] as did the First Battalion Ranger and Air Force Special Tactics QRF [quick-reaction force] who went in to secure the crash site and extract the American casualties."

The 10th Mountain troops were well aware of the events that happened on the ridge, and knew about the Americans lost in the 17-hour gunfight, including Jason Cunningham and John Chapman (U.S. Air Force Special Tactics), Neil Roberts (Navy SEAL for whom the ridge was named after), Matthew Commons, Bradley Crose, and Marc Anderson (75th Ranger Regiment), and Philip Svitak (160th Special Operations Aviation Regiment, SOAR). "But to my young and overwhelmed mind, either it didn't register—the significance of the ground we were preparing to walk on—or I was so deep in my muscle memory of preparing for my first mission, that it didn't strike me until long afterwards the significance of what we were about to do."

A mission like this, securing a mountain top, was in 10th Mountain Division's DNA. The division traces its history back to World War II when it was charged with offensives in the Italian Alps. Despite the legacy and unique mission alignment, Fort Drum, New York, has no mountains. While upstate New York does have snow and freezing cold, it is barely above sea level. No one in that company with whom Knippel inserted in the shadow of Takur Ghar was mountaineering qualified, or had any significant mountain-warfare experience.

The force was not equipped for this mission either. The soldiers were utilizing heavy IBA (Individual Body Armor)—oversized flak jackets whose securing straps fold laterally like a suit jacket—layers upon layers of excess material holding steel plates instead of Kevlar. "We took so many pictures using disposable cameras, but the only picture of me that survived is when I'm laid up in a fighting position on the ridge, wearing that ridiculous flak jacket; you can see where I had used ALICE clips to fix ammunition pouches to the front. No one had functional MOLLE rigs yet. I looked like an absolute 'boot' in that one photo."

A recurrent theme in this work has been the role of the new types of radios used by FACs in unexpected environments. The invasion of Afghanistan was the first time the PRC-117F radio had ever seen combat. Previously, for controllers to have comms across the different frequencies—VHF/FM, UHF, and HF (the latter being the only option for beyond-line-of-sight until SATCOM)—they would have to carry three separate radios, each one weighing around ten pounds. "We used the PRC-119 SINCGARs[3] for VHF/FM, to talk on Army nets for ground C2 [command and control]. Then there was the PRC-113, which only did VHF/Hi and UHF for talking to aircraft, and the PRC-104 for HF long-distance comms." The PRC-117F changed all of that, allowing controllers to put all their nets—including SATCOM, which needed far less power and replaced HF—into a single radio, allowing operators to switch between nets as needed.

The force set into Shah-i-Kowt, beneath Takur Ghar, an entire company of 10th Mountain soldiers plus the two Air Force TACPs. They flew in on 160th SOAR MH-47s. For a conventional force, flying on helicopters piloted by the Army's premier pilots (and, arguably, the "best pilots in the world") was a novelty which Knippel would not appreciate in this moment; conventional forces almost never flew with the exclusive 160th, whose expertise was formed to provide airlift for the elite special-operations units.

The MH-47s were at maximum capacity, inserting at 12,000-plus feet, an elevation for which no one was prepared, and it was blisteringly cold. Most of the men on those birds had never been to that type of elevation before. The pilots could not set the helicopter down due to snow, opting to do a lip landing. This is when the ramp is lowered, the rear wheels contacting the ground, but the rest of the aircraft remains aloft over a vertical drop. No one was stepping off; instead, they jumped, fell, slid or otherwise ignominiously flopped into several feet of snow. They had brought plastic cargo sleds, similar to SKEDCOs,[4] loaded down with supplies, and a lot of mortar rounds. As men fell out the back of the helo, one of the sleds slipped past the catchers on the ground, and started sliding down the snowy embankment, scattering mortar rounds everywhere.

"I'm not a big guy, at the time I think I weighed about 140lbs, and I prepared for this mission by packing out a Blackhawk Raptor backpack, which was touted as a jumpable ruck alternative to the ALICE packs. It didn't have a frame or anything, just a giant square pouch with straps on it. Somehow, I managed to get over 100 pounds of shit into that bag. When I hit the snow, I was immediately stuck and couldn't even roll over to get out of the way of more dudes exiting." No sooner had the first waves of Americans left the helicopters then the force began receiving machine-gun fire from a fighting position on the ridge. It was far enough away that the rounds were not effective in direct-fire mode, which was the only good thing. Had the remaining insurgents utilized plunging fire—elevating the gun barrel so the rounds would hit on the descent from their arc, that would have been far more effective and likely produced casualties caught in the open. "This fighting position was a small tent, or at least a framed tarp, so it was easy to see, especially with the muzzle flashes and smoke coming out of it. But it was just out of effective range of an M4, and with as chaotic and scrambled as our infil was, getting our mortars set up was not feasible."

Knippel had set in on the first helicopter, and the enlisted terminal attack controller-qualified TACP hadn't landed yet. The task organization was such that the two Air Force TACPs were manifested on different birds, so that if one of the fires personnel was shot down, it wouldn't cripple the entire force for utilizing air support. "I was the first one on the deck and, at the time, the Army hadn't learned the difference between qualified controllers and their ROMAD/FO assistant, so the company commander turned to me and yelled 'Air Force! Put some bombs on that DFP [defensive firing position]!'"

When lacking experience, military personnel revert to training and muscle memory. In these chaotic moments, his first gunfight, Knippel decided to confirm authorization to do anything kinetic with aircraft, since he wasn't ETAC-qualified. "I got on my PRC-117, plugged in my SATCOM antenna, and called back to the ASOC [Air Support Operations Center] at Bagram, which was still in a tent. All good ROMADs memorize every frequency for every mission, which was beaten into me from the beginning of my career. In the later years of the war, you preloaded entire mission packages onto radios from the Comms shop and didn't memorize anything. But in 2002, there weren't that many frequencies. I had every uplink and downlink for the SATCOM channels memorized, their three-digit channel identifiers, and all of the line-of-sight frequencies committed to memory. Everything was so incredibly analog back then that it is hard to fathom for later generations."

The Army personnel on that mountain top hadn't seen the 117 in action yet, and the radio had features not before seen on radio sets, including the detachable faceplate, called a KDU (keypad display unit), remotely mounted to the front of a user's kit using a fiber-optic cable. "The Army guys yelling at me thought that this green, three-inch square aluminum box was my radio, and I tried to explain that it was part of the setup so I could remotely control the radio settings. But that simply confused them amidst bullets flying and people yelling. I had the old-school expanding 'coke-can' antenna, with the arms you had to extend and the spider web filaments that became taut when you had the thing fully opened." This antenna is not omnidirectional and requires the operator to know the take-off angle (vertical slant of the antenna mast) and azimuth for the satellites in orbit. "In the middle of everything, I'm unfurling this huge antenna and trying to point it in the right direction. We did not have the Key-CO switches so that the SATCOM cable could be routed into the base of the UHF antenna either, that came years later. I had fabricated a cable that mounted to the housing of the radio, and the other end had the connector for each of the UHF line-of-site antenna, and the SATCOM, which was zippered into my ruck." The sight of their Air Force TACP unfolding a ridiculously sized antenna and carefully manipulating the apparatus in a particular direction while talking into a tiny "green box" was undoubtedly an absurd spectacle for the 10th Mountain soldiers, who were continuing to consolidate equipment and personnel while attempting to return fire on the fighting position above.

The ASOC monitors the joint air request net (JARN), which is doctrinally allocated for all FACs to request immediate CAS sorties when in contact. The JARN is also used for occasional air-mission tasking changes. The ASOC is manned 24-hours a day, with personnel always monitoring the JARN. Knippel would raise the ASOC on this SATCOM net amid the unfolding chaos. "We were taking fire and, strangely, I wasn't scared, because I was so deep into my repetitive patterns from training, I was just going through my checklist. I didn't even ask the ASOC for more aircraft, we had Marine AH-1 Cobras on station, but I relayed that we were taking fire—'troops in contact' wasn't a formal label yet—and I passed a general grid and told them the other fires personnel had not landed with the force yet. Then I simply asked, 'Am I good to call for fire?' The ETAC who was monitoring the JARN just said, 'Yeah, man.'"

With authorization confirmed, Knippel undid the SATCOM antenna, plugged back into the line-of-sight UHF antenna, and called up the AH-1s, quickly achieving good two-way comms. He passed a nine-line, which is most often employed with fixed-wing fighters and bombers, not rotary wing attack aircraft. By doctrine, however, Marine fire-support helicopters train to nine-lines as well as call-for-fire "five-line" briefs. If the force had been supported by Army attack helicopters on this mission, it could well have confused them due to the unfamiliar format. Serendipity and luck met in those moments, and the Marines did not skip a beat; "Send it."

Lacking an IP (initial point, Item I on the nine-line template), as they were flying directly overhead, Knippel instructed them to simply look out the window for friendly positions to vector their initial attack heading. It would be the easiest talk-on of his career, although certainly not his most proficient attack. "They opened up with the 25mm, and I was not prepared for the hot brass to start falling right on top of me. I kept staring at them, instead of simply saying 'Cleared hot' and letting them get after it. In 2001, we trained for something called 'positive control'—this was before Type I, II or III engagements, the fallout and doctrine changes from the Udairi Range incident [see Chapter 10] hadn't been implemented yet—I just kept staring straight up at them to keep control measures for the attack." The AH-1s led with multiple gun engagements, and followed up with AGM-114 missiles; the fighting position was reduced beyond a doubt. "I just happened to be the guy who was there at the time and didn't freeze up under pressure. It should be acknowledged that, in hindsight, those rotary wing assets were organic to us and I didn't need to be ETAC-qualified, and those aircraft could have just as easily engaged in defense of the force, so I wasted valuable time."

They had landed about a thousand feet below Takur Ghar, while another 10th Mountain company down in the valley, at the base of the mountain, had been engaged by some straggler Al Qaeda (AQ) fighters. These enemy personnel were sacrificial stay behind fighters meant to harass any follow-on forces after *Anaconda* but, by now, most of that valley and the surrounding areas had been cleared. But several of those fighters' remains had been found with American weapons, some night-vision devices, a PSN-11 Precision Lightweight GPS Receiver, and other equipment.

Following the initial engagement, things mellowed out, and they began to climb Takur Ghar. "We are loaded down with gear, and it's cold and snow is covering everything. I'm a TACP, surrounded by Army guys, so I'm not about to let them see any weakness, and I'm not going to embarrass the community by falling out. I'm going to attack this stupid walk up this stupid mountain. I thought I was out of shape, and it pissed me off that I literally couldn't catch my breath, but it was the altitude and lack of acclimation." Early in the climb, one soldier would slip on a snow-covered rock, breaking his leg—now they had a casualty. The first order of business was to cross-load all the equipment, with Knippel volunteering to take more gear. "The injured guy had a fucking pillow, Vienna sausages and fruit cups in his pack. Meanwhile, I've got a ruck full of batteries, targeting equipment, all kinds of things that I don't want, but need, and this clown had snacks and camping gear in his bag. We rat-fucked what little actual gear he actually had, and I called in *Dustoff* to get him off the mountain."

Summiting the ridgeline, on Roberts Ridge, the company came face-to-face with *Razor03*, the Chinook shot down during *Anaconda*. The ASOC hadn't called in the airstrike to reduce the wreckage yet, and all the carnage was untouched. It reminded them of pictures from a World War I battlefield: burn marks, brass everywhere, and scorched earth. Once the force had consolidated at the top, they set in an observation point and began patrol-base operations. From their vantage, they could see "The Whale," the key ridge that forms the edge of the Shah-i-Kowt

The western edge of Takur Ghar. (Peyton Knippel)

Valley which special-operations teams had occupied to coordinate air strikes before the *Hammer* and *Anvil* pincers began. There was a handful of villages down below, and they could also see the second helicopter crash site from *Anaconda* near one of the villages—where the SEAL team had attempted to reinsert to the ridge to recover Neil Roberts. "There was an Australian SAS [Special Air Service Regiment] team in the valley near that other crash site, and we were all sharing the same fires net, which made comms pretty congested."

The other company had the two TACPs, as well as an air liaison officer (ALO) who inserted with the command element. This ensured the TACPs could remain with the maneuver elements while the ALO assisted with command and control, as well as managing airspace and monitor comms. The ALO, Air Force Major Schmitt, temporarily assigned to the 20th ASOS and hailing from the B-52 community, happened to be listening to the fires net when the SAS team below had been trying to call in an airstrike on the ridge observation point. Even on the shared net, it had not been clarified that Knippel's company had moved to occupy Roberts Ridge. "This was about dusk, so you are dealing with thermal crossover, the light does weird tricks up in the mountains, it is easy for that type of misidentification to occur when no one is cross-talking. Major Schmitt just happened to be listening in on the net during this time while the other TACPs were resting or rehabbing radio batteries." Realizing a fratricide was about to unfold, Major Schmitt jumped onto the JARN, calling the ASOC and establishing an NFA (no-fire area) over the mountain top. He then immediately contacted the SAS over fires to let them know of the updated friendly positions. It wasn't until the end of this sequence that anyone had been able to jump on the net to let the Australian controllers know, due to the net being so congested with traffic. "I don't think Schmitt has ever been properly recognized for what he did, but he prevented another major fratricide incident in those early months of the war."

This lack of deconfliction and lack of awareness happened far more than is recorded during those early months, the result of no one knowing how to perform joint-force operations. The invasion of Afghanistan tested these procedures across every medium. "We knew that we needed to go in and smack the enemy, but putting so many different units—special operations, conventional, and Coalition partners—in such a rugged and austere area, from staging areas as far away as K2 and Bagram, there was no way to keep everyone informed with that type of analog command and control." The ASOC knows how to do air-support operations—allocating aircraft assigned to missions in the Air Tasking Order (ATO) to the controllers out forward—but it had never been a verb of "ASOC." The men manning the ASOC function did tremendous work during *Anaconda*, but had never seen combat and now supported some of the most intense air bombing the war in Afghanistan would ever see. What was not implicit in the joint-force paradigm was the critical role the ASOC would have to play in friendly battle-tracking in such a congested area.

"We [the entire joint force] didn't know what the fuck we were doing. We didn't understand how to distribute communications across the battlespace, or at best we had not rehearsed in a functionally relevant exercise environment. The lessons of conflict are derived from conflict, right? You learn those things in training, but even the best training can't replicate reality. Maybe that SAS unit just wasn't switched on, or ignored the information, or their operations center hadn't told them, who knows. I do not want to be reductive, but it all boils down to communication. And that is one thing we were not good at in 2002—communicating and information sharing across the force."

Potential tragedy averted, and with waning daylight, the ground force closely examined the battlefield around *Razor03*, and the caves Al Qaeda had made their stand in. It would feel like an eerie Civil War historical site when one walks the path of the battle. Spent brass littered the ground everywhere. There had been two bunkers connected by a comms trench, which Knippel went into alongside several soldiers. Al Qaeda had antenna wires strung between the two bunkers, tarps hung up for walls, everything up there that "belonged" to them had been carried by foot or donkey, 12,000 feet up to the top of a mountain. The audacity of outfitting a cave atop a mountain made for an utterly surreal spectacle. "They even had a potbellied stove for heating and cooking."

There were remains of the Al Qaeda fighters in those caves, those who had not been recovered by the terrorist group after *Anaconda*'s bombing campaigns. There was one that stood out to Knippel as he investigated one of the bunkers, an individual with an unfortunate connection to Jason Cunningham, the pararescue jumper who gave his life during *Anaconda*. Before that fateful operation, Cunningham had become certified to carry live blood for emergency transfusions. He carried blood bags with him and had several on his kit when he was killed. Cunningham's death was later attributed to his refusal to receive care for his own injuries from those very same blood bags, while he was saving the lives of wounded Rangers.

"I had never seen a dead body, or any sort of human remains, until this point. One of the bodies in the cave, an AQ fighter, he had joined the 'canoe club'; it basically looked like someone had taken a spoon and made a perfect furrow right through his skull, but what was weird about it was that he had a Gore-Tex bivy sack wrapped around him, and a blood transfusion bag ineffectually inserted into him. This confounded us. The only explanation we could determine was that the insurgents had somehow acquired one of the blood bags Cunningham had been carrying, and they tried to use it on this insurgent, who was all but certainly expired before ever getting back to the cave."

More bodies were strewn across the crest near the cave entrance, the redoubt layered in death. Walking through the ruins, Knippel would trip over what he initially thought was a small animal, though this seemed unlikely at such elevation, cold, and recent carnage. "It was the top half of an AQ fighter's skull."

"At one point, I stepped on a landmine, an old Russian landmine that had been buried under some rubbish, and I heard a weird crunch. Fortunately, it was completely corroded through with rust, otherwise I certainly would have been dead."

Outside one of the caves, they found a tree with some bullet holes in the trunk at chest-height. It wasn't the bullet holes that drew their attention, but some bindings several feet from the ground. "I have no sure way of confirming this, but I believe this is where Neil Roberts was executed after he had been overrun by AQ fighters late into that first gunfight. Again, this was our presumption. To us, it looked like he had been tied up to this tree and executed; looking at the site, you could easily make that inference. That is why I don't feel the slightest guilt after seeing what happened in the caves."

This mountain top was a strategically pivotal piece of terrain, easy to see in every direction, with every vector of approach coverable by overlapping fields of fire. For the Rangers to have assaulted straight up into the channelizing terrain during the peak ferocity of *Anaconda* was incredible, and humbling for Knippel and the 10th Mountain soldiers to examined in review. "We walked that same path they did, and it was just brutal, trekking up that peak with all our stuff. But we didn't face a fraction of the intensity of enemy fire. AQ had dug holes, reinforced fighting pits, and each one held hundreds upon hundreds of rounds of ammo, RPG boosters, everything they needed to sustain blistering volumes of fire. It's a miracle the Rangers were able to fight up there and into the bunkers to extract the dead Americans. I do not know how we could have missed how many AQ were up there, or why it wasn't cratered with a B-52. I'm sure there was a reason that the task force didn't use pre-assault fires on that mountain peak before sending ground forces in, but this single piece of terrain utterly dominated the valley. Mistakes were made during the JIPOE (joint intelligence preparation of the battlespace), some of those brutal lessons that you can only learn in blood."

For the duration of their time on the ridge, Knippel would have the only consistent, reliable comms beyond their element, the Air Force radios serving as the company's only lifeline. The company soldiers tried to set up an OE-254 omni-directional antenna on the side of the mountain using the guide wires as anchors to the rocks, a behemoth mast with six two-foot-long prongs. But the huge antenna would not support line-of-sight communications. Soon enough, the Army increasingly utilized the ROMAD for all comms, including ground force command and control, in addition to the existing need to stay active on air nets. "I was more proud of this success than anything else. I kept plugging in frequencies. The 1st Brigade commander, 10th Mountain, was flying around the battlefield for command and control, probably to avoid the coordination problems that happened during *Anaconda*. I ended up being the company's entire communications to the headquarters element. The brigade commander would later land on the mountain top, where our mission turned into a dog and pony show. He made a big speech and, of course, made sure to get his picture with the downed helicopter. This was followed by some rousing speeches and flying a U.S. flag in front of the wreckage."

The company would spend the rest of the night in overwatch on the valley. Down on "The Whale," they could easily see flashing lights going back and forth, almost certainly residual Al Qaeda coordinating with each other, but they couldn't get an airstrike lined up to disrupt those activities. This went on long into the night. In the early morning hours, more unexpected and inexplicable events transpired, leaving them on edge in an eerily quiet redoubt. "There was a van doing huge circles around one of the villages down in the valley, and at one point the fucking thing just blew up—no one had called in CAS, no friendlies were near this village, the van was just driving around and then suddenly blew up."

It was cold and windy through the night, and there was nothing they could do about either. This reality would produce an odd second- and third-order affectation of the War on Terror. "That's probably the reason Carmex became so prevalent: and you could find boxes of it on any FOB [forward operating base] in Afghanistan. Dudes came back from *Anaconda* and *Polar Harpoon* with lips that would be so dried, split and cracked, with blood dripping and freezing, breaking, and dripping and freezing again. You couldn't talk because your face and mouth hurt so much. This injury was one of the most consequential things that could happen short of an actual casualty. If I couldn't talk on the radio—which was my entire job—well then, I'm not combat effective. Sunscreen and Carmex: two of the most important things you don't think you need in combat, but that's some of those things you only learn the hard way."

The rest of this deployment would be decidedly mellow and uneventful for 10th Mountain and their Air Force enablers. Different components kept the pressure on, but for now, the "job" was done, and the question of what came next hadn't been asked, let alone answered. But this was the beginning of a life-spanning journey that would see men like Knippel returning to Afghanistan time and time again. "I was there every year from OEF 1 [Operation *Enduring Freedom*] through OEF 4, every single year I kept deploying back there. I got an award for the novelty of my rank and this mission, the other TACPs who had gone in received awards for winning the battle. If a TACP got an award for every time he called in a bomb, he'd never be able to pick up his blues jacket from the weight of its ribbon rack. We got those awards for the novelty of being some of the first people in, not so much for the things we did at the time. Getting my first call for fire by stepping off the ramp on my first mission, with Marine AH-1s no less, was pretty amazing. And I don't know how many or if anyone else has set foot on Takur Ghar since we left it, and the war just went on elsewhere."

***

"This last bit will bother me until the day I die. This was my first deployment, first time overseas, and I had brought a bunch of those Kodak disposable cameras. I thought it would be cool, capture images of being there, and, of course, the significance of capturing the battlefield. Going up there to re-take Takur Ghar, at least I had the wherewithal to know it held significance now and for a long time and I wanted pictures of that. I had a ton of photos of Roberts Ridge."

The time came to exfil. The rest of the Coalition forces were continuing the pursuit of what little Al Qaeda remained in the mountains. The company loaded the MH-47s for exfil, a slightly less-chaotic gaggle of men surging on the machines. Knippel had the camera in his cargo pocket. "There was an Army major who got on late, I don't remember his name, but he made me move from where I was sitting because, as a very young airman, apparently I didn't rate the seat I had taken. We were all tired anyway, so I guess he just didn't want to suffer on the floor while the Air Force guy had a bench seat. Regardless, somewhere in me shuffling across the back of the helicopter, the camera fell out of my pocket. I even went back to the aircrew after we had disembarked and asked them if they had seen it, nothing."

"I had taken pictures of everything I told in this story, all of it. Photos of the immediate aftermath, probably some of the only evidence of what the ridge looked like after AQ had been pushed out, and before the JOC [joint operations center] had ordered a kinetic strike to reduce the helicopter wreckage."

"I didn't play a huge role, all I did was my job. I happened to be the guy at the time. Other ETACs did so much work during those early months, and I came in at a strange time. So I guess that my claim to fame is that I was the youngest TACP in the entire country, and I got to call in an airstrike. Other ROMADs were out there too, guys who stepping off the ramp and immediately controlling medevacs and helping their ETACs in the middle of absolute air-power chaos. After the mission, we all got together at the 'Motel 8,' the old Russian barracks near the air-traffic control tower in Bagram. Everyone was just so tired, exhausted in their bones after the things they went through."

"There is something I took away from the experience, a bit of wisdom that was passed to me by a former 2/75 ranger named Jericho Denman: 'Yeah, man, war was awesome, and it's okay to be okay'; a lot of guys have gone over there, and maybe they think that they need to be fucked up from the experience. It is ok to not be bummed out that you went through this hellacious experience, something that tests the very fabric of your humanity, and yet you still come out okay and not fucked up in the head. War was awesome when you killed the bad guys and kept your people safe."

"I did a lot of missions after that, more conventional deployments, a long time on the SOF side working with Rangers, but that first mission will always stand out to me for how significant it was to be standing on that ridge. But I'll forever recall how aggressive and violent combat is, and how it isn't romantic, it's real with real consequences. There was this incident that just made this twenty-year-old kid feel amazing after landing back at Bagram. It was a two-hour flight over some of the worst terrain on the planet; in retrospect I probably should have been scared shitless but I wasn't, I was just enjoying the ride. We offload the birds, walking across the tarmac, and these British commando dudes are coming towards the helos we had just offloaded, and this dude gives me a high five. I thought it was the coolest thing that had ever happened, it felt like I had arrived."

"There were a lot of mistakes that air controllers made during those early months and, rightly so, they are criticized and publicized. Even during *Anaconda*, there were some ETACs who did not perform well, and the career field very quickly culled those dipshits. There were the incidents like the bomb that almost killed Karzai a few months before—no one knew or had experienced the fact that this piece of equipment, the PLGR GPS, displayed the user grid, and not the last target grid—when you powered up after the batteries had died. We just didn't know these things, and those were hard lessons that could only be learned the hard way. I'm not trying to immunize or vindicate the guys who fucked up either."

"But we got better as a community because we learned those lessons fast, and every time, any time, something went wrong, we immediately set about fixing it across the controller community. Udairi range was another example; dudes died because there were no positive control techniques like a Type I—when you as the controller must maintain your eyeballs on the aircraft and the target when weapons come off the rails. After Udairi, and after some of these mistakes in Afghanistan, we had to rewrite the J-Pub [Joint Publication] and standardize positive and procedural controls to prevent these mistakes from happening again."

"Some of those lessons are written in blood and experience. It's a hard fucking job, you are the only one of the ground force that never takes a break. You're on the mic from start to finish, and you don't get to fuck up, because if you do, you just created another lesson in blood. There were also lessons that could have, but didn't involve blood, because we just had the right guys—like Major Schmitt—on the radio at the right time and the awareness to stop a mishap before it happened, during combat."

PART II

A New World War

Iraq, 2003

We resolved then, and we are resolved today, to confront every threat from any source that could bring sudden terror and suffering to America ...

As Americans, we want peace. We work and sacrifice for peace. But there can be no peace if our security depends on the will and whims of a ruthless and aggressive dictator. I'm not willing to stake one American life on trusting Saddam Hussein.

Failure to act would embolden other tyrants, allow terrorists access to new weapons and new resources, and make blackmail a permanent feature of world events.

This nation, in world war and in cold war, has never permitted the brutal and lawless to set history's course. Now, as before, we will secure our nation, protect our freedom, and help others to find freedom of their own.

GEORGE W. BUSH, OCTOBER 7, 2002

CHAPTER 8

The Pivot

A War on Terror becomes Global

Iraq is not the sole root cause of the failures of Afghanistan, but it deserves the lion's share of the blame for policy failures in the early chapters of the War on Terror, when the transition of combat capabilities left American and Coalition forces unable to press their initial advantage over the Taliban and Al Qaeda. It began the cyclic strategy sans policy of limited ways, means, or reasons for the mission's continuation. While latter years of the war in Afghanistan were perpetuated by the return to familiarity in favor of hard decisions, this phase of limited capability in Afghanistan was the result of adventurism at its worst—faulty intelligence, bent to the whim of policy makers whose ambition to make dramatic geopolitical changes to the Middle East's power brokerage created the cracks in an otherwise hopeful foundation.

While the purpose of this book aims to examine how the unique battle spaces in the Global War on Terror helped foster the unique success and ultimate faux intractability of close air support (CAS) as the primary tool of American warfighting, Iraq, as much as Afghanistan, deserves review for its influence on how the upper tiers of command and control evolved as the War on Terror opened new fronts on a regional scale.

The broader view of Iraq mirrors the same aspects of battlefield supremacy as in Afghanistan—after the initial invasion, there was no significant force that posed a threat to American dominance outright—and early tactical gains, the rapid employment of technological capabilities, and the near unanimous support of global partnerships gave the false impression of indomitable capacity. Meanwhile ends-based policies never enabled a strategy to achieve a successful outcome. To use analogous terms, the panoply of American and Coalition war power dove into the second course of a meal before the first course had been completed, only to try returning to the former long after it had grown cold, stale, and was turning rancid.

Iraq challenged the capabilities of the United States as did Afghanistan in many regards—like environmental conditions, although in Iraq most cases of environmental complexity lay in the scattering of dense urban battlespaces, rather than the rugged and indifferent Afghan landscape. Iraqi geography was no less efficient at concealing insurgent forces behind murder holes and complex cover and concealment. The cultural complexity was equally riven with discord, but more stigmatized by the Ba'ath Party's Sunni minority's ruthless subjugation the majority Shiite and Kurdish demographics under the Hussein regime. Neighboring power brokers, Iran and Syria (whose second-order influence from Moscow requires acknowledgment as well), further fomented a hyper-complex environment which defied presumptions of American war power after the invasion achieved early success. With uncontested borders east and west, the exodus of Iraqi fighting forces, who would return as part of the insurgency, had easy access to sponsors of terror in the Assad and Khomeini regimes.

The overwhelming early success of American war power created its own monster that would haunt the region in the years to come. With counter-terror fostering a new, hybrid architecture of prisoner detention and blurred lines between criminal actors and enemy combatants, the Coalition was forced to contend with detainees who failed to coincide with standard cordons of due process. Thus, the horrors of several detention facilities, including the infamous Abu Ghraib prison complex, housed a variety of actors from the former Iraqi military, as well as malicious players of the surrounding states who bore great antagonism to American forces.

It is within the shadows of this detention facility network, allegedly at Camp Bucca in Umm Qasr (Basra Province), that Abu Bakr al-Baghdadi fomented his radical beliefs; he would eventually lead the meteoric rise of a new Caliphate in Iraq and Syria, to be known as ISIS. Though the Islamic State would eventually span multiple continents with its disaggregate cell networks, it was born in Iraq following the U.S.-led invasion and, later, the failed nation-building occupation. In 2004, after the Iraq pivot had reached fever pitch, Abu Musab al-Zarqawi established Al Qaeda in Iraq (AQI), with the aim of destabilizing the U.S.-occupied Iraq state in its early goings. Two years later, Zarqawi was killed in an American airstrike, creating a new leadership void, to be filled by Abu Ayyub al-Masri, who would go on to declare the establishment of an Islamic State in Iraq (ISI), with Abu Omar al-Baghdadi as its leader.

Years of insurgency, spilling Coalition and Iraqi blood, would pass. American-led raids and airstrikes ultimately removed Abu Omar al-Baghdadi and al-Masri by 2010. In the leadership lull for the two organizations, compounded by the anticipated American withdrawal from Iraq in the near future and the relative stability of the Coalition-supported Iraqi government, Abu Bakr al-Baghdadi became the new leader of the Islamic State, seemingly unifying elements of the heavily fractured ISI and AQI during a variety of complex attacks and prison breaks across Iraq. Following increased government pressure against the insurgent campaign, al-Baghdadi relocated the bulk of ISI to Mosul, biding time and consolidating as chaos broke out in Syria following the civil war, the rise of the Nusra front in Raqqa, and the vacuum to be created by the American withdrawal in Iraq.

Iraq enjoyed economic development in many categories which Afghanistan did not. Oil reserves, for example, made Iraq a far more lucrative ambition for international interests, by way of resource security, than did Afghanistan's limited agricultural export (excluding opium production, a component of the underpinnings of global motivations that perpetually evaded Western attempts to reduce). Iraq's location, the birthplace for much of civilization, placed its sand and soil above some of the world's most critical lifeblood, and enough ink has been spilled about the Western motivations for regime change in Iraq as it relates to black gold.

Iraq was far more infrastructurally developed than its Global War on Terror counterpart to the east. Further, its proximity to a host of American allies in the region made the logistical and sustainment challenges less imposing by a wide margin. After all, the United States had led a Coalition invasion just over a decade prior in the Gulf War and had maintained an air-led deterrence mission (Operations *Northern* and *Southern Watch*) through most of the 1990s. The battlespace was institutional knowledge to many American and allied partner militaries. Saudi Arabia, Turkey, Israel, Kuwait, and Qatar all had close ties to the American military, and hosted an assortment of U.S. capabilities on near-permanent bases at the onset, and throughout, the War on Terror.

The combination of economic, resource, financial, and, to a much smaller degree, geopolitical factors are components to the decision to divert resources from Afghanistan. After such a swift defeat of the Taliban, the pressure by policymakers to make intelligence and political theorizing justify an invasion, makes the pivot away from Afghanistan seem, in this historical context, par for the course of 21st-century geopolitical events. This shotgun marriage of military might, public opinion, and economic motivations was further calcified by the rapid overthrow of the Iraqi armed forces by a massive coalition force, once again leading military strategists to ask, amid the settling dust of a successful invasion, "What now?"

Having failed to account for the inability to develop constructive policies that would support the long-term development of a stable state from its preceding negligence in Afghanistan, the U.S.-led Coalition moved to begin another nation-building fiasco in Iraq where, once again, the ability of American military precision and speed—buoyed by the incredible success of CAS and the foundations of a future kinetic strike capability—would falsely conflate the tactical successes with strategic improvements at the scale of policy making. The double-edged sword of this new tool in the warfighting panoply would, in later years, betray the very stark reality of the battlefield environment: that an employment method of precision fires, delivered in close proximity to friendly forces and civilian infrastructure, was achievable to its exponential degree of success only because of a wholly dominated battlespace in most, if not all, domains.

CHAPTER 9

The Battle of Debecka Pass

Lance Maguire is quite possibly the last person one would suspect of being one of the most accomplished forward air controllers of the 21st century. A tall, gaunt man with an effortlessly relaxed demeanor, his unique vocal timbre and deeply analytical expression of thought conjure up mental images of a successful financial expert nearing the end of a long career in corporate finance, not the warrior of renown within the community. The unassuming character is anathema to the prolific career he enjoyed in the United States Air Force (USAF).

Lance's name is well known across the community. Speaking to other members of the joint-fires community throughout this book's writing, the consensus among the countless stories of close air support was that his contributions to the career field were a critical part of the community's legacy. In fact, it was a conversation with Lance and another USAF JTAC in the spring of 2020 that prompted the idea to draft this manuscript, or, as was often said in JTAC units all over the world, "Someone has to start writing this shit down."

What follows is Lance's account of the Battle of Debecka Pass in northern Iraq in March 2003.

Maguire was at Fort Bragg (now Fort Liberty), then Fort Lewis, collocated with multiple Army special-forces groups (SFG) in the days leading up to September 11, 2001. After assessment and selection for SOF TACP (special-operations forces tactical air control party) while stationed in Korea between 1998–99, he would return to North Carolina, promoting to technical sergeant and taking a leadership role over all SOF TACPs aligned with the 3rd SFG. The invasion of Afghanistan would double the manning requirements for forward air controllers (FAC) at line units, due to the rapid increase in demand for close air support (CAS). He would transition to Fort Lewis where the 5th Air Support Operations Squadron commander placed him in charge of the operational detachment supporting both Special Forces (SF) and Ranger platoons.

"Because TACPs are right there with their customer, I was able to do the spin-up training with 3rd Group twice, 7th Group once, and 1st Group prior to various deployments."[1] Regularly, Maguire's experience and expertise would lead various units to quickly evolve standard operating procedures, adding planning steps to the fires battle drills, CAS training with the teams themselves, and, starting in 2004, planning and executing CAS training trips with the Army's emerging SF FAC programs. As a result, he would be in charge of allocating Air Force and Army controllers to teams preparing to deploy based on his intimate knowledge of the capabilities of those under his direction.

As air-power experts, people entrusted to integrate those capabilities into the ground force scheme of maneuver, FACs have to think about how tactical problems—and their proposed solution to the ground-force commander—will have an impact on the broader strategic situation. It's much more complicated than being a rifleman in a platoon. Because SOFs function at the tactical level but must consider the effects and outcomes at operational and strategic levels, they cannot afford to lose focus in those tactical problems—the gunfight of now. That relationship between the controller and the ground commander is magnified in these situations, especially when a single Army SF A-team might have an entire indigenous battalion under its guidance. This often means the mission planning has to factor those maneuver forces into the equation—mortars, artillery, communications, and their plan of attack.

In the 2003 Iraq invasion, 10th SFG led CJSOTF–North (Combined Joint Special Operations Task Force–North) and, later, CJSOTF–Iraq during the 2007 surge. In both cases, Maguire deployed with units under those commands, as well as covering teams from the 3rd and 1st Groups, due to the shortage of FACs available for pivotal objectives in northern Iraq. In March 2003, he would support two SF A-teams under 3rd Group during the invasion.

"I had what was a fairly standard loadout at the time. I wore the same uniforms as my Army counterparts, body armor, rucksack, and personal protective equipment. For comms, I carried a Harris PRC-117F manpack radio [12lbs] with extra batteries [1.3lbs each], including the full antenna suite—FM and UHF/VHF line of site, SATCOM 'coke can' expandable satellite antenna—and I always carried a KYK-13 cryptological fill device. My A-team comms sergeant gave me a Thales PRC-148 MBITR [multiband inter-team receiver] loaded with line-of-sight frequencies for CAS coordination and inter-team backup. Neither radio ever failed me on five deployments. I always rode with the team commander in vehicles, and we backed each other up on battle tracking, target nomination and prioritization, and direction of organic fires. Because we never had a joint special operations aviation liaison, I always planned and requested fires support through the land component commander coordination channels using the joint air request net. Those requests were routed through the Battlefield Coordination Detachment, deep inside the Combined Air Operations Center (CAOC) and, with the help of a SOLE (Special Operations

Liaison Element), would process and fill my requests according to the allocation and apportionment plans for the entire country."

The Battle of Debecka Pass serves as a key example of when things go right using CAS to support the Army's objectives, and how FACs are responsible for much more than simply calling in airstrikes. Leaving the United States with two teams to support, Maguire would bring along another TACP, Todd Gannon, to support two additional A-teams. An important point to make as it relates to this timeline—March/April 2003, with the strategic bombing or "air war" beginning on March 19, 2003—was the lack of fire-support experts available at the tactical maneuver level. For the SF construct, the battalion is not a maneuver element, it is the higher headquarters supporting element. The operational detachments—8–12-man teams—are the maneuver forces. Air-power integration and indigenous forces are the only capabilities that give SF teams the ability to shift a battle. By design they are small, nimble, and low-profile. In 2003, with how few FACs were available to support the number of teams serving key roles of the invasion plan, CAS integration would be exponentially critical.

Just before the invasion, Maguire and his teams forward staged in Romania with 10th Group headquarters, planning the invasion of northern Iraq. During the buildup of forces, the U.S. State Department and Headquarters Army were negotiating with leaders in Turkey to host the 4th Infantry Division (4ID) out of Fort Hood, Texas. The division would provide much of the fires capabilities—artillery and long-range rockets, and rotary wing gunships—which would be critical assets for the A-teams well ahead of the main invasion force. It was a mechanized unit, utilizing M1s (Abrams main battle tank) and M2s (Bradley infantry fighting vehicle). The original invasion plan would be a massive push from the north across Iraq's highlands from Turkey, serving as a counter-thrust to the forces coming from Kuwait in the south.

However, the negotiations with Ankara broke down, and high command shifted 4ID to Kuwait with the rest of the main invasion force. This left two battalions of 10th SFG and 3rd Battalion, 3rd SFG (Forward Operating Base 33), alone in the north with Peshmerga indigenous forces (Kurds) to secure northern Iraq. In late March, the Army also set in motion the plan to airdrop the 173rd Airborne Brigade out of Vicenza Airbase, Italy, into Bashir airfield, a few miles from Erbil. The 173rd would provide no assistance to the SF teams, however, as the airborne operation would limit the available combat equipment the ground force at Bashir could insert with—no artillery or rotary wing support would be available. "We never saw any of them; they 'built combat power' for the next two months. When my battalion landed in Erbil and met up with the Peshmerga, we never saw anyone from the 173rd. They got a combat jump out of that, yet they were probably a good hour away from the green line, on the friendly side no less."

CJSOTF–N was charged with figuring out how a handful of A-teams would achieve the impossible and defeat more than half the Iraqi Army in the north, and was now forced to do so without 173rd Airborne and 4ID support. The 10th Group's commander, Colonel Cleveland, decided the teams would do the northern push alone. It remains unclear years later what purpose the 173rd Airborne was supposed to have in this battle; though they seized Bashir Airfield, they succeeded in little else during this phase of the operation.

With massed maneuver forces no longer available and, with it, a loss of enabling combat power (armor, infantry, aviation, surface fires), conditions were further muddied by a lack of coordination between the conventional and SOF units in the north. "And this is an example of how things involving the integration of CAS can go wrong, even before the actual mission had rightly begun." The disparity between air and ground did not lie with any air controller or SF team, but at the higher echelons. Those large maneuver forces failed to effectively integrate plans for the cohesive fusion of these different teams with conventional units.

By the end of March 2003, teams had already inserted into northern Iraq, linking up with Kurdish forces and moving to their assigned zones with clear objectives: break the Iraqi strength along key routes and staging areas while the blitz from Kuwait kept the Iraqi high command's attention focused south. It was a bold, high-risk plan, and could only have been entrusted to highly trained, specialized operators who thrive in austere, unclear, and variable extremes: the exact environment for which Army SF are trained. "You have SF troops already on the ground, when the decision is made that the mechanized armor division who were supposed to support, is not going to be a part of the scheme of maneuver. Can you imagine what went through our heads?"

"At this point, we were already fully immersed with the Peshmerga, teams were deep into their foreign internal defense [FID] and irregular-warfare activities. As the air-power guy on the ground, I had to ask myself 'Now what?' Tenth SFG A-teams did the majority of FID mission with the Peshmerga. Meanwhile, my 3rd Group teams had specially modified light tactical vehicles [LTV: a flatbed semi-truck dubbed the "deuce-and-a-half"]. These could be resupply vehicles, but they were armored and equipped them with defensive weaponry, so we would be the actual closing force and assumed the role of offensive maneuver—a role that would have been performed by the 173rd Airborne."

The A-teams were briefed that two-thirds of Iraq's Army was in the northern third of the country. The plan consisted of three SF battalions—two of which were rolling around in completely unarmored Land Rovers, and only one battalion prepared to do battle—facing nearly two-thirds of Iraq's Army. "Although that intelligence turned out to be inaccurate, over the course of our time in the north—10th SFG teams ended up facing an entire Iraqi division, while 3rd Group faced two total Iraqi infantry brigades. For the most part when we invaded, and the Iraqis saw that we were going all the way to Baghdad, their Army went home. Not to say that fights didn't happen, they did, but it wasn't *Desert Storm*'s version of how things played out. Much of their Army just evaporated." The ones who stayed, what remained of the Iraqi Army—a professional, well-equipped national fighting force—were the ones who were going to fight and die no matter what, and who the A-teams would face in the coming days.

There was a decisive point in the Battle of Debecka Pass where CAS literally made the difference. There is a terrain feature called "The Green Line" (not to be confused with the "Green Zone," the secured area inside Baghdad after the invasion). The Green Line ran along the mountainous arch running from Kirkuk to Mosul in a southeast-to-northwest line. North of this terrain is the traditional indigenous region which the Kurds called home. To the west and south is the Kirkuk–Mosul highway, where the Iraqi Army was dug into prepared fighting positions. The Kurds were predominantly isolated on their side of the line, making the Green Line a distinct demarcation between two regions of the country. "Our goal, as Colonel Cleveland had explained to us, was that we needed to take the Kirkuk–Mosul highway, and then take Kirkuk and Mosul from the Iraqi Army. Debecka Pass was a decisive point where we had to break the Iraqi Army's hold, in order to gain overwatch of the Green Line, and from there push into the cities." The terrain is not prohibitive for infantry and light-mobility packages, yet there are few ways through it. The few passes through the rugged terrain feature were critical to the plan.

The Debecka Pass is a highway that goes through that major terrain feature which ultimately leads to Erbil, a Kurdish redoubt. It is the only major route through the Green Line. "Considering the fact that we expected to face a major concentration of Iraqi mechanized infantry, off-roading wasn't likely, making that pass absolutely critical in the broader scheme of maneuver."

There were two significant limitations for employing CAS for this mission. The first was that northern Iraq was a sideshow to the big push to Baghdad, despite the assumption two-thirds of the Iraqi Army was thought to be in the north. In the days leading up to the assault on the Green Line, the teams lost a great deal of sleep trying to sort out this problem. They were far enough north that the only supporting firepower would be their own mortars, or fixed-wing aircraft operating at extended ranges. This meant the only aircraft available came from partner bases, aircraft carriers in the Gulf, or long-range bombers originating from well outside the region performing beyond-the-horizon launch and recoveries.

"The prioritization simply wasn't there because so many resources had been allocated to the southern push. This fundamentally changes how a JTAC [joint terminal attack controller] performs their job because typically you go into a mission relying on reactive fire assets and the variety of assets and capabilities inherent to a full inventory of air platforms. In 2003, EW [electronic warfare/non-kinetic effects] was not available to us either. The Navy had some EA-6B Prowlers, but those were focused on the surface-to-air threats closer to Baghdad, nothing going north for us.

Attack helicopters couldn't reach us, depriving us of anything quickly reactive, and ditto for AC-130 gunships."

They would make do with whatever was available. Unlike later in the war, when SOFs had the predominance in asset allocation, in the early phase of the war, aircraft would be tasked haphazardly based on need. For this mission, command and control and requesting aircraft was indeed haphazard. "We were told that we would get CAS by contacting CJSOTF–N, who would then prioritize requests and submit those directly to the CAOC, who would allocate assets against the entire invasion forces' prioritized requests. We didn't use the direct line, the Air Force air request net, which would later become the JARN (joint air request net), a beyond-line-of-sight satellite frequency." Instead, they would use a separate, independently allocated SATCOM channel to communicate with CJSOTF–N. Within the CAOC, there was a SOLE who would receive those requests, but once Lance and the other controllers sent the data to CJSOTF–N, there was nothing to do but wait for aircraft to check in on their strike nets, hoping the request had been filled. The SOLE, embedded in the CAOC and manned by SF personnel, were there specifically to help the CAOC prioritize their assets to support SOF missions. "They did a really good job early on in the invasion of Afghanistan—but it was a growing process a year and a half later and in March 2003. I got two pairs of F-18s and a B-52 for Debecka, Todd Gannon got a four-ship of F-14s that were loaded for close air support, unlike their typical air-interceptor loadout."

The assault on Debecka Pass would happen regardless of dedicated aircraft support. Before any aircraft arrived, the Peshmerga prepared to attack a section of the ridgeline deemed viable for overwatch. The force approached from the north; of Todd Gannon's two Operational Detachment–Alphas (ODA), one would secure Debecka village itself, the other was going after the Iraqi forces on the ridgeline further south. Lance would provide CAS for ODA395 and 394. "We had been waiting for CAS or any other assets to begin our push and kept waiting. The Pesh saw our gun trucks, with M2 .50 calibers, Mark-19s [40-mm grenade launchers], and organic mortars [60mm], and said they thought that would be enough firepower to take the ridge along with their personnel." The Kurdish Peshmerga had several flatbed, two-and-a-half-ton trucks upon which they had installed ZU-23/2s (a Russian twin-barrel 23-mm anti-aircraft cannon). The indigenous forces believed their organic firepower might be enough to break the enemy's hold on the ridge. All eight of the American gun trucks lined up abreast the ridgeline and began the ascent. Within two kilometers of the ridge, the M2 and Mk-19 gunners opened up on the Iraqi positions visible on the ridgeline. Those dug-in positions returned fire with DShK 12.7-mm machine guns. "We pushed forward, on-line, until we got about a mile [1.6 kilometers] from the ridgeline itself, then one of our gunners was able to clearly affect those fighting positions."

While this movement happed, Maguire worked out the nine-line for when aircraft arrived, realizing that, as they identified more fighting positions, there was roughly one dug-in Iraqi redoubt for each of the trucks. "I anticipated that backside of the ridgeline is where the preponderance of the Iraqi fighting personnel are, at least that's what I would have done. I plotted all eight of the DFP's [defensive fighting positions] that looked like they were sandbagged, covered, with those DShKs fully mounted and fixed to achieve overlapping fields of fire. And then on the map and imagery, which at that time was just FalconView topography, I picked identifiable points on the backside of the ridge to use as reference points for when aircraft came, something they could visually acquire."

They were under effective fire this entire time, from the moment the trucks began advancing on the ridge, and it was absolutely withering. "My particular gun truck was equipped with an M2, and our gunner was in a duel with a DShK gunner. He was hammering the living fuck out of that position when, all of the sudden, in front of us, I saw a white poof, which I called out over the net to the other trucks, who acknowledged." That white poof of smoke was the unmistakable signature of heavy artillery. A few seconds later, 122-mm artillery began raining down in between, in front, and behind the trucks. They could not stop, as this would give the mortar positions a fixed target, forcing them to withdraw, chased by artillery the entire way. They retrograded until they could put a terrain feature between them and whoever was calling in those artillery shots on the Iraqi side. As they moved to a defensible position, Maguire coordinated with the truck commanders on one radio, and waited for aircraft to check in on the other radio, simultaneously directing gunners at targets on the intended axis of advance, all the while working out the targeting solution for CAS.

The Pesh learned the hard way that they couldn't take the ridgeline with the gun trucks, so they waited behind a large spur, restocking ammunition. American deuce-and-a-half trucks coming up from the rear provided the sustainment. "Third SFG really thought through logistics and support, 10th SFG wasn't as sharp on resupply. As a side note, everybody was pretty shaken, we had all gotten our bell rung by the 122mm, it's an extremely unpleasant experience. This wasn't a couple indirect rockets or sporadic artillery either; 122-mm rounds weigh 45 pounds each and, at the rate they were firing at us, I'm not sure how many guns they had on the backside of the ridge, but it was miraculous that none of us took a direct hit as the vehicles were weaving at varying speeds up, and back down, the approach." Unlike a handful of mortars lobbed by insurgents in future years, 122mm were artillery pieces operated by the professional Iraqi Army in fixed positions, with overwatch from a key piece of terrain. Competent gun crews on these systems can sustain four to six rounds per minute, and all of these were firing on the American–Peshmerga force.

The formation of eight gun trucks and Peshmerga vehicles was set at open intervals, covering a one-kilometer battle line, and had approached to within a mile of the fighting positions. American doctrine states that all artillery fires are 600 meters for danger close, so there was no element of this force that was not considered danger close by these enemy fires throughout the entire advance. "The dispersal pattern is really hard to ascertain when you're right in the middle of the receiving end of that kind of hate, but it was all around us even as we made our retrograde to a concealed location."

Resupply complete, one of the A-team leaders got a call from higher echelons, telling them that they had two sorties of F/A-18s on the way, "So I said, 'Great, I've got targets.'" In the meantime, the Peshmerga commander asked what the aircraft can do to enable the assault. Maguire knew these aircraft would be limited on munitions, meaning they would have to prioritize targets; not every enemy position could be struck. "So I asked the commander his priority of targets, showing my map and imagery, everything that I had plotted based on my assessment of the terrain, and he agreed with the judgment. He picked two of the fighting positions, and a third which he believed to be the C2 [command and control] node for the forces embedded on the ridge. The thought process here was that, if we could at least take out those three positions, that would provide a lane for the Peshmerga to traverse the ridge and seize dominating terrain." They mounted up and retook the advance, halting about two miles from the ridge outside of the effective range of the DShKs. By this time, the artillery had stopped, but they remained in cover behind a small rise in terrain to avoid being spotted again. The first set of F/A-18s checked in, each armed with a single GBU-32.

The GBU most often arrives over a gunfight as a 500 or 2,000-lb GPS munition, the GBU-38 and 31, respectively. The 1,000-lb version is utilized exclusively by the Navy, dubbed the GBU-32 (GPS). Other 1,000-lb variants are the laser-guided GBU-16 and the unguided Mk-83. With only two bombs available, Maguire chose the two fighting positions at the highest point of the ridgeline; by the time he had passed the first set of nine-lines and the pilots were setting up for their attack, the second set of F/A-18s showed up. This second sortie had one GBU-38 (500-lb GPS), one GBU-12 (500-lb laser) and one Mk-82 (500-lb unguided) on each bird. "For this second pair, I briefed on the C2 node and a fourth fighting position that I assessed would have the most effect on the Peshmerga as they made their way to the ridgeline. I told them to employ the guided ordnance on those predetermined targets, wanting to hold onto the Mark-82s. Since the fighting positions ... aren't going to move, I kept the 82s in my pocket ... for when we moved over the ridge, where I anticipated there would be a mass of troops in the open, the contingency infantry there to provide a counterassault to our advance." The two unguided bombs were equipped with a DSU-33 radar sensor in the nose, which detects the weapon's distance to the ground, and an FMT-152 fuse in the tail, which triggers the weapon. These systems were phased out of the weapons inventory soon after the Iraq invasion. Both the DSU-33 and FMT-152 are activated when the weapon is released, sending out a brief radar-return signal. When the sensor detects a certain altitude above the ground, the FMU-152 detonates the munition, creating an "airburst" effect.

Airburst munitions detonated by a tail fuse are particularly effective. However, by removing the nose-detonation fuse in this construct, there is no ignition redundancy, meaning a higher potential to "dud" (fail to explode upon impact). Typically, unguided bombs have two fuses to ensure ignition of the explosive material. With the nose sensor creating that single point of failure for ignition, the advantage gained from a five-foot-long bomb with a tail-fuse ignition is that, when the fuse goes off, it begins the explosive chain from the back to the front as it falls. Therefore, this tail-down ignition across the weapon's surface drives explosive effect straight down towards the target. "The shrapnel pattern is positively fucking lethal, as opposed to nose fusing creating a nose-to-tail explosive sequence, where you would send the fragmentation up and away from the target."

The Mk-82s offered a superior fragmentation option for the infantry counterattack which waited on the other side of the ridgeline. The F/A-18s opted to rework their formation as a four-ship in order to execute simultaneous coordinated attacks. But there would be challenges doing so: not all of them were equipped with sensor pods such as the ATFLIRs (all-terrain, forward-looking infrared). Only the flight lead for each two-ship showed up with the sensors. But, as each aircraft had a GPS-guided weapon, and a laser-guided weapon, there wasn't a need for all aircraft to have an ATFLIR. The pilots worked internally to sort which aircraft would employ what bomb in sequence, to achieve the quickest desired effects for the ground force.

Prior to the F/A-18s dropping their weapons, a lone white Land Rover with three 10th Group soldiers approached Maguire's truck with news of a B-52 inbound; they could not reach the forward team over the command net. Maguire revised the air plan with the F/A-18s, based on the inbound B-52, wanting to utilize the first attacks as a visual queue for the behemoth bomber. After another quick discussion, the Peshmerga commander delayed his force's attack until after all aircraft engagements were complete, at which point all ground forces would assault the ridge and clear through everything.

When the F/A-18's came in, Maguire passed "Cleared hot" and immediately began briefing the B-52. The battle-damage assessment from the F/A-18s called the two fighting positions from the first nine-line destroyed, the C2 site reduced to rubble. When the force took the ridgeline, there was nothing but a smoldering hole. The other two fighting positions were not destroyed due to slight differences between targeted coordinates and actual impact points but were effectively reduced to the point of being unusable. The final bomb impacted at a cross point between sites atop the ridge, preventing anything from being able to traverse the ridge from the backside. The F/A-18 pilots reported a large group of personnel on the backside of the ridge, on-line, at the base of the terrain, just as Maguire had anticipated.

Those remaining enemy forces would be the target of the bomber, and Maguire briefed the B-52, which checked in with two dozen Mk-117s and 16 CBU-103 cluster munitions. The former is an older, unguided 750-lb bomb from previous decades, something the B-52s used to carry regularly in Vietnam. The latter weapons were the Wind-Corrected Munitions Dispenser variant of the CBU-87 cluster munition—yielding 202 BLU-97 bomblets dispensed via GPS guidance. The B-52 released its payload of Mk-117s on an axis between reference points briefed by Maguire. Each weapon was staggered by milliseconds, from the start to the end of the target corridor along the full axis of Iraqi forces behind the ridge as reported by the F/A-18s. The bomber carried the Mk-117s out on its wing struts, offering a staggered offset for the release pattern. "Talking with the B-52 bombardier, I asked him to string them a half a mile in each direction from the cross point that was hit by the F-18. I wanted no effects gaps. He said that was the perfect dispersal. I revised the two anchor points based on the F-18's input, and picked two spots that were at the base of the ridgeline's backside, each one a half mile from that new center point."

The B-52 would expend all its Mk-117s, but Iraqi personnel remained en masse. At this point, Maguire directed the B-52 to conduct a reattack with the CBU-103s slung in the internal bomb bays. The 3,232 bomblets would eliminate the remainder of the Iraqi forces preparing to counterattack over the ridge. Cluster munitions would have a brief career in the Global War On Terror, almost exclusively being used in the Iraq invasion, with occasional employments after, until being phased from Central Command's inventory around 2016.

"I still can't see any of this, I can't see the start or end points, the bomber didn't even have a sensor to 'see' the points I was plotting, so the bombardier is checking the terrain imagery on his FalconView as I'm passing grids for him to correlate. It was a very deliberate talk-on, it wasn't 'big to small,' but references to very definite points that none of us could effectively 'see' since we were both working off of imagery and coordinates." This was also the days before the 'bomb on target' or 'bomb on coordinate' method of attack, but for all intents and purposes this was a bomb on coordinate without guided weapons. "If you do math really quick, a mile is 1,760 yards; so, convert that to meters, which is what all weaponeering solutions are based on, that gives you about 1,600 meters. Now put 24 of those weapons at intervals in that space, that puts one bomb every 69 meters—at this point I've dropped 26,750 pounds of munitions—absolute hell-on-earth devastation. Additionally, somebody at Barksdale Air Force Base in Louisiana, where these B-52s came from half a world away, had thought this through. The weapons folks had set those Mk-117s to airburst fusing. Those weapons in all probability completely eradicated the battalion of Iraqi infantry on the backside of that ridgeline waiting to counterattack us."

Between the single ODA on the north end of the green line and the Peshmerga aligned with them, the size of the assault force trying to take the ridge was approximately ninety personnel, a company-minus of indigenous forces at best and a handful of SF soldiers with one FAC. With the aid of air power, such a force in lightly armored pickup trucks fought against an Iraqi infantry battalion, fully arrayed in defensible fighting positions, between five hundred to six hundred professional soldiers. "By the time we reached the top of the ridge, the Peshmerga took about twenty Iraqi soldiers captive, that was it. Air power crushed them. For anybody that doesn't think that precision munitions and good old-fashioned overwhelming firepower doesn't work, then they've never seen air power in combat."

Maguire, after the battle atop Debecka Ridge (March 2003). Here, he compared weapon impact points against the coordinates he had plotted mid-gunfight. (Photo provided by Lance Maguire)

"When it was all said and done, my driver yelled at me 'Hey, Lance, come back and sit down in your seat (the front passenger seat).' I went back and sat down and looked out the windshield to see a DShK round stuck in the plexiglass. My Army teammates, the gunners especially, knew their business. We never got within a mile of the ridgetop during that initial assault, because they knew the DShK can't outshoot the M2 but, from a mile away, even though we would take DShK plunging fire, where the trajectory of the gun is tilted upward so the bullets fall in an arc, our gunners could still employ direct fire. Were it not for the ground guys being absolutely dialed in to their jobs, I couldn't do mine. So, yes, there is the CAS team, whose purpose is to provide aerial fires, but the mission is about everyone doing their job, and doing it well, and, wouldn't you know it, sometimes luck is involved, exemplified by the cracked bulletproof glass between my face and a 12.7-mm Iraqi bullet."

***

"While perhaps physical fitness is the one human-performance tier over which the servicemember has supreme control, the other three tiers reside largely in the hands of the spouse/partner, who remains at home for months and years at a time. Thus, if any member of the CAS team, and indeed the entire national-defense enterprise has a direct impact over every echelon of the battlespace, it is the ones who remain at home while their loved ones volunteer to go into harm's way in service to the ideals that this nation upholds as supreme."

"Having lived through Grenada, Panama, Gulf War, Somalia, the Balkans, Afghanistan, Iraq, Syria, and deployed or watched everyone deploy unexpectedly, our wives make or break the relationship based on how well they hold up under stress, and how well they can handle everything at home alone. I saw the same thing in the year I was in Korea."

"Regardless of how good one's marriage or relationship is, very often time stood still at home for the next four months, six months, or year for the family. It takes a strong, patient, and at least semi-independent woman to be able to handle it. It takes a phenomenal wife to stick with it through multiple assignments and deployments. A support system is necessary but, honestly, unless the in-laws cohabitate for that deployment, the spouse is alone and doing nearly everything."

"My wife had been in America for two years, we had been married for 15 months, and we had a three-week-old son on 9/11. Her English vocabulary measured in the hundreds of words and the closest relatives, my parents, were a six-hour drive away. Timewise, I had 18 years in service and was looking forward to retiring in two years. On that Tuesday (September 11), 20 years ago, it was such a long day in everyone's life. Me and my Army brethren planned all day at the unit. When I got home, well after dark, AK (Ae Kyoung) looked at me with Spartan determination and stated what happened (as if I didn't know), said it was going to take a long time for this to be over (as if it had really even started), and that I wasn't going to retire in two years, I was going to fight! I deployed five times over the next six and a half years. You'd never guess she was Korean, not Spartan, because she basically told me to come home carrying my shield, or on it! We've been together since November '98, married in June '00, still going strong, and honestly I just don't think I can take any of the credit."

CHAPTER 10

Type of Control and Method of Engagement

On March 12, 2001, just a few months prior to the invasion of Afghanistan and the two decades of close air support (CAS) that followed, a pivotal and scarcely reported incident occurred at the Udairi live-fire range in Kuwait, killing six military personnel and wounding 12 more. On that day, U.S. Air Force TACPs (tactical air control party), a New Zealand forward air controller (FAC), a U.S. Army Special Forces contingent, and several members of the Kuwaiti military were conducting live-fire training in doctrinal CAS procedures. They were supported by U.S. Navy F/A-18s, who were employing Mk-82 (500-lb unguided bombs) on target sets designed to simulate the conditions of a combat mission. The section of F/A-18s, callsign *Lion71/72*, was joined by an F-14, callsign *Latch41*, whose pilot was an FAC–Airborne (FAC–A), a terminal attack control-certified pilot.

According to the post-incident investigative report instigated by Central Command's (CENTCOM) commander, General Tommy Franks, there were no extraneous issues with the aircrew (medical, training readiness, or technical) preventing safe execution of this training mission. There were minor equipment discrepancies with the incident aircraft, including an issue with the head-up display and night-vision goggles (NVG) used by the pilots, but none resulting in a 'grounding designation' or deemed a high-enough risk to the mission. For the ground party, the location, known as OP10 (Observation Point 10), was properly manned, with more than the minimum requisite of ground personnel current and qualified to perform CAS as directed by regulations and range instructions. Further, the use of overt and covert marking devices—as well as the minimum-required equipment for communications, target marking, and night-vision devices—were on hand, and the investigation reported that non-NVG-equipped personnel confirmed the use of an overt white strobe light fixed to one of the nearby vehicles for marking purposes.

In summary, the investigation report[1] noted: That numerous personnel occupied OP10 throughout the day of the incident, but SSgt Crusing (the lead TACP and Range Control/Safety Officer) maintained a highly professional atmosphere. The number of people did not adversely affect his performance as the GFAC (Ground

Forward Air Controller) or ECAS (Emergency Close Air Support) trainer. SSgt Crusing was not over-tasked on the day of the incident because the responsibilities of OIC, RSO and RCO are inherent in performing GFAC duties. During the pre-mission planning and coordination, the Air Support Operations Center had mis-assigned callsigns to certain aircraft, including LION71, who the ground party understood to carry live munitions, but this particular aircraft had been assigned LION71 by mistake. This was attributed to "administrative errors." Further, while the main GFAC had agreed to integrate the FAC-A, contradictory mission planning had presumed that the aircraft would be supporting a separate ground element conducting training on an entirely different part of the range, well clear of operations associated with OP10. The main GFAC and all ground party at OP10 knew and understood that LION71 would be flying with live ordnance, as did the aircraft of the same callsign. The primary GFAC had conducted a range clearance pass with LATCH41 to ensure the absence of the Bedouin tribes who frequently transited the area, per range instructions, and that as the mission went on, did not assess that additional clearance passes from other aircraft would alter or change this assumption due to the increasing darkness of nightfall and the persistent employment of aircraft earlier in the day.

It should be noted here that, in the calendar year prior to this incident, Udairi range had experienced CAS exercise mishaps with aircrew misidentifying the target and engaging twice, and, in the third instance, improper clearance from the GFAC to the aircraft resulted in munitions impacting within one hundred meters of a Bedouin tribe who had not been cleared of the range. Per the investigation: "That identification of OPs and the target area, and differentiation between the two, have been documented problems that have contributed to previous range incidents. That despite four documented incidents in the past eight months, and attempts to improve conditions, OPs and targets remain hard for pilots to see day or night." The incident pilots described the target location as "a cratered, blackened out area with indiscernible vehicles vice a defined target array," while OP10 included a tower with a white-painted roof, situated on a ridgeline two kilometers south of the impact area.

On the night of the incident, the GFAC had agreed to split controller responsibilities with the FAC–A, where the GFAC would maintain "positive direct control" for observing and orienting the aircraft as well as "final clearance authority" for weapons release. The FAC–A would conduct aircraft check-ins, situation update and vectoring, and enhanced target talk-ons for the attacking aircraft—for the purpose of understanding target and friendly locations. Prior to the incident, a two-ship of F/A-18s (callsign *Sniper*) had conducted successful CAS attacks on intended targets with the GFAC at OP10. However, it was noted in the investigation that *Sniper* did not receive a standard nine-line CAS briefing, nor did they request one. Eighteen separate descriptive calls between the controller and *Sniper* occurred for target correlation, and the aircrew for these F/A-18s acknowledged difficulty in acquiring both the intended target and the friendly location prior to the first weapons release. Further, the FAC–A was using non-standard CAS brevity ("Good nose position"), while *Sniper* provided the doctrine-mandated calls of "Target in sight, Friendlies in sight" prior to making their "In" call before requesting clearance from the ground controller.

Lion71 and *72* would check in after sundown, and again did not receive a nine-line brief. The incident report noted that, while the standard attack vectoring template for fixed and rotary wing aircraft performing CAS, doctrine did not mandate the use of the nine-line as a requirement. The pilot for *Lion71* acknowledged required calls for identifying friendlies, targets, and restrictions provided prior to the attack. The pilot identified the OP during his pass over the range before the attack, but did not identify the target location and the OP at the same time to ensure segregation of the two points. Fourteen descriptive calls were passed between the ground controller and the FAC–A, and the relaying of these comms and confirmatory remarks from the attacking aircraft led the ground party to believe *Lion71* understood the intended target from the relay.

As *Lion71* departed the initial point and proceeded inbound, his aircraft was oriented on the OP, not the target. The ground controller had momentarily stopped assessing the attacking aircraft while conferring with another member of the ground party who was correctly marking the impact area using an infrared pointer device. Upon reacquiring the attacking aircraft, the ground controller observed three aircraft (*Lion71* and *72*, and *Latch41*) and requested confirmation that *Lion71* was inbound, which the attacking pilot confirmed. *Lion71* never briefed "Target in sight, Friendlies in sight," and yet again *Latch41* provided non-standard comms, stating "Good nose position." *Lion71* hit the "pickle" button, releasing the three 500-lb bombs with a trajectory terminating at OP10. As soon as the weapons were released, the GFAC passed clearance to include the method of target mark: "Cleared hot on sparkle [brevity term meaning infrared pointer to indicate target]," but *Lion71* transmitted over "sparkle" when acknowledging clearance.

Too late, the ground party realized *Lion71* had been errantly targeting OP10, and the bombs impacted within fifty meters of the OP, killing four American personnel, including TACP Jason Faley, and the New Zealand special operator, while 12 others were wounded from the blast and shrapnel. The four vehicles on site were significantly damaged. None of the ground party were wearing personal protective equipment, including Kevlar helmets or body armor, as it was not required by regulation.

The injured and deceased were evacuated later in the night after every first aid and emergency care was attempted on site, with credit to the FAC–A and ground controller who began medevac procedures immediately following the incident. CENTCOM surgical care had been alerted and scrambled to aid, but the extent of injuries was extensive enough to be beyond hope for the fallen. The investigation's conclusions asserted the attacking pilot's, FAC–A's, and the ground controller's actions, as well as the conditions of the range, were all contributing factors to the misidentification of the target—which included errant comms, failure to assess aircraft vectoring and positions, and assumptions of both responsibility and clarity among the CAS team—added to the missteps that resulted in six dead and 12 wounded.

There were other incidents that had a profound impact on how procedural CAS would evolve in order to prevent fratricide, including the Tarnak Farms incident where a misidentification of ground fire from an F-16 resulted in a laser-guided bomb killing four Canadian soldiers and injuring eight more. It would not be until 2004 that the need to brief distinguishing "types of control" and "methods of engagement" were required pieces of information in the now-mandatory nine-line attack brief, intended to clarify procedural sequencing of aircraft and controller actions leading up to the release of ordnance.

There are three types of control, each specific to the battlefield circumstances and conditions of the mission. According to close air support reference manuals,[2] Type I "control is used when the controller visually acquires the target and the attacking aircraft at the point of weapons release. This type of control is used when the controller needs to visually analyze aircraft geometry in relation to the target to ensure the aircraft are attacking the intended target."[3] Simply, Type I controls are those circumstances where the JTAC (joint terminal attack controller) must see the target and be able to assess the aircraft simultaneously, and provide deliberate clearance based on visual cues. The aircraft must also be able to see and acknowledge the target and friendly position in real time prior to, and through, weapons release.

Type II is used "when the controller cannot visually acquire the attacking aircraft at weapons release or cannot see the intended target. The JTAC must either visually acquire the target or acquire accurate targeting information from another approved source."[4] Despite the lack of mandate to visually acquire targets or aircraft, the JTAC will still make every attempt to do so. Type II controls are typically performed when the JTAC is confident the targeting information (grid, explicit terrain feature, aircraft designation) is a high-confidence target vector that has been verified by the attacking aircraft; the parameters for confirming safety to ground forces remain paramount through additional confirmation.

Both Type I and Type II controls are single-clearance engagements, meaning every time an aircraft is "in" for an attack, the ground controller must provide individual clearance to the aircraft releasing a munition.

Type III control, according to the doctrine upon which close air support reference manuals are based "is used when the JTAC requires the ability to provide clearance for multiple attacks within a single engagement subject to specific attack restrictions, and any or all of the following conditions exist: JTAC is unable to visually acquire the attacking aircraft at weapons release; JTAC is unable to visually acquire the target; the attacking aircraft is unable to acquire the mark/target prior to weapons release."[5] Type III controls are much rarer, but not infrequent. Often, this type of control would permit the JTAC to release an aircraft for multiple attacks without delaying the kill-chain sequence by providing subsequent, individual clearances. However, each Type III attack requires explicit constraints to restrict effects to a specific area, desired effect, or ground-commander limitation. Thus, Type III should not be misconstrued as "carpet bombing" or the erroneous release of aircraft to unnecessarily reattack a single target to the detriment of the mission.

At the time of the Udairi incident, there were still three types of control, but Type I was simply defined as "direct control" (JTAC–aircraft), Type II as "indirect" (incorporating additional assets or targeting) and Type III as "reasonable assurance" (uncertain targeting info).

There are two methods of engagement which dictate or influence which type of control a JTAC selects for a CAS brief—bomb on coordinate (BOC) and bomb on target (BOT). There is no "right" or "wrong" application of these labels, and one—coordinate-driven—should not assume a higher degree of accuracy or precision; it is merely the quickest employment method within safety considerations. From Joint Publication 3-09.3: "A BOC attack is used when the JTAC determines that he can create the desired effects against that target with CAS aircraft and ordnance employing on a specific set of coordinates."[6] Thus, if a JTAC or aircrew is able to determine specific coordinates with a relative confidence in their accuracy, then the JTAC will request aircraft employ munitions on a specific location on the battlespace, making for a relatively swift CAS brief. The parameters of the type of control endure regardless of the method of engagement.

For bomb on target: "A BOT or self-derived targeting requires that the aircrew is tally/contact/captured the JTAC's intended target or aim point."[7] This method is most readily applicable in the climes of Afghanistan and Iraq, where enemy combatants are not fixed to a grid in many circumstances, requiring the JTAC or FAC–A to conduct target correlation with the aircraft—target talk-ons and confirmatory comms—because the controller is unable to ascertain a specific grid coordinate.

The preceding technical information is complex to be certain; understanding its role in how CAS was achieved is difficult for anyone to grasp at first read, let alone understand how to apply in the middle of a gunfight. Its inclusion in this chapter is intended, like so many of the introductory vignettes in this work, to express the sheer complexity and specificity required to perform CAS in a combat or training environment. The production and implementation of these tactics, techniques and procedures (TTP) were standardized in the September 2003 JTTP for CAS (3-09.3), the precursor doctrine manual to Joint Publication 3-09.3. Further, the changes began distribution across the community by inclusion as a Headquarters Air Force-directed read file for JTACs prior to conducting CAS training. Ultimately, these requirements were revised to become part of the CAS standard-template briefing in order to ensure safe execution of CAS.

Close air support is undoubtedly the most dangerous activity American service members undertake in warfare as it deliberately employs the most destructive weapons ever designed for tactical-level confrontations in close proximity to the friendly elements engaged. While mistakes were made, sometimes at great cost, these revisions would be the first of many intended to ensure some measure of improved safety in the most difficult and dangerous thing these men were asked to do.

CHAPTER 11

Shock and Awe

Haditha Dam, April 1, 2003

Chief Master Sergeant Tommy Case (ret.) holds a special and distinguished place in American military history, being one of a select few U.S. service members who has been awarded not one, but two Silver Stars for gallantry in combat. His story of the two separate incidents resulting in his receipt of these distinguished citations is one he has told often; "I'm actually a little sick of telling these, because I've done it so many times." His name echoes across the JTAC community and, like a few others, he saw service throughout the entire timeline of the War on Terror. Chief Case, or "TC" as he insists on being called by all who talk to him, is like every other JTAC who interviewed for this work: recounting the selfless service, calm collection under fire, and sheer relentless determination to rise to any occasion—always qualified by some version of the statement "... but I was just another guy doing my job, it wasn't that big of a deal."

This work would be incomplete without the exploits of TC, who, by luck and circumstance, would be one of so many JTACs who participated in historically significant events that significantly impacted the strategic impact of the War on Terror. In this case, it was deployed alongside U.S. Army Rangers on one of the most harrowing missions in the 75th Ranger Regiment's history: the seizure of the Haditha Dam during the invasion of Iraq on April 1, 2003.

Case would deploy many times, but only twice to Iraq. For both, the timing and circumstances were incredibly significant: his first trip was at the very front lines of the 2003 invasion, and his last was during the closedown and withdrawal of U.S. forces in 2011. Even in a community of men who exude uncommon valor and innovation, his career is almost without peer.

His first deployment was in May 2002. When 9/11 happened, most of the TACPs (tactical air control party) around Case, most of whom were senior in rank, geared up and invaded with the Rangers. Case would miss the Afghanistan invasion but would more than make up for it. "When some of the guys came back, several of them had collected sand in a bunch of little jars from different locations in Pakistan and Afghanistan."[1] Fate's unpredictability meant Case often became a TACP of circumstance: right/wrong place at the right/wrong time, "… however you want to look at it. It seems like everything I did going forward turned out to be pretty lucrative as far as doing what we trained to do as JTACs."

One key thing to make clear, especially when discussing Case's role during the raid to seize Haditha Dam, is that it wasn't just him executing air power. There were several others who were as deeply integrated into enabling the Army's success on the ground. Close air support (CAS) is achieved in a collaborative fashion, even though the final sequence comes down to a sole individual clearing the skies for air strikes. The invasion of Iraq would be his first time truly employing airpower assets; "Iraq in 2003 was the 'put me in coach' moment early in my career."

Case would leave the United States embedded with Bravo Company, 3rd Battalion, 75th Ranger Regiment, headed to a forward-staging base close to Iraq. This too was the product of circumstance; another controller had been assigned to Bravo Company but, during the training spin up for the invasion, had a negligent discharge of his weapon—a cardinal sin for the Ranger Regiment where weapons discipline is sacrosanct. "It sucked for that JTAC, but that's what resulted in my opportunity. We were in Saudi Arabia for what seemed like forever, just rehearsing to jump into Saddam International Airport. I am so thankful we didn't, because I wouldn't be telling this story if we had jumped in, that was going to be certain death for most of that assault package."

Bravo Company staged at H1 Air Base in southern Iraq, hours before the invasion was slated to kick off. H1 had already been seized by Alpha Company, 3/75, completely bombed out, and was largely unchanged from the First Gulf War. "There was nothing there but a bunch of goat shit and a huge runway that was big enough for C-17s. This was late in March, and it was cold those nights in the desert. I was huddled up against the company FSO [fire support officer] and FSNCO [fire support non-commissioned officer] trying to stay warm the night we arrived." The next morning, the Rangers awoke to guidance from the Special Operations Task Force—a vague FRAGO (fragmentary order) ordering them to drive north towards Syria, and conduct VISOPs (visual operations)—looking for targets of opportunity near Iraqi border-control checkpoints. "It wasn't going to be challenging, but for certain it would be a controller's wet dream, where all I would need to do is match infrared (IR) sparkle with the aircraft and go to town."

The mission changed quickly, and Bravo Company spent the next night driving across the open desert, and linking up with a Special Forces (SF) reconnaissance team as they made their way north from the border. They stopped next to Objective *Roadrunner*, another desert landing strip which 3/75 Rangers had jumped into and secured in the prior hours of darkness. There, Case would link up with his then-supervisor and veteran of the Afghanistan invasion, Eric Brandenburg. "He would be on the net with me, controlling aircraft on this mission. I was relieved to see him. I'll admit I was feeling a little overwhelmed at what we were about to do, and having another Air Force guy there who happens to be my supervisor was a comfort in a place where comfort was not readily found." The combined company force got a couple hours of sleep and then immediately turned their efforts towards hasty planning and rehearsals for the new objective.

Their updated task and purpose: take the Haditha Dam—no other force on earth is better suited for seizing key terrain than the Ranger Regiment. When the SF reconnaissance team was briefed on the new objective—seize the dam—the recon operators were taken aback. "There is a brigade-sized element of the Iraqi Army guarding that facility, including elements of the fanatical Republican Guard and Iraqi Special Forces." They would be decisively engaged from the moment the first trucks came into view of the dam. The company commander, Dave Doyle, got on the SATCOM radio and was communicating with the Central Command operations center, voicing his concerns about the size of our force relative to what the reconnaissance team relayed was at the dam. General Tommy Franks came back over the channel and told Captain Doyle, "Your mission is to seize Objective *Lynx* [the code name for Haditha Dam], and that is what you are going to do."

The Rangers were using Garmin eTREX GPSs during mission planning; this was before the CJCS (Chairman of the Joint Chiefs of Staff) directive which mandated all American forces had to use issued military GPS systems for targeting. The J2 (intelligence section) at the Joint Operations Center was passing dozens of relevant grids for targets, infil routes, and all manner of other points of interest, and Rangers were rapidly hand-jamming these into their commercial GPS devices.

The day before Objective *Lynx*, the men of Bravo Company could see the contrails of B-52s passing high overhead, vectored straight towards Baghdad and the dam. Those strike packages were the battering ram that would clear their path to Haditha. As they drove in that night, everything around their infil route was burning hulks—remnants of the Iraqi Army. To have attempted a movement to contact without the air war opening this corridor would have been certain death had the company-plus-sized element tried to fight through that much defense—armor and anti-aircraft artillery pieces were in layered defense but smoldering wrecks now.

"I'm sitting in the back of the gun truck as we make our way to the objective, and all I have for navigation is a 1:250k JOG [joint operational graphic] map. I don't have an easy-to-read 1:50k MGRS [military gridded reference system] map, from which I can quickly pull grids for targeting. This behemoth map is all in lat/long. I had this thing unfolded and was staring at it under my red lens headlamp, looking like an old man at a park reading a damn newspaper. We had F-15s escorting the convoy, and I'm trying to pass them lat/long coordinates for our frontline trace, which was slow and atrocious. Back then we didn't have codified brevity or worldwide standards for terminology like the later years of the war. This invasion is where those TTPs [tactics, techniques and procedures] would be developed in real time. So, when it came to sensor tasking, I just told the pilot to keep one sensor on the lead vehicle, and the other sensor to scan ahead. This would go on to be labeled "Neutral posture" in future tactics manuals but, in the hours of darkness on April 1, 2003, I just made it up because it seemed reasonable."

When they got to the dam, attack helicopters from the 160th Special Operations Aviation Regiment buzzed overhead, as the F-15s peeled off. The Rangers thought this could have ended up just being like a raid in Afghanistan: a few pop-shots, take the objective, slam a Rip-it and everybody high-fives at the end. "It was a little more exciting than that."

Case was with the company's headquarters element, which was labeled "CP Black" in planning and identified as such in all ground and air communications. CP Black set up an austere C2 (command and control) node right on the spillway, which worried Case. "I was a little concerned about that, because the reason we were sent in to seize the dam was to prevent the Iraqis from blowing the dam and causing a catastrophic humanitarian crisis." Haditha Dam held 2 cubic miles worth of water, and rupturing the dike would have submerged Baghdad, impacting millions of people and, most importantly for the invasion, stalled the 3rd Infantry Division's advance to take the city. "So, yeah, I was a little worried about where we set up—TACPs don't surf unless you're stationed in Hawaii." Rangers would set up blocking positions (BP) at the eastern and western ends of the dam, and Brandenburg would go with BP West while Case remained with CP Black on the spillway.

Immediately, the anticipated pop-shots began, but the gunfight grew louder and louder, reaching a crescendo in short order and quickly becoming a full-on battle. Iraqi soldiers started coming out of the cracks and crevices, many of them leaving the control center and outstations and immediately engaging the BPs on both sides. "Bodies were being stacked like cordwood, it was unreal. Brandenburg and I had an internal radio net, so that we could confer with each other to deconflict airspace and airstrikes, and I could hear from his comms that he was in the fight of his life at the BP. But over the net, he's so casual: 'Hey, man, can you send up the request for more assets? It's super busy up here.'" Posted at one of the gun trucks where they had SATCOM set up with an X-wing antenna, Case grabbed the handset for the truck radio and came up on the joint air request (JARN) net, "This is *Striker*, located at Objective *Lynx*, request immediate air support, heavy contact on objective." He heard nothing on the net in return. He would revert to instinctual radio operator drills: check "ABCs" (antennas, battery, connections). "On the X-wing antenna, one of the array blades was broken at some point, shot off sometime between rolling into the objective and setting up CP Black. I didn't want to dig through my shit in the middle of this fight to pull out my AV-2125 coke-can antenna, the one you needed to expand and pull out the little winglets and soft-antenna arrays, so I tried a shot in the dark." He picked up the handset and repeated the request over SATCOM, and added "If anyone copied this transmission, key your handset twice." After a few seconds of waiting, he recalled distinctly hearing a "click-click" over the net.

A few minutes later, F-16s checked in. For the next five days, they had assets overhead 24 hours a day. Haditha Dam would be one of the most CAS-centric battles of the war, exceeding any of the battles ahead of the 3rd Infantry Division's push to Baghdad proper. As soon as the F-16s finished checking in, Case tasked them to Brandenburg. No sooner had the Ranger force set in place to begin clearance than the dam began receiving mortar rounds from multiple MFPs (mortar firing points), tiny islets on the reservoir on the other side of the dyke. "Trying to talk an airplane onto any of these little islands, with those old-school sensor pods and the pilots unable to identify the smoke plumes from 25,000 feet, it was tough as hell. Brandenburg and I both tried doing talk-ons to get the aircraft tally of those mortars, and we didn't want to just start blowing shit up and risk missing the mortars entirely either. And then a ranger had a brilliant idea."

One of the squad leaders pulled out a Javelin missile launcher from their weapons stock, a newly issued tool the regiment had yet to employ in combat. "This dude sends a shot, and it impacts one of the islands with an MFP on it, and the pilot immediately tallied the 'spotting round.'" One CAS brief and one bomb later and the first MFP engaging Bravo Company was neutralized. Case would have the distinction of using a Javelin anti-tank missile to mark for CAS in extremis.

This had all occurred within the first hour of taking the dam. Brandenburg had taken the priority of fires up to this point, being in the best position to see and direct aircraft, as his element was up on the dam itself. The forward air controllers (FAC) would conduct friendly centric CAS briefs over and over late into the night and the next day.

The gravity of the spectacle was not lost on either man, something Case took note of in a brief, quiet moment. "If you've ever been to Vegas and seen the Hoover Dam, it's impressive. The Haditha Dam is every bit as impressive as the Hoover Dam but, unlike the latter, the former is so wide and deep it has a four-lane highway on top." Haditha had been designed by the Soviets in the 1960s and built in the 1970s. At the time, it was one of the biggest in the world, and powered nearly a third of Iraq. "We are still dealing with contact all around, and suddenly an Iraqi LMTV [light medium tactical vehicle] comes barreling down the highway, stopping and picking up Iraqi soldiers from the superstructure in the middle of the causeway. Now it's sandwiched between the two blocking positions, loading up with dudes and then starts rolling towards one of the BPs."

When the LMTV was identified, Case was controlling a two-ship of F-16s, callsign *Darby54*. Of the dozens of aircraft types and different callsigns actively utilizing their airspace over the days spent on the dam, *Darby* is the only name Case would recall from this mission. "I'll never forget that one. I passed an attack brief for this truck, asking for 20mm because we certainly couldn't risk putting a bomb on the dam, but this truck needed to be neutralized immediately before it could hit the BP at speed. The F-16s made their approach, calling 'in from the north.' I'm looking up into the daytime sky trying to find the aircraft." For those who have never seen CAS in person, there is a delay between sound and visual when aircraft fire their guns. Depending on how far away the observer is when the pilots pull the trigger, it might be several seconds between seeing the shells sparking and impacting the earth and hearing the report from the cannon. "We held everything fixed wing at medium altitude, or more than 15,000 feet above ground level, due to the assessed surface-to-air threats. I never see the aircraft, but I hear the rip of the 20-mm M61A1 Vulcan cannon, and I look where the rounds are impacting. That first pass engaged BP East, and by the grace of God nobody got hurt from that gun run. Those Rangers at the BP are sitting there shaking their fists at the enemy and screaming 'America!' thinking this is the greatest thing, but I'm utterly mortified knowing how close they came to being a near fratricide."

Case had never given the F-16s clearance for that pass. Once confirming no Rangers had been harmed in the errant gun run, he immediately told the pilots of the near fratricides, that they had done so without the controller providing clearance. His next action was directing them to depart the airspace and contact the Air Operations Center for routing and follow-on actions.

"This is my first time controlling fixed-wing CAS in combat. My heart is sunk into my stomach at this moment. And Captain Doyle looks at me and says 'Tommy, I heard everything, I know that wasn't on you, I need you to stay on the horn and keep controlling CAS.' That was hands-down the single most important moment of my life because that company commander didn't look at me as some Air Force guy, he didn't think of me as some dude that just talks to airplanes on the radio, he called me by my first name and made it clear that he trusted me to keep doing my job. That was the biggest boost I've ever experienced. Up to then, I was pretty confident in doing my job, I've been doing it for a long time. I knew I hadn't done anything procedurally wrong, but that mistake by the pilot shook me to my core."

The next set of aircraft came in and the mission continued apace. Brandenburg and Case got into a rhythm, holding all aircraft to the north in their assigned blocks. Brandenburg had everything to the south and west along the river, while Case had all targets on the reservoir and east. Out on the reservoir itself, the Iraqi Army was using patrol boats equipped with DShKs and other heavy machine guns, never getting close enough for the Rangers to engage with organic weapons, but they could certainly affect the Americans posted on the dam. Case was working with a set of F-14s at this point, working feverishly to get the Navy fighters talked-on, but several different iterations of target correlation couldn't get a head-up display lock, due to the waves breaking line-of-sight and no ability to generate a return from using the ground-based laser designator. During this ordeal, a pair of British Harriers checked in. Pivoting to these slower aircraft, who were able to see below better than the F-14s, Case passed a nine-line brief with an area-focused attack profile, and the British jets employed a Mk-82 airburst munition over the formation, successfully neutralizing several boats zipping around the lake. "From the battle damage assessment, they hit seven of the big PT boats, and an additional couple of smaller zodiac-type vessels. These smaller craft had one dude on the motor and another dude firing an RPG. It was beyond believability what the Iraqis were throwing at us in this phase of the mission."

Case and Brandenburg would not be alone in striking priority and time-sensitive targets. The Ranger reconnaissance element, that had forewarned Bravo Company about the overwhelming Iraqi forces on the dam, were continuing to conduct reconnaissance nearby, staying in comms with the Rangers on Haditha. "We were consistently getting harassed by 152-mm artillery. I'm not sure how many times it impacted around the dam; we stopped counting after 150 or so had landed nearby in the first night. Artillery shells landing near you absolutely sucks, to put it bluntly. You feel so utterly helpless, because you can't do anything about it, and it was made worse by the fact that we didn't know where it was coming from. We were taking cover in the concrete pillars along the causeway, trying to control aircraft or shoot at the enemy, and after so long I'd have to swap a battery or some other necessary tasks. What else can I do but run to the truck and grab a resupply while rounds are falling? This barrage included white phosphorus [WP], either being used as marking rounds or simple illumination for the Iraqi ground forces attacking us, but the entire Coalition was utterly paranoid about the threat of chemical weapons. So when one of these WP rounds would explode, everyone would freeze, wondering if that was the first CBRN [chemical, biological, radiological, nuclear] shot, and then you'd see some mangy dog run past it unfazed, and get back in the gunfight."

After some of the shells impacted, Brandenburg and the FSNCO ran to the crater to do a hasty reverse-trajectory calculation of the distance and direction of the artillery rounds. It is a rare skill, but possible to ascertain from a fresh artillery impact, though not precise by any means. But rudimentary calculation could not ascertain usable data for vectoring aircraft to go look for the firing point, especially not while still actively fighting the battle for the dam.

The FSO and Case opened up the 1:250k JOG map and began scouring for likely locations, ultimately identifying a small airbase depicted about thirteen kilometers away. Knowing the capabilities of the enemy inventory, it was the only reasonable location within range of those types of artillery pieces. Case relayed this information to the Ranger reconnaissance unit. A few hours later, the FAC with the recon team called back, confirming they had eyes on active artillery pieces which matched the pace of continuous incoming fire. Case tasked the next set of incoming aircraft to the recon team, who successfully destroyed the Iraqi artillery.

This mission would be the first time these controllers had employed JDAMs (joint direct attack munitions), and these were dropped from a bomber at 20,000 feet. Neither Case nor the other controllers had formally trained on the use of these GPS-guided weapons in a CAS scenario, beyond what had been discussed internally in the team room back in the States. "This is a big deal because it was 'only' two years after the … incident in Afghanistan which had almost killed Hamid Karzai. JDAMs as a CAS tool was brand new, and for anyone to think that there weren't huge risks involved would be wrong. But we were sent there to do a job, and were given these kinds of tools, so we had to figure it out under the most stressful and dangerous conditions imaginable. We didn't have quick-reference manuals like the JFIRE or any other type of TTP manual back then. The techniques we used out there on the dam, other than some basic procedural terminal attack control tactics, were things we came up with on the fly. To the bystander, or someone who isn't familiar with the intricacies of CAS, maybe it seems incredible. I don't think of what we did as incredible; a lot of what we did simply became the TTPs and future doctrine … in the JPUB [Joint Publication]. We employed these tactics out of simple necessity."

There was a combat controller (CCT) who jumped in the truck with Case when the force left H1; "As we were about to head out on this crazy mission, I asked him what his deal is, and he said 'I'm a combat controller.' At this young stage of my career, all I knew is TACPs aren't supposed to like CCTs; I'd seen these guys at the big Ranger multi-lateral jump exercises, didn't really know what they did, and hadn't bothered to find out either. There was a lot of tribalism between the two different Air Force career fields back then. Now, before raiding a giant dam in the middle of Iraq, it seemed as good of a time as any to find out. I asked what he was responsible for here, and he said, 'I'm responsible for HLZs [helicopter landing zones], drop-zones, and resupply.' 'Cool, man, I'm a TACP and I do airstrikes.' High-fives all around and we rolled out."

"While we were in the middle of this massive battle, after about a day into it, I asked him if he was TAC-qualified, and he responded, 'Yeah, dude, I've just been waiting for you to ask.' This ended up producing an absolutely lethal TGO [terminal-guidance operations] team; we literally burned up the three SOFLAMs [Special Operations Forces Laser Acquisition/Marking Device] that we had brought with us out to the dam." The men would take turns on the radio and the laser designator, one marking targets while the other was controlling aircraft, then swap, over and over and over. The Ranger FSNCO was in this rotation as well. "We would split our little AO [area of operations] within the broader ROZ [restricted operating zone], each of us controlling a set of aircraft on individual radio nets; but with us standing right next to each other, we could easily deconflict airspace, and we already had an established 'be-no' line between our half of the airspace and Brandenburg's. By day three, after burning through those SOFLAMs, the smoke and haze from all of the bombing was so thick that we couldn't use the lasers anymore. The laser spot would just refract off of all the particulates in the air."

The Air Force team came up with a variety of airspace-management control measures during this mission, none of which had ever been utilized in combat or training. Over the course of the mission, the dam would have anywhere from 10 to

15 callsigns checking into the ROZ, totaling 20 to 30 individual aircraft at a time. As these flights would check in, the newest callsigns would circle the target at the top of the "stack," while the ones being actively employed would be the lowest. "We didn't have JAAT [Joint Air Attack Team] doctrine, the battlespace was just too tight and congested. But as Brandenburg or our group would Winchester[2] a flight, they'd depart, and the whole stack would 'elevator down,' both to get the next flight on targets, and to make room up top for more aircraft arriving." The technique worked so well that future generations of controllers would learn of the "elevator-down" method, which is solely attributable to Case and Brandenburg.

At night, the Iraqis would probe the Ranger force's positions using the cover of darkness, which the BPs took in their stride because it meant the enemy pushed right into the killing zones. But the constant harassment after several days began to wear on the men, regardless of their stamina and proven battle prowess. The company commander asked Case to do something about interdicting the harassing attacks so the BPs could begin a work–rest cycle. The probing attacks during hours of darkness was a constant occurrence; sleep deprivation was beginning to take its toll. "So now I have to come up with a solution, which prompted the use of the GPS weapons. I suggested to Captain Doyle that we could request a bomber with JDAMs, and he asked me what I knew 'about those GPS bombs.' I told him, in a fit of hilarity, 'I know they are GPS-guided, just like you, sir.' That got a chuckle from everyone who heard it, and he approved the plan." Case contacted the ASOC

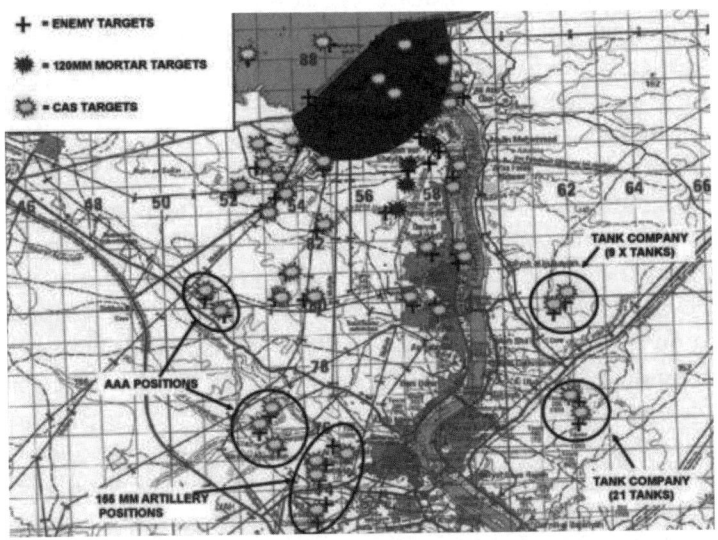

A post-mission graphic depicting some of the joint-fires engagements from Bravo Company, 3/75's seizure of Haditha Dam. (Photo provided by Tommy Case)

[Air Support Operations Center] over JARN via SATCOM and requested a B-52 but got a B-1 instead.

"I learned something that night: if you planned on expending two or three dozen GPS-guided munitions, it's going to take a hell of a long time to execute." In 2003, all read backs of the target locations for GPS-guided weapons had to be performed in latitude/longitude, because the software in the aircraft targeting systems didn't support locations in MGRS grids. Case and Army Sergeant Lund, the FSNCO, sat there for what seemed like hours plotting every key point for where they wanted the bombs to hit, over two dozen impact points.

Passing target locations takes time when using grids, and longer when passing lat/long coordinates. "When you pass a grid over the radio, it sounds like this: '38 Sierra, Kilo Charlie, five-six-three-eight-six, eight-eight-four-seven-five.' That's a grid for the dam itself and it takes about seven seconds to say it out loud over the radio and another couple of seconds to be read back by the bombardier or pilot. For that same grid, in lat/long, you would say 'North, 34 degrees, 12 minutes, 31 decimal eight-six seconds, East, 42 degrees, 21 minutes, 21 decimal zero-nine six seconds.' It takes several more seconds, and there are a lot more explicit digits that must be conveyed correctly, and they have to be read back and, most importantly, input into the weapon correctly. Lat/long is more precise than MGRS, but it just takes longer. If you're reading one or two, it's not that difficult. But for the number of targets we were pinpointing, this took forever, and getting one single digit wrong could mean the weapon impacting hundreds of meters from the intended aim point, risking us, the dam itself, infrastructure, or, worse, civilians."

The process to pass all coordinates and successfully read them back took precious minutes, blocking positions being harassed and gunfights continuing apace. They were deep into the night, and the darkness was oppressive, save for the occasional flashes coming from Baghdad to their south. "It's pitch dark, and I passed approval once I got the nod from the company commander and had pushed all the other aircraft to safe offset positions. The B-1 calls up '*Bone1*, in from the north.' I was so used to F-16s or A-10s, where the time from 'cleared hot' from me to 'weapon away' from the pilot is just a few seconds. For this bomber run, I passed clearance, which the B-1 acknowledged, and a full seven minutes passes before I heard the 'weapon away' call."

The men on the dam could barely hear the rumble of the massive jet overhead, all of them looking through their night-vision goggles for the indicators of bombs falling. After minutes of eerie silence, the entire night sky turned to a vibrant red and orange as the weapons impacted along an axis, perpendicular to the dam, along the reservoir. Case had told Captain Doyle to relay to the Rangers that they needed to get behind cover, because the FACs couldn't realistically account for how tremendous of an effect this many munitions would create.

Those bombs impacted exactly where Case wanted them to, to the point where Brandenburg and Case opted to abort the last five weapons in the run to avoid hitting any buildings unnecessarily. The nighttime probes trailed off dramatically after this pre-planned use of air power. This would be one of the final airstrikes called in for this part of the invasion. A company-plus of Rangers and three Air Force FACs had successfully captured Haditha Dam, seizing it from an overwhelming force that outnumbered the Rangers several times over.

***

"There is an important dynamic that needs to be captured here, discussing the divide that exists between different JTAC tribes—TACP and CCT for example. The older generation of TACPs, the ones I looked up to, had a divisive mindset: 'Fuck CCT,' fuck anybody that wasn't part of our tribe. And it was reciprocal. But then 20 years of combined, joint operations across the entire JTAC spectrum really healed a lot of the underlying misgivings between those tribes."

"Haditha Dam was pretty incredible because, quite simply, you and 120 of your best friends went into some of the most heavily defended terrain on Earth and defeated an entire brigade of professional enemies. That included 30 tanks which we engaged at various points throughout the mission. We controlled everything you can imagine from the 2003 inventory: A-10s, F-14s, 15s and 16s, American and British Harriers, bombers, attack helicopters from AH-6 Little Birds to MH-60 DAPs, literally everything the Air Operations Center had available to task, at some point, ended up in our airspace and decisively engaged the enemy. On this mission, and this will forever astound me, we barely had any casualties. My rucksack had shrapnel pieces lodged in it, and I wasn't even aware of it until days later in daylight. One ranger was shot in the midsection, but it miraculously didn't pass through the guts. We had another ranger who got a piece of shrapnel in his head, causing seizures and loss of sight in both eyes."

"This mission was such a strange 'gunfight at the OK Corral,' we were outmanned, outgunned, but certainly not out-trained. But it wasn't just wanton killing, we ended up taking a ton of prisoners from the dam. The enemy who we detained were treated for wounds and processed respectfully. Those we couldn't detain would face a much darker fate. We would discover later that a lot of guys who weren't killed or captured by us would go back to their unit commanders, and have

Case, 2003, in between missions. "We had no windows in the crappy hooch we lived in, so I took spray paint to (humorously) add a touch of home with a view." (Photo provided by Tommy Case)

their ears or noses cut off for perceived failure to defeat us. This was done to them by their fellow Iraqis as a lesson to their comrades."

"The sheer brutality of the Hussein regime, and the Iraqi Army itself was real, there is absolutely no denying that. Political opinions notwithstanding, we went there and fought an enemy that had no semblance of humanity, and I was fortunate to have been out there during this pivotal episode. I was okay at my job, but that is not a reflection of me, but of everyone before me who trained me, TACP and ranger alike."

Haditha Dam became one of the most historically significant Ranger actions of all time, the regiment carries names like "Haditha Dam" with an immeasurable weight of pride, and Air Force FACs were a part of that. "And just the sheer volume of effects we employed to achieve mission success—CAS from fighters and bombers, HIMARs [High Mobility Artillery Rocket System] and our own artillery—if you can name it we used it. And we achieved synchronized communications across all elements of the battlefield; tribes, uniform, or beret color, none of it mattered out there."

"It was some of the most intense combat I ever experienced over the course of my 20-plus years deploying. Maybe not as episodic as other rotations with how often I dropped danger close. But as terrifying as that artillery was, you find a coping mechanism, no matter how bad things get."

"I remember sitting there with my Ranger brethren, looking out past the spillway, and near a bend in the river you could clearly see this orchard of palm trees. And we'd all just stare at that during a quiet moment, and someone would say something like 'Damn, it's really pretty and serene over there.' And you'd laugh for no reason, and then get back to slinging bombs."

CHAPTER 12

Chasing Saddam

A Different Kind of War

Iraq would present new dynamics that would challenge the close air support (CAS) paradigm in ways Afghanistan would not, forcing forward air controllers (FAC), aircrews, and ground-force maneuver commanders to adapt year after year. This was complicated by policies and grand strategy that would never manifest coherently. Electronic warfare would feature much more significantly in the Iraqi battlespace, owing to the proximity of more advanced adversaries and aggressor actors with a vested interest in thwarting American efforts whenever and wherever possible. Iran would be, and remains, a key cog in the wheel of destabilization that clouds any Middle East future involving liberal democracies. Syria under the Assad regime would host Russian military capabilities in the future to proof and test new warfare capabilities, and a variety of chemical weapons and human-rights atrocities by the Syrian Government would open a future Pandora's Box of battlefield conditions which would challenge and force evolution of American air power in the decades to come with the Syrian Civil War and subsequent rise of the Islamic State of Iraq and Syria.

Iraq would feature its own manifestation of a seemingly inevitable insurgency, one that was even more violent, bloody, and chaotic than Afghanistan. The fingerprints of the Iranian Republican Guard, and in particular their Qods Force under the direction of General Qassim Suleimani, would become evident in the years to come, but, at this phase, all public branding of the Iraqi insurgency would point directly to Al Qaeda's resurgence in the Middle East. That the insurgency would be swallowed under the wave of counter-terrorism strategy and ignore the policy realities in failing to understand the Iraqi culture, its political and demographic particularities, and the external conditions which fomented continued unrest, would prove to be the justification for reliance on American force-projection capabilities on a tactical level—this meant ground forces enabled by the rapid integration of air power in the form of ISR (intelligence, surveillance and reconnaissance) and CAS.

The Iraqi insurgency would be difficult in its own right, owing to the much more densely populated urban congestion of critical Iraqi cities with Sadr City (Baghdad), Fallujah and the broader Anwar Province, Mosul, and Kirkuk being some of the bloodiest and most ruthless battlefields in the entire War on Terror. Urban locales challenge the employment of CAS for a variety of notable factors, chiefly, the presence of civilians in extreme proximity to aerial-delivered effects. Much like the dense vegetation in Afghan locales, the overlap of buildings from dense metropolitan sectors to the underdeveloped squalor of the lower-income portions of these cities—structures, alleyways, intersections, and rubble—provided countless points of cover and concealment for insurgents to hide, conduct ambush and complex attacks, and egress objective buildings during Coalition missions.

The decision to invade Iraq came on the heels of a swift and sudden success in Afghanistan, one that may have ultimately proven a false indicator of American primacy in a new arena of warfare. Despite the policy and strategic failures that led to a two-decade quagmire of foreign intervention, the tactical successes and infrastructural build-up achieved in the two theaters was nothing short of incredible.

"I'd rather get shot in the face, than shoot a friendly by mistake"

Robert Zackery would see the War on Terror from its beginning to its end and, as every chapter of the war would be underwritten by JTACs, 'Zack' too would be one of those lucky (or unlucky, depending on perspective) legacy JTACs who would have the distinction of invading both Afghanistan and Iraq; as the community likes to say about such men, Zack was one of the OGs (original gangsters) whose experience bridged so many aspects of the timeline. For his second interview, given during the 2022 Annual TACP Reunion in San Antonio, we would discuss a mission that, unknown to so many, would feature another JTAC well ahead of the main force, deep behind enemy lines, as the Coalition aimed to cut the very head off of the Iraqi snake, before the 3rd Infantry Division had even made the push into Baghdad.

***

Just before invading Iraq, the preponderance of Joint Special Operations Task Force units staged at regional airfields. There was tension with American forces staging across the Middle East for attacks into Iraq a decade prior (this serving as motivation for Osama Bin Laden's fateful formation of the Al Qaeda terror group). At this point in Zackery's career, he had transitioned from supporting U.S. Army Special Forces A-teams to working with Alpha Company, 2nd Battalion, 75th Ranger Regiment, based out of Fort Lewis in Washington State (he would also support the battalion's reconnaissance detachment on multiple missions). This Ranger force was supported by a variety of entities, as well as a battalion from the 82nd Airborne Division at Fort Bragg. "Our first mission wasn't sexy, but it was relevant and set conditions for what would come soon after, especially with regards to joint-force relationship building. Alpha and Bravo Companies, 2/75, were tasked with escorting the HIMARs [High

Mobility Artillery Rocket System] packages over the border to be able to conduct pre-assault fires for the invasion, to affect 'shock and awe.'"[1] Strategically, maneuvering those long-range fires assets into position would prove critical for the invasion (and were subsequently utilized by men like Eric Brandenburg and Tommy Case on the Haditha Dam raid). But for the Rangers, escorting a conventional force and HIMARs wasn't "sexy" or their anticipated first foray into Iraq. "Nothing exciting happened during that mission. But we were one of, if not among the very first Coalition forces to cross the border into Iraq, long before the big push to Baghdad."

They returned to the staging airfield, soon receiving intel that Saddam Hussein had moved to the Presidential Palace on Lake Tharthar, approximately fifty miles northwest of Baghdad. The potential to take the "Ace of Spades" from the Coalition targeting deck was invariably a risk which Coalition invasion planners were willing to attempt. As special-operations forces (SOF) are uniquely trained and equipped to operate in areas beyond friendly control, Rangers would be selected for this high-risk, high-reward mission. Even if the target would turn out to be a "dry hole," it would achieve tremendous psychological effects: "We would show Saddam that there was

1st Platoon, Alpha Company, 2/75 Rangers, Zackery, front row, far right. SSG Ricardo Barraza (back row, unshielded), and Sgt. Dale Brehm (front row, unshielded) would be killed in Iraq, March 18/19, 2006. (Photo provided by Robert Zackery)

nowhere on earth he could hide, nowhere that our air power would not find him. And not just air power, but because of that air power, we could put boots on the ground right on top of him or his cronies."

The task force sourced multiple Ranger assault packages to hit priority targets simultaneously. There were three targets prioritized over all others: the H1 airfield in southern Iraq, the Haditha Dam, and the Presidential Summer Palace. With so many special-operations units going to so many targets, the anarchy of moving pieces and people scrambling to get mission planning done in short order made those last few nights of peace a blur. The helicopter assault on the Presidential Palace would be the longest helicopter infiltration ever conducted by American forces to date, three and a half hours, just to get to the target.

During the planning event for the raid on Lake Tharthar, "It was the who's who of the U.S. SOF: Army, Navy, three-letter agencies, a bunch of specialized folk who were there in civilian clothes but were part of the real exclusive clubs." Unfortunately, some of the SOF tribalism reared its ugly head. "Out of all these joint-force personnel, there were two known, visible Air Force guys—me and a combat controller (CCT)—and we started butting heads about 'Who is the better ETAC [enlisted terminal attack controller]?' while planning airspace coordination. We had to sort out who was going to control what assets, as both of us were manifested for this operation." The stack over the target would consist of A-10s and MH-60L DAPs (Direct Action Penetrators) to provide direct support for actions on target. During infil, they would have a combat air patrol of F-15s and F-16s leading the helicopter-assault package into the target area, conducting pre-assault fires on surface-to-air missile (SAM) sites and key infrastructure. "But the argument was who was going to be the big dog in charge once we got on the X, boots on the ground at the palace. We were expecting Saddam to be there, with his entourage and a whole shit-ton of fanatic guardsmen, so this was going to be the gunfight of all gunfights. And I told the CCT 'I don't care how many scuba dives you have, you ain't a better controller than me.' It got pretty heated, and soon the whole house was watching us getting in each other's faces. Then suddenly some dude in civvies walks up to us and said, 'Knock this off, here is what is going to happen: CCT, you'll have control of the DAPs out to 500 meters from the target, TACP, you've got A-10s and everything from 500 meters and beyond the compound and further.' We didn't know who this guy was, but he spoke with authority and everyone in the room seemed to defer to him, so me, being a foolish young staff sergeant, I rogered up. Found out later, that was TACP Chief Master Sergeant Eddie Mireles, a living fucking legend."

The assault package would be flown in on 160th Special Operations Aviation Regiment MH-47s and MH-60s, Zackery being manifested on one of the Black Hawks. While the palace teams walked to the flight line to board the helicopters, Rangers from Alpha Company, 3/75, were rigging parachutes to jump in on their target (the H1 airfield seizure). "I gotta say, I was a little jealous of my brethren who were going to get their mustard stains;[2] when you're a young bad-ass dude, you want to do the jump, not fly on a helicopter, but it is what it is. We all wanted the best for each other, and I'm glad those guys were able to do what they did. I was going to be with the initial assault element on this HAF [helicopter-assault force], so the Black Hawks would be the first on the deck with the MH-47s close behind."

As with all other components of this invasion, the task force did not know whether Saddam had chemical weapons at the palace, leaving the Rangers with uncertainty for how to equip themselves for that possibility. "You can't put dudes in their full J-list suits [MOPP gear—Mission Oriented Protective Posture, i.e., biological-warfare suits] and stuff them into a helicopter for three and a half hours, and then expect them to be combat effective. You sure as hell can't move fast wearing those giant rubber-ducky chem boots either." Further, they did not know how long they would remain on target, leaving more questions on how to sustain themselves if they could not be extracted or resupplied. "We ended up prioritizing lethal inventory, doubling our ammunition, batteries for equipment, and, for actual sustainment, only a handful of Rangers took rucks, and those were packed to the brim with more ammo, food and water." Regarding CBRN (chemical, biological, radiological, nuclear) concerns, they wore base wool socks, and two layers of Gore-Tex socks over those with standard-issue boots. The thinking was that, if they needed to wade through any chemical or biological grime, they would have some kind of insulation and vapor lock around the skin of their feet. For uniforms, they wore regular combat trousers, a MOPP-jacket, and body armor over that. "Because we would be spending much of the flight over the water of Lake Tharthar, we wore the B17 life preservers. We also carried our gas masks on us in those ridiculous giant carrying pouches."

For this mission, Zackery utilized two PRC-148 multiband inter/intra team radios (MBITR), one on front for the team net and the other on his back. The second radio was connected to a power amplifier for talking to aircraft, increasing the transmission power from 5 watts to 20 watts while transmitting. "The MBITR amp was a relatively new gizmo, the first-generation type that needed to be tuned in order to propagate correctly, otherwise it was just eight extra pounds of gear you couldn't use. We knew our equipment so intimately, I knew exactly how many extra batteries I would need for a given number of hours on target, based on how quickly they drained power; we knew things like tuning the amp, and could do it blindfolded. Muscle memory just knew which way the switches and toggles needed to adjust. Something to be said about being a real fucking professional, that's what made TACPs so successful: attention to detail and knowing your equipment."

Getting the assault teams into the helicopters was a challenge. Already pressed for space inside, the assault force had to figure out how to get eight fully kitted operators inside with all of this extra equipment. They would fly nearly all the way with doors closed to prevent additional drag from compromising the carefully-calculated fuel reserves against the extreme distance. Closing the doors made it exceptionally congested inside the helicopter. "And if those seats are removed, where do you park your ass? Right on that hard floor and you tuck your legs up under you as best as you can." The MH-47s, carrying the bulk of the force, would keep seats installed, making for a much more comfortable ride into this new war.

The force lifted off from the staging field in the evening, as they would have to get to the target well before sunrise in order to be clear of the Baghdad air-defense zone. For the first 30 minutes, all operators were riding high on adrenaline, "We're rolling out to capture or kill fucking Saddam Hussein, man. And then I peek at my watch and realize 'Shit, we still have two and a half hours to go.'" The adrenaline wore off quickly. "We keep flying, sitting there curled up in your gear, my ass has skipped past being numb, now I just can't feel my legs. We didn't get go-pills back then, that simply wasn't a thing; so, we had no stimulants of any kind besides the shitty coffee pot back in the TOC [tactical operations center]."

After more flying and the constant thumping of rotor blades in the pitch black, suddenly the entire helicopter started twitching and vibrating. Zackery was seated all the way to the back, closest to the left door. Looking out the window to the right he can see the other Black Hawk in formation, seemingly elbow-to-elbow. The helicopters were setting up for an aerial refuel, which is what was causing the sudden shuddering—the turbulence from the MC-130 just ahead of them buffeting the smaller helicopters. "I closed my eyes again, because the vibration woke me up thinking some shit was going down, but I'm gonna try to get some sleep. It's pitch black, and then all of the sudden, night turns into day in an instant."

The whole sky illuminated, and the helicopter made a violent pull back and immediately banked hard to the left. "I'm looking out my window when this happens, and I'm looking straight down at the ground from the helo being pitched over so hard. When I do so, I vividly see two black holes surrounded by bright orange and white rings—two MANPAD surface-to-air missiles had been fired at the passing MC-130—heading straight up towards us. I know that it was a man-portable system, because if anything bigger had been fired at us, like an SA-6, which Saddam had plenty of, we would have been dead." The spectacle of night turning into day was the MC-130 popping flares as the two MH-60s broke off from the fuel lines and pulled away in opposite directions. "I look up and see the MC-130 rolling away too, they didn't even have time to reel in the refueling hoses coming, the helos just pulled back from the baskets, and everyone scattered."

"I remember thinking that I should do something, but this all transpired in a couple of seconds, kind of like when you get a football tossed at your face and you know that you need to flinch or reach a hand up, but it hits you in the face anyway." The two missiles missed the helicopter, one "above," and the other "below," as it appeared to Zackery while they were rolled over sideways. "Now think about that MC-130, those motherfuckers didn't even have time to retract the hoses and baskets. And those goddamn things leak JP-8 jet fuel, now they're popping chaff and flares to evade two SAM launches, shit got really real, really quick. It's one of those things where, if you saw this in a movie you'd be like 'Man, that's bullshit, of course the missiles barely miss the plane and helicopters,' but it happened. Truth is stranger than fiction. And we still have an hour and a half of flying, the actual mission hasn't even begun yet."

The combat air patrol (CAP) escorting the HAF package comprised six F-15s and six F-16s; the A-10s and MH-60L DAPs would remain under the assault force's control, but were holding back to avoid early detection. The fast movers were well ahead of the assault package, engaging a series of pre-designated targets on known SAM threats—the big ones that could be planned for—which posed a known risk to the HAF along the helicopters' infil route. "These guys were literally ripping a seam through Iraqi air defenses and clearing a path for us to get to the presidential palace. This was precision carnage, truly impressive and overwhelming stuff to see in the distance, every time they shacked a target, we just kept flying."

The fleet of helicopters passed over the water of Lake Tharthar, low and fast from the west, with the palace soon dominating the view ahead. Zackery disconnected his headset from ICS [internal communications system] and plugged back into his primary MBITR, listening to the F-16s on the primary strike net. Those fast movers were identifying and sorting targets for pre-assault fires, focusing primarily on the Republican Guard bastion on the lake shore nearby. The F-16s had already been granted release approval, so as the pilots correlated dynamic targets with pre-approved target packages—meaning when they saw SAMs or other known targets where they were expected to be—they immediately engaged. "Based on the intelligence we had available, it was a pretty sure bet that they didn't have SAM threats just floating on barges out on the water, but any other ingress route was assessed to be thoroughly covered by air defenses, which is why this huge air package and pre-assault fires was necessary to get us to the target."

The spectacle was one Zackery would never forget; even amid the hundreds of CAS missions he would conduct over his 26-year career: the CAP engaging pre-planned targets was a volume of fire unlike anything he had ever witnessed. "There is no amount I wouldn't pay to go back in time with a Go-Pro camera to record what we saw on the flight over the lake." As the force was on short final, slowing to lower into the palace compounds after an initial flyby, the doors were thrown open; the lake seemed so close that one of the operators could have leaned over and touched the water with his fingertips. They flew low as a last effort of evasion against any remaining anti-aircraft systems guarding the palace, the low level kept the aircraft out of radar-acquisition slants. The air-mission commander ordered the gunners to hold fire until the last second because the Iraqi defenders still had no idea that Rangers were about to land inside the palace. "I can hear the F-16s sorting targets and prosecuting on the fires net, and it looked like World War Two on both sides of the lake, the sky is absolutely alight. There is countless AAA [anti-aircraft artillery] fire arching up into the darkness, like giant illuminated octopus arms waving through the night sky. We had literally kicked the hornets' nest, you'd see those octopus arms arching through the darkness and, seconds after, a bomb from the F-16s would impact; they were utilizing proximity fuses, so many times those would be airburst effects and a fireball would totally illuminate everything for a split second. This was the craziest laser light show ever seen."

Zackery heard the "One minute!" call from the MH-60 pilot, leading him to contact the A-10s on his radio. For the ground assault, they had been allocated three sets of the vaunted "Hawgs," whose callsigns were *Rambo*, *Pistol*, and *Colt*. Zackery and the CCT were on separate nets, as the operational plan tasked the DAP attack helicopters to the CCT and the palace itself, while Zackery would control the "outer cordon" where the main threat of counterattack would originate from. Any airspace deconfliction between assets was going to be handled by the aircraft themselves; ensuring both FACs could simultaneously prosecute fire missions if necessary, in case everything went awry inside and outside the palace.

The palace itself was on a jut of land on the water, with one access road built on a levy; it was unmistakable even in the dark. There were two massive towers hemming in the road, which served multiple purposes: an entry control point for forces transiting from the mainland to the peninsula, and as living quarters for the personnel posted there as part of the security apparatus. "You couldn't miss these two giant fingers rising up out of the water, and the entire complex behind it covered the island, with towers at each corner of the giant compound." Before the force finally landed, the DAPs engaged the flat open area, with flechette rounds loaded into their miniguns, directly where the assault package would land. This was done because intelligence suspected the open pathways and grounds had been booby trapped, so the engagement was meant to set off any explosives or traps buried which the Rangers would have set off upon traversing.

"I don't have enough hands, I'm trying to talk on my radio, I'm trying to undo my snap-link safety tether on the floor, and I've got two Rangers next to me, who will be the first ones on deck and pushing to secure the key buildings once we go wheels down. The ranger closest to me, we called him "Griff," yells at me to hold his plate carrier, because he's untethered and just suspended on the lip of the helo, so I grab him, but I'm also still coordinating with A-10s who are calling out targets. More crazy shit is happening on the shore and surrounding areas, and I'm still trying to unclip my damn tether. I yell at another ranger to grab Griff for me so I can unhook, which he does. It's not a smooth ride in, we're banking and jiving and pitching, and at one point we banked so hard that I thought we had gone wheels down. I glance up and see that Griff is gone, so we must have landed right?"

But they had not landed, and were still roughly 10 feet off of the ground. Though the Rangers were using night vision, they could not see clearly in the haze. "I realize that Griff left the bird and we haven't touched down yet. I look across the courtyard and see Griff running, stumbling and moving very awkwardly, but hauling ass all the same, so now I'm thinking he broke his leg in the fall or is otherwise injured." They finally touch down, sharply, and the assault teams leapt off the helicopter and attempted to sprint towards Griff's position, only to stumble the exact same way that he is—tripping and swaying. The flechette rounds which the door gunners put in the courtyard had completely obliterated the pavement, leaving small craters ranging from a couple inches to several feet in width and depth. "You don't think about these details when you're prepping for the mission, but trying to run through that torn-up pavement was miserable."

Based on all the available intelligence, they fully expected Saddam Hussein to be there, with his personal bodyguard and the ceremonial palatial guard dug in. It was already confirmed that an entire battalion of Special Republican Guard was at the security depot less than a kilometer away, ready to react to the sudden arrival of American helicopters. "We expected the firefight of our lives. I'll say this about what goes through your mind in those seconds before crisis, and it's a reflection of where our society is today in terms of social issues—if you're carrying a gun, and out of fear of the situation, you pull the trigger on someone who is potentially an innocent civilian rather than taking a bullet and saving an innocent life, then you need to find a different job. That's a decision you must make beforehand: 'Would I rather take a bullet if it means not hurting or killing an innocent person, or am I going to shoot first and figure it out later?'" As he moved towards their objective building, Zackery led a fire team of Rangers to first cover on the side of a small structure. Peering down his gun's optic, he spotted a human silhouette with a gun in hand a few meters away, through the dust of the helicopters hovering above. "I drew down, painting this person with the AN/PEQ-2 IR pointer on my rifle, finger on the trigger, but I did not know if this was friend or foe. And it seems hyperbolic, but I thought to myself 'I'd rather get shot and die right here, rather than shoot a friendly.'" After another second, more silhouettes stack up behind this first one—Rangers moving to enter a separate building. That's the reality of being in a gunfight, split-second decisions change the outcome, and if the individual can't make those calls correctly, it can mean catastrophe of the worst sort: fratricide.

Zackery's element was tasked with clearing one of the palace towers, first for security, second so the TACP could get to higher ground in order to employ the A-10s on outer cordon while the rest of the assault force searched for the "Ace of Spades." Once his team was stacked on the entry, the element froze in place after the first Rangers breached the doorway, but no one knew why. Initial entry is the most dangerous step in the clearance sequence. "I'm trying to figure out what's going on inside because now we aren't moving. Soon as I get through the door, I see what's wrong." Inside the foyer is the entry to the elevator shafts, but the Iraqis had blown the elevator itself, leaving it suspended between floors. When Rangers are trained to conduct building clearance, they clear dynamically—each operator flowing in and finding the next room. The first few assaulters walked right through the elevator opening, and three had fallen into the elevator shaft, not realizing it wasn't an actual room. The clearance became held up as the next wave of assaulters was trying to pull these three out of an elevator shaft. "We had no fucking reason to prepare for the elevator shaft being open, or for the elevator to be compromised, so that's just a reflection of how crazy this kind of mission can get. This shit ain't *Call of Duty*, and we don't have blueprints or 3-D scans of the building, we just have to get in there as fast as possible and react faster than the enemy."

They finally managed to continue movement through the foyer, and began clearing the stairwell to the second, third, and top floor. But as they proceeded deeper into the building, their numbers dwindled. At every room, assaulters peeled off the main element to secure entire floors. By the time they reached the third floor, only Zackery and a couple Rangers remained, the latter breaking off to secure the floor. So now, to get up to the balcony and finish clearance, Zackery was alone. "You never clear a room by yourself, but there isn't shit I can do right now, so I pass through the final threshold and I'm up on top of the tower. I remember yelling back down the stairwell 'You motherfuckers better not leave me,' and they called me on the radio asking for my position. 'I'm on top of the tower where I'm supposed to be, where the fuck are you guys?' 'Not where you are, ETAC.' 'No shit, you better not leave me up here.'"

Once the top floor was secured, Zackery moved to the windows to get eyes on the enemy force marshalling across the water. But the aircraft couldn't hear him on the strike net, due to antenna propagation in the building. Structures of any kind impede an antenna's ability to propagate the signal and, to make matters more complicated, his equipment set up was not ideally suited for controlling atop the tower. "They couldn't hear me when I'm facing out with my front, so what do I do? I break the window on the top floor, and literally hang my ass out the window so that the amplified radio on my back can propagate the signal. And sure enough, now I have great comms. I start going to work with the A-10s on targets across the water from us, but I'm peeking over my shoulder, trying not to fall out of a three-story building. Lesson learned: figure out a better way to mount radio antennas so that I don't get shot in the ass next time I have to climb up on a fucking rooftop to call in airstrikes."

In the time it took the assault force to offload the birds and secure the first set of buildings, the Special Republican Guard had mobilized and were loading up en masse to counterassault the palace. From his perch, Zackery could distinctly see three large flatbed trucks laden with armed Iraqi soldiers, en route from the security depot to the levy, the only means of accessing the palace from the shore. Additional vehicles with heavy machine guns drove behind those flatbed trucks. "So I'm passing this information to the A-10s, and I'm reaching over my shoulder with my IZLID

IR pointer trying to mark this convoy for *Rambo*. I passed a very abbreviated attack brief because, at this point, we have mere minutes before we are about to be heavily outnumbered and outgunned on the ground. *Rambo* comes in from the west, almost directly overhead, and I hear the 30-mm burp. But I don't see any effects, and I'm thinking to myself 'Those fuckers missed the goddamn convoy.'" In the rush, with seconds feeling like minutes, the separation between the sound of the GAU-8 Avenger cannon erupting directly above and the rounds impacting seemed an eternity. But the A-10s did not miss. The depleted uranium rounds in the GAU-8 cannon aren't designed for soft-skinned vehicles. Rather, they are designed to punch through tank armor, then explode. The flatbed trucks weren't solid enough to set off the fuses and, as such, the shells did not detonate until they had passed through the trucks and hit the pavement underneath. A second after impact—another seeming eternity under such duress—the entire causeway lit up, and the trucks were quickly reduced to burning wreckage. A few more reattacks with the guns would destroy the convoy and effectively block the levy so the Republican Guard couldn't bring forces to bear against the Rangers, who had nearly secured the palace.

"Once that crisis was sorted, I started laying waste to the Republican Guard complex, which was just an absolute anthill of the enemy trying to mass forces and counter-attack. It's a blur now, I didn't have time to write down my attack briefs, but we just kept hitting the compound over and over. I went at it with all three sets of A-10s for a solid 45 minutes, employing everything they had."

The Rangers had been on the target for just over an hour, and determined fairly quickly that Saddam was not there. This left precious minutes in which to decide on, and then prepare for, a quick exfil. The extraction would be different from infil, as the assault plan had separate MH-47s staggered from the insertion package, waiting for the call to recover the ground force. The retrieval Chinooks approached, one at a time, picking up the assault force in sequence; Zackery's element would be the last team off the target. "I kept yelling to my team 'You sons of bitches better not leave me behind,' but I'm completely consumed with controlling the helos in and out while continuing to engage targets with the A-10s. It seemed like no matter how many times I brought in the A-10s, more Republican Guard kept appearing from thin air. Finally, it's our time to get out of dodge." The last Ranger team swiftly proceeded down the stairwell, filing into line and sprinting across the courtyard, once again stumbling through the craters left by the flechette rounds. As Zackery stepped onto the ramp, he told the A-10s they were approved on any armed individuals surrounding the palace, or near the Guard complex, as there were no friendlies left in vicinity, and they needed covering fire for the last helicopter. Once again, the sky came alive with aircraft engaging targets, but this barely registered with the men watching the palace disappear into the dark below.

On the way out, the last MH-47 took small-arms fire, registered by a distinct 'whump-whump-whump' into the side of the helicopter. The men inside could hear the rounds impacting clearly, despite the volley of fire being laid down by the A-10s nearby. Once again plugged into ICS, Zackery heard the pilots making the preparatory calls for CSAR (combat search and rescue). "I thought to myself 'It's a three-and-a-half-hour flight, if the rescue birds left the forward bases right now. So if this bird goes down, we have to survive at least four hours before anyone can come help us.' And we just kicked one of the biggest hornet's nests in Iraq trying to find public enemy number one; this is going to be a long night." Somehow, the MH-47 stumbled and stuttered the entire flight back, thanks to the brilliance of the 160th pilots and crew. "But unlike the ride in, I don't get to crash off of the adrenaline, I'm at full tilt for the rest of the night, not knowing if we're going to crash behind enemy lines or not."

"So that was my 'second' mission of the Iraq invasion, April 3rd, 2003, before the force had even gotten into Baghdad. I was with Rangers, well ahead of the invasion force, and we thought we had Saddam Hussein ready to roll up. But that was only the beginning of this rotation, it would continue to be the adrenaline climb and dump the whole way."

***

"Soon after Lake Tharthar, we began planning to jump into BIAP [Baghdad International Airport]; that's what Rangers do: seize airfields. We began rehearsing for that mission with an additional brigade from the 82nd Airborne augmenting nearly the entire Ranger Regiment, and the idea was that we would seize the heart of the country in the first minutes of the war—that's about as decisive of a blow as you can strike. I was at one of the big planning conferences, all of the players were there including the airlift planners, the 'other color agencies' [named intelligence assets], and I was getting pumped up about getting my 'Mustard Stain.' The plan called for ten C-17s to carry the entire package—that's a lot of badasses loaded up for war. During the intel portion of the brief, we were told to expect three of those C-17s being shot down before getting jumpers over the target. I thought to myself, 'Hmm, I want a Mustard Stain, but maybe not that bad.' Further, the expectation was that, after green light, once forces had been inserted into the airfield, an additional two to three C-17s would be shot down on departure."

"So the expectation based on available intelligence was that we would lose 30 percent of the force before anyone hit the ground, planes and all souls on board, and an additional 20–30 percent of the air package would get shot down after inserting paratroopers. Fortunately, it was decided that maybe we should let mechanized infantry take that airfield, that's kind of what they're built for, and that is why 3rd Infantry Division [3ID] has such an important piece of the story of the invasion. They were the literal Battle of Baghdad heroes; it was a much more rational decision for them to take BIAP rather than use losing half or more of the task force."

Zackery (left) with Pat Tillman in Baghdad, 2003. (Photo provided by Robert Zackery)

"What a lot of people don't know about seizing BIAP, is that after 3ID had taken the airport, it wasn't clean and over. There were subterranean rat holes and tunnels surrounding the flightline, and around many of the hangars. These were just big enough for Iraqi soldiers to poke a machine-gun barrel out of, and impossible to spot unless you're looking for them specifically. Once Baghdad had been taken and secured, we moved in and began running ops out of the auxiliary hangars across the runway from the terminal, and I could only imagine what it might have been like if we had jumped in there with those murder holes giving perfect fields of fire at every angle."

"We spent weeks looking for remaining Ba'ath party members and, of course, still trying to find Saddam and his sons. The Ranger Regiment and 3ID got really tight during that rotation, they loaned us a mechanized vehicle package and those guys became our Uber, for lack of a better word, and I don't mean that pejoratively. We had a really close working relationship with them, and it enabled us to hit the ground running, working targets and pushing deep into Baghdad, much sooner than we initially hoped."

"One early mission of note, we had intelligence on the alleged whereabouts of the U.S. Navy pilot who had been shot down and missing since *Desert Storm*, Captain Michael Speicher. We would raid a prison west of Baghdad, riding in M113 Bradleys with our 3ID brothers. Every so often, you'd hear plinking on the side of the vehicle, small-arms fire. Better to be in that Bradley than a soft-skinned Humvee, otherwise my brains would be plastered on the wall. We hit this prison complex, stacked up, begin to clear, and, while moving down a hallway, one of the Rangers near me is on a knee and then immediately starts cursing up a storm. The dude took a knee in a huge puddle of human waste. The conditions in that prison were surreal. The longer we went on, we started hitting barricades and barriers, and ended up breaking down gates and barricades with the M113s. It's some crazy shit that you can't anticipate or plan for, you just react. To our tremendous regret, once we got there and finished clearing the entire damn complex we didn't find anything on the pilot—dry hole. That prison turned out to be notable later in the war for the wrong reasons—it was Abu Ghraib."

"There wasn't any CAS on that specific mission, but I bring it up to emphasize how much planning went into things of historical significance, and how, at every single major event throughout the war—in Afghanistan, and Iraq—there was guaranteed to be a forward air controller who was central to the planning, which accounts for 85 percent of the mission, and the execution, which is the other 15 percent. Iraq in 2003, there was a lot of chaos with very occasional and intense close air support. But we—the forward air controller tribes—were there every step of the way."

CHAPTER 13

Dragging a Nation out of a War

"This is the end of combat operations"

Afghanistan became a forgotten war after its early successes—fracturing the Al Qaeda infrastructure, training camps and safe havens, uprooting the Taliban, and establishing an early network of seemingly pro-American Afghans in positions of transitional power. It was an apparent foregone conclusion when Hamid Karzai was nominated by the Bonn Agreement to take the reins of the fledgling Islamic democracy in 2002, and the apparent spontaneous chain of successes created an environment where American policymakers had already turned their eyes to Iraq, Africa, and beyond. That protraction of resources, close air support and intelligence, surveillance and reconnaissance collection, as well as the logistical support, medical evacuation, and theater assets (refueling and airborne command and control and battle management) meant, despite the enduring charge to pressure and capture Al Qaeda leaders in their remaining safe havens, assault forces and their supporting air-power experts had limited resources with which to do so.

Further, the post-invasion phase gave rise to the reconstruction efforts that ultimately served no better purpose than the perpetuation of corruption and a pit into which international funds disappeared forever—yet those efforts commanded a great deal of what little air power remained in Afghanistan as the colossal defense apparatus moved west into the second Iraq bout. As international aid—workers, equipment, non-government, and international government organization sites—and politically sensitive environments grew, the ability to wage offensive operations gave way to an increasing amount of presence patrols, and large operations to stabilize entire village complexes/networks; sometimes entire valleys became subjected to Coalition named operations. Relevant though these efforts may have been at the time, it provided a lucrative target roster for Al Qaeda operatives and the shadowy early insurgency of Taliban fomentation, meaning the opportunity to apply pressure became an exercise in reactive defense with air-power capabilities stretched to their limits and, in many circumstances, unable to support.

The dearth of air-power resources was attributable to the shift into Iraq to topple the Saddam Hussein Sunni regime, and ultimately attempt to rebuild a stable, democratic Iraq. Two months after the American-led coalition utterly dominated the morale-deficient Iraqi Army, then-Defense Secretary Donald Rumsfeld declared "This is the end of major combat operations," coinciding with President Bush's assertion of "Mission Accomplished" from the deck of the aircraft carrier USS *Abraham Lincoln* on May 1, 2003. At this time, a mere 8,000 American troops remained in Afghanistan, while one of the most comprehensive military forces ever assembled presided over the fractured remains of Iraq.

For the American-led mission to be standing over the skeletons of the Iraqi and Taliban regimes, there was one singular component which made the difference—air power and air dominance. But both war zones would prove to be far more complex than simply invading a foreign state and enabling the implementation of a new government and social order. As Afghanistan saw the ebb and flow of Taliban and Al Qaeda forces seizing the advantage of the border-crossing areas in the Federally Administered Tribal Areas between Afghan and Pakistani territory, Iraq would see the rise of its own brutal insurgency, borne of factional and sectarian foundations. In both circumstances, air power would be called upon time and time again to sustain the Coalition dominance of the battlespace.

In Iraq, much of the southern reaches of the nation would barely register on the international radar, as Coalition forces blasted through those large swaths of territory on the drive to seize Baghdad. Iraqi cities like Fallujah, Karbala, Mosul, Tikrit, and Sadr City (within Baghdad) would be isolated worlds within the Iraqi theater, as each would gain renown and infamy for the bloody and savage house-to-house warfare conducted by Coalition forces against a rapidly swelling insurgency.

Iraq remained an intractable fixture in American foreign policy well into the previous century. In the 1950s, the burgeoning American clandestine-intelligence apparatus began sowing the seeds of discord, chiefly by its assistance in the overthrow of the Iraqi monarchy at the direction of President Eisenhower's chief advisors led by then-CIA director Allen Dulles. Concerns over growing communist influence in Iraq, and across the region (notably including wayward misadventures in Iran), would lead American clandestine interventions there, shaping much of the West's presence in the region for the duration of the century. In the 1960s, after Abd al-Karim Qasim, leader of the post-coup Iraqi Government following the monarchy's overthrow, expropriated 99.5 percent of the American and British-owned Iraq Petroleum Company's concessionary holdings, President John F. Kennedy authorized plans for another clandestine intervention in Iraq. This would lead to a decade of exceptional sectarian violence led by the Ba'ath Party, who would purge communists (both real and alleged) and ultimately seize power in the 1970s. With changing American administrations, increasing clandestine operations would be authorized by the Johnson, Nixon, and Ford White Houses, with varying degrees of attribution and contextual awareness.

This would include confusing and erratic swaying from one position to another on whether or not to deepen ties with the violent regime in power in Baghdad, or working to overthrow it through unconventional means. This would be an early entry into the American utilization of the indigenous Kurdish people to undermine and destabilize Iraq—using Tehran as an interlocutor to funnel weapons and supplies to the Kurds who would foment discord—especially after a 1971 cooperative agreement was signed between Moscow and Baghdad resulting in the Soviet Union providing significant weapons and military technology to Iraq. This close fusion between Iraq and the Soviet Union would lead to increased American support for Iran, which would once again make an abrupt turnaround when Iran and Iraq engaged in a bloody and violent conflict in the 1980s. The American position of support (for Baghdad, now ruled by Saddam Hussein) during this decade is easily explainable, citing the Iran hostage crisis and the failed rescue mission known as Operation *Eagle Claw*. Millions of dollars of weapons, aid, and other financial commitments would see American weapons enabling Saddam Hussein's forces in a protracted and violent conflict with Iran, while the fateful sidebar agreement to swap weapons for hostages (the Iran–Contra affair) would occur near-simultaneously.

This would bring the U.S.–Iraq dynamic to the doorstep of the First Gulf War, where air power would prove a decisive factor in defeating Iraq's Army, one of the largest and most well-equipped in the world. The remainder of the 1990s would see air power employed as a security and containment tool during missions such as Operations *Northern* and *Southern Watch*, grounding the Iraqi Air Force and ultimately setting the air-war conditions for the 2003 invasion, where forward air controllers would find themselves at the pivot of countless critical moments in a decisive war, decades in the making.

CHAPTER 14

Rescuing Jessica Lynch

On March 23, 2003, a convoy of U.S. Army soldiers from the 507th Ordnance Maintenance Company based out of Fort Bliss, Texas, conducted a patrol in Nasiriyah in southern Iraq. Following a fateful wrong turn, the "Humvee" carrying Private First-Class Jessica Lynch, 19 years old, drove straight into an ambush, resulting in the detainment of Lynch and seven other American soldiers by Iraqi militia. For several days, the whereabouts of Lynch and her squad mates remained unknown, until an intelligence tip from a CIA source would initiate a rescue mission comprised of U.S. Army Special Operations Forces, U.S. Marines, and multiple Air Force forward air controllers (tactical air control party and combat controller). The mission was conducted at the Nasiriyah hospital where Lynch was being held alive, although severely injured. The remaining U.S. service members would also be found at the hospital, although tragically it would be too late to return those individuals alive as they had been murdered while in the grasp of Iraqi militias.

The rescue of Jessica Lynch and the recovery of her fellow soldiers' remains for dignified transfer home was no different than other high-risk missions performed by the operators involved, albeit a far more emotionally traumatizing and harrowing moment in their lives. Another key point captured in the following interview is the intensity of the human experience that goes far deeper than the intense adrenaline of a gunfight or a call-for-fire mission. The depth of this intensely emotional event manifests in multiple subsequent pieces of the anthology (like the mission to recover the U.S. service member remains following the shoot-down of Extortion17 in 2011, or the August 2021 withdrawal); there is a difficult-to-qualify dynamic which passes through the minds of the operators whose job was to see the battlefield from a detached, three-dimensional perspective while remaining engaged in the gunfight at hand: the JTAC is unable to process the crisis of the moment, as the sheer complexity of their job requires them to bury the emotions and weight of that immediate crisis, because the rest of the assault force requires the air controller to remain wholly plugged-in from before the mission starts until well after it has ended. There is no respite for the JTAC on a given mission, no chance to "zone out," there is always a myriad list of tasks that require absolute concentration.

Senior Master Sergeant Abel Martens (ret.) would be one of those controllers assigned to integrate air power into the most highly publicized rescue mission of the early years of the War on Terror. Martens, like several others who interviewed for this book, is among the rare company of service members who invaded both Afghanistan in 2001 and Iraq in 2003 as a TACP. He would later cross-train to become a combat controller in 2005, deploying multiple times as an air-power expert of multiple tribes. The following interview highlights a key narrative of this work that emerged early on in the composition and remains a pivotal point worth denoting here: at every single key event of the Global War on Terror with strategic impact and force multiplication, there would be a forward air controller managing aircraft to enable the ground force to conduct a sensitive and difficult mission.

Martens was new to Team One at the 17th Air Support Operations Squadron—what would become the 17th Special Tactics Squadron—aligned with 1st Battalion, 75th Ranger Regiment, at Hunter Army Airfield in Savannah, Georgia. He had already been to Afghanistan in 2001, embedded with Army Special Forces (SF) as part of the invasion force with Robert Zackery. After the Afghanistan invasion, Martens left Fort Bragg for Georgia in early 2002. "The senior TACPs on the team—guys like Kevin Vance, Mark Hurst, Matt Nugent, Troy Lundquist—they had already been in some pretty gnarly stuff, places like Takur Ghar, and their experience combined with the professionalism of the men at the 17th helped me prepare for what would come next in my career."[1]

Embedding with the Ranger Regiment, after previously working with Army SF, was a stark change in tactics and mission sets and, with it, a steep learning curve. "Having done some urban-combat training while I was a conventional TACP aligned with the 82nd Airborne Division at Fort Bragg, as well as having completed Ranger School, I had an inkling of how Ranger did business, but that is wholly insufficient when it comes time to be a forward air controller supporting the regiment. You must become an expert on Ranger SOPs [standard operating procedures], the 'speed, surprise, and violence of action' that is the Ranger mantra."

Martens had the benefit of a brief rotation with the Rangers in late 2002 to Afghanistan, during the winter. But in that theater, ahead of the Iraq invasion, the Coalition was engaging against guerilla tactics, often five or six insurgents fighting from well-covered areas, maneuvering in extremely rugged, mountainous terrain. Most of those missions weren't kinetic. But while in Afghanistan, they started hearing whispers about "the big show," and while it remained RUMINT (rumor intel), they were fairly certain the whispers from on high—White House level—meant this "big show" could be nothing else but Iraq. "This was based mostly on George W. Bush's comments about the 'Axis of Evil.' Iran, too, was considered by everyone across USSOCOM [United States Special Operations Command], but our confidence in Iraq as the next event was high."

Despite his experience downrange, it was sobering to consider the potential of an invasion against a professional military with modern capabilities would mean American forces would soon be squaring off against an enemy that, unlike the Taliban and their Al Qaeda partners, would not be so easily overwhelmed by the shock and awe of American firepower. "My experience with real world close air support [CAS] remained in its infancy, at least when considering how air power might be employed in a force-on-force kind of war. This relative lack of experience was despite having two deployments under my belt. That was the effect that Iraq had on the CAS community: that it was going to change the depth of our role in this new kind of war we were still figuring out. You have to keep in mind, at this time, Saddam had one of the five biggest armies in the world, and he had already gone toe to toe with Iran before all of this. So that is the reality, the mindset that starts permeating through everyone in the community: this next phase is going to be much more of a legitimate fight than chasing the Taliban through the mountains. In 2001–2002, we had all of the momentum against that particular enemy, the tides didn't shift until after everything pivoted to Iraq."

In February 2003, the "big show" buzz was at full steam, and the atmosphere across the regiment was shrouded in a thin smoke of obscuration, but the Rangers and their Air Force enablers knew what was coming, "… though it wasn't being said out loud. Iraq became the sole focus, and the rehearsals took on a new intensity: far more exercises focusing on flatland/desert training. We only had a few weeks between getting home from Afghanistan around Christmas in '02, and the spin-up to invade Iraq."

As did most of the special-operations forces (SOF); Alpha Company, 1/75 (Martens's aligned Ranger cohort) staged just over the border from Iraq, a mix of experienced veterans and new forward air controllers (FAC) who were facing their first downrange experience. It was a lot of waiting, with occasional *Scud* launch alarms which would send all of them scrambling to put on MOPP (Mission Oriented Protective Posture) gear, for fear of NBC (nuclear, biological, chemical) attacks. Alpha Company was guarding a Patriot missile battery, which would send occasional volleys into Iraq. Finally, the gears of war began to grind. Within 48 hours of the first Tomahawk missiles being fired from the cruiser USS *Bunker Hill* on March 20, 2003, used to open the massive pre-assault package and initiate the invasion, Alpha Company would cross the border to seize their first objective.

"There was a great deal of chaos during those early days, when forces first crossed the border. We got the call to launch force, Mark Hurst and I went with A Co 1/75 and, as we're crossing the actual boundary, everyone is totally jazzed up. We were one of, if not the very first U.S. special operations forces to invade this sovereign nation, and our intel has reported that we would be coming face to face with the Special Republican Guard, allegedly eight divisions worth, riding around in the T-72 tanks which TACPs have spent entire careers training for. All the foundational air controller skills and tasks: visual reconnaissance, enemy force recognition, massing of fires, everything you've ever read in the pubs or worked through in a training scenario on a range, now it's all jumbling through your mind in the back of a Humvee. Emotions were running high to say the least."

As soon as they crossed the border, they were on edge, expecting a massive ambush, when one of the vehicles broke down. "So, no shit, there we are, a company of Rangers, cross loading equipment and hooking up a tow-bar to a hard-broke Humvee, young Ranger privates smacking hammers on this tow-bar screaming 'Fuck this piece of shit,' and it's strangely comical to be helping them move rucks and ammo in the middle of this chaotic event in our lives." In rehearsals, this goes smoothly every time, but at that moment, they were all "… wearing clown shoes. Of course, if we had gotten ambushed in that moment everyone would have gotten on-line, returned fire and Rangered up, but this would serve as a strange out-of-body moment of hilarity that none of us anticipated."

Alpha Company's first objective was a small landing zone (LZ) which had been codenamed *Coyote*, roughly twenty kilometers into Iraq. After the force left their staging base, they traveled up Highway 80, which would go on to become known as the "Highway of Death," turning west soon after crossing the border onto Route 22, which took them to LZ *Coyote*. "This would be my first observing the dirt landing zone capability come to fruition, the routing and sequencing of aircraft into austere environments. This was something that we simply didn't get exposed to in Afghanistan—what combat control did—so it was really eye-opening for me." Alpha Company seized the objective, which enabled the combat controllers (CCT) to bring in the air train with logistics, resupplies and follow-on forces. This all took place during darkness and, once the sun came up, they began clearing many of the buildings surrounding the landing zone. As the Ranger force maneuvered around the local area in their vehicles, someone noticed the entire surrounding area had been hit with cluster munitions during the pre-assault phase; many of those munitions remained unexploded. "How we missed them, I'll never know. These weren't mines, but the unexpended bomblets whose proximity fuses had failed to detonate. So we might not have been in immediate danger but, still, a UXO is a UXO [unexploded ordnance], and we were completely surrounded by them on our first objective in Iraq."

"That was one of the first times that it occurred to me that the enemy is not the only threat out there, the dangers of being in a war are far more complex than simply getting in a gunfight with an adversary. This would also be the first time I put eyes on significant numbers of dead enemy soldiers. My experience in Afghanistan was that of small skirmishes and limited numbers of enemy combatants—Al Qaeda and Taliban fighters. In this war, we were up close with the enemy and, at this time, they weren't hiding amongst the civilian population, we were coming face to face with them."

The force pushed deeper into Iraq, following the border going towards Syria. After the seizure of *Coyote*, their task and purpose was to capture and degrade small border outposts which intelligence assessed were housing Special Republican Guard units. This westward arc would set the "noose" for the main invasion force's push into Baghdad from the south via Kuwait and prevent the dispersal of Iraqi forces, as well as those trying to evade capture into Syria. One of the primary objectives in this sweep was Al-Lasaf, a strategic positioning post for the Republican Guard deep in the hostile desert, far to the west of Baghdad. Its significance was its proximity to Highway 1, which was a critical supply route for the Iraqis, but for the Americans, reaching that highway would serve as a phase line for Coalition planners, proving the reach and speed of the ground forces.

As they prepared to clear through Al-Lasaf, they stopped at an objective rally point (ORP) waiting to roll in. The ORP was just out of range of mortars and artillery, which the Iraqi Army had plenty of, but close enough that the attached Ranger reconnaissance detachment (RRD) could launch their small UAS (unmanned aerial system, sUAS) and conduct reconnaissance into the objective. "We knew we were on the right course, because when RRD recovered their sUAS, it had bullet holes in it. And we were close enough that the time it would take our force to close with the target was going to be short enough to render their ability to adjust artillery fire moot."

As the company performed last-minute hasty planning, greasing up the crew-served weapons, and waiting for the call to launch, Martens looked out on the horizon and saw the sky getting dark. "We had no weather technicians with us, just broad operational data about potential inclement weather, nothing detailed enough for us to adjust our plan. From where we sat, the sky kept on getting deeper shades of brown. It sure as hell wasn't a tornado, this was horizon-to-horizon. By then, we had enough collective sense to realize this was one of those famed Iraqi sandstorms. From first 'contact' with this storm until it was right over the top of us couldn't have been more than 20 minutes. You can't appreciate how quickly those storms move in until you've seen it. Call it my inexperience, or naivete, but I assumed this would hit us and then blow right on passed. We all had goggles, Ranger is never going to slouch on wearing proper personal protective equipment [PPE], thanks to every sergeant major who fretted over those 'little details,' so we donned our eye-pro and waited. The storm, however, did not just blow over; this was exactly the kind of flesh-eating violent storm you see in movies. We had trucks, but these Humvees were not up-armored, many of them had open beds, nothing like the fully enclosed vehicles of later years. I had a seat in the back, but the back end of the trucks was totally exposed to these elements, so there wasn't any point in sitting there. After an hour in this absolute brown-out, I grabbed my poncho-liner out of my ruck thinking 'Wow, this is really inconvenient,' and picked a spot alongside the Humvee, putting the poncho-liner behind my helmet and rolling it over my body into a makeshift tarp."

Alpha Company remained there for 24 hours straight. The storm itself blew on for about 36 hours total. During that time, they received word that an Iraqi force was detected via signals intelligence maneuvering on the American position, using the storm as cover. "So, towards the end of us waiting out this sandstorm, we think that we have to be ready to react to contact. That ended up never materializing, but as we're preparing for that and the raid we've postponed, that's when we realize all of the 40mm and .50 calibers are down—completely gummed up with sand and grime and totally dysfunctional." The next short interval was spent trying to get the guns back up for the raid, and it took nearly all of their water supply just to get 50 percent of the crew-served weapons back to functional. Once the guns were up and ready, the recon team launched the sUAS again, confirming the enemy up ahead.

"We hit the barracks at Al-Lasaf, and it was the first time special operations ended up on the news. There is a recording that made it back to major media soon after, and I believe it was the first time footage of U.S. special-operations forces made national broadcast. I'm sure the video is still floating around the internet somewhere, but for anyone who vividly remembers the news broadcasts in early 2003, the video [makes] reference to SOF personnel raiding a key enemy stronghold. That was us in Al-Lasaf, Rangers and a couple U.S. Air Force TACPs. You can't tell much from the video, but it's a nighttime raid with tracer fire going back and forth, but we did make contact with the Special Republican Guard. I had seen dead Taliban in Afghanistan, but the greater societal impetus in Afghanistan was one deeply rooted in anger at 9/11, and our gambit in 2001 and 2002 was vengeance. That enemy were comprised of extremists and terrorists. After the raid in Al-Lasaf, I saw the dead bodies of uniform-wearing Iraqi soldiers we had squared off against in battle. It's an unsettling mirror—that guy I'm looking at is clean-shaven, wearing a uniform, and we just rolled into his country and kicked the shit out of his Army. It almost made you think about them as more human, there was still respect for the Iraqi soldiers we fought, and you treated everyone humanely—no exceptions. The Taliban, despite that anger, were still worthy of respect for their fighting prowess. But the insurgency in Iraq soon after this invasion would change everything you felt about the monsters who dominated the battlefield after the invasion."

"It's important to emphasize the divergence I felt then between the two theaters. Each one was so uniquely different, and affected those of us who went there very differently. It seems as if people think about GWOT [Global War on Terror] as one large Middle East problem set, they don't consider much difference between the Afghan theater and the Levant. But those were two completely different worlds. It's almost like three different wars sequentially fought in very short order: first the Taliban and Al Qaeda, then the Iraqi State, and then the insurgency."

After securing Al-Lasaf for follow-on forces, Alpha Company was ordered to return to the forward post, a 12-hour drive, towing the broken Humvee the entire way.

Once they returned and refit the force, Company command received word they would be participating in the Jessica Lynch rescue mission. "We're all chomping at the bit for this, and for a few days immediately after the initial dust of the invasion settled, this was the only story, the only mission." There are several accounts of this mission, and Martens's is but one perspective, but what has gone largely unreported in posterity is the role of Alpha Company, 1/75, which was tasked with securing the hospital complex in order to set conditions for the team that would locate and secure Private Lynch. The company would roll in with the first-phase clearance and establish the blocking positions, ensuring no one got out of the hospital, and that no one else could get in. In preparation, the force moved up to Talil Air Base, about twenty-five kilometers west of Nasiriyah, where Lynch and her team had been captured in an ambush and where she was being held in the hospital.

They were given information about the battlespace, which included a high-probability risk assessment of contact with Saddam's Fedayeen forces. The Fedayeen were not like the renowned Special Republican Guard, whom they had encountered days prior. The Republican Guard were, in essence, the Iraqi equivalent of American SOF. The Fedayeen, rather, were like the Iraqi paramilitary equivalent of the American CIA's "Ground Branch" division—specializing in clandestine operations, subterfuge, and other shadowy missions. "So, for all intents and purposes, the ones guarding Lynch—as far as we knew—were supposedly Iraq's most highly trained operatives; the types who didn't wear uniforms, conducted clandestine operations and the like. There was an obvious connection to be made between the Fedayeen and the rising insurgency. And these guys all lived in the suburbs surrounding the hospital." Previous engagements by the Marine regiment that "owned" the Nasiriyah battlespace had been so intense the Marines had been forced to regroup outside the city.

Alpha Company would link up with two Marine Corps M1 Abrams tanks, which would escort them into the city and provide additional outer-cordon security. But no guidance or location for the armor support was given to Alpha Company leaders; they only knew that somewhere in Nasiriyah—a sector of the battlespace allocated to a Marine Corps regiment—were the Marines and heavy armor needed for the mission. "We loaded up and drove from Talil to Nasiriyah. As we approached the city from the south, our introduction to this part of Iraq is the biggest landfill I have ever seen. Driving through it, all you could see was piles of burning garbage. We had to stop right in the middle of this landfill, and comms echoed back through the team net that we are on a short halt, having 'linked up with friendly forces, hold fire.'"

The Marines had set up shop in the middle of this burning wasteland; a place that made the Rangers think of a literal hell on Earth. While awaiting force consolidation, the Rangers looked left and right, and could see foxholes in this rubbish—the Marines had dug themselves fighting positions and were bedded down in this location as a patrol base for missions into Nasiriyah. "First thought that popped into my head when I saw these poor bastards was 'Holy shit, no wonder the Corps retention is so bad.'"

The combined force left the landfill and met up with the other special-operations units on the northern outskirts of the city. Tensions were high, as each operator knew the eyes of the Coalition, and most of the Western world, were watching and waiting for what would happen this night. "We had a full stack of aircraft overhead, performing various route scans, looking for possible ambushes, barricades, anything to indicate that our approach was compromised." Air deconfliction would be a non-traditional method for this mission; there were multiple SOF FACs with the various joint teams. But as Nasiriyah belonged to the Marine Corps battlespace owner, the controllers would coordinate airspace deconfliction and sequencing of aircraft with Marine ANGLICOs (Air Naval Gunfire Liaison Company) at the regimental headquarters and the airspace requests would be routed through the Marine Direct Air Support Center rather than the Air Support Operations Center. Despite the complexity, they would not have any problems managing the dense skies over the city during the mission.

The infil route was Highway 16, an east–west road on the north side of the city; immediately to the south, between the highway and the urban centers, was a huge canal that framed the entire city outline. The canal and dam works ran through the city itself, as the Euphrates River essentially cut the city into northern and southern halves. There were 15 vehicles in the convoy, led by one of the tanks, the SF team driving four Pandur II armored personnel carriers, and the remaining trucks being driven by Rangers (Martens being in the last of these). The second tank brought up the rear.

The mission would be supported by national assets, including those sourced by highly classified components of the American clandestine service. "One of the three-letter agencies had coordinated to have the power to the entire city cut as soon as we began our ingress into the city proper. That was essentially our launch call from the release point at the edge of the city—once we saw the lights go out, we would turn south on Route 7 and make our way into the heart of Nasiriyah." They would cross the Euphrates and, once on the south side of the canal, turn east, taking a circuitous route. A head-on approach was likely to tip their hand early. The airspace was jam-packed with fires and intelligence, surveillance, and reconnaissance platforms. "We had F-15s conducting pre-assault fires on known insurgent checkpoints and strongholds, while the convoy was escorted by MH-60L DAPs [Direct Action Penetrator] Black Hawks on an offset position, and a whole horde of additional aircraft."

For the scheme of maneuver, Alpha Company, 1/75, would drive into the zone surrounding the hospital and establish a blocking position (BP) on the east side of the hospital complex, while another Ranger force—Bravo Company, 1/75—would conduct a helicopter infil to another major road just south of the complex and move by foot to set up BPs along the hospital's west side. Once the isolation and containment was set in, the SOF would enter the hospital and secure the hostage. "When the lights went out, it was utterly surreal, something straight out of a movie. Words fail to convey the sensations that coursed through all of us in that moment. Try to imagine being in a major city, the ambient lights illuminating everything, and then it all goes dark, absolutely pitch black." At this point, no one on the mission had slept more than a few hours in the past week, owing to the variety of priority targets under SOF purview, or the long transits necessary to coalesce into this rescue package in Nasiriyah, far in Iraq's eastern quadrant.

Martens spent the first stretch of the blacked-out drive reviewing the map data as the convoy passed through checkpoints and phase lines. In 2003, air controllers and ground commanders didn't have smart phones with live-imagery, or even GRGs (gridded reference graphics) for terrain correlation; everything was done using a 1:50,000 topographic map, if those were available. "But at least the maps we had of Iraq were up to date on the geodetic reference datum, unlike the ancient Russian cartography we were still using in Afghanistan." The head of the convoy made a left turn, and the convoy followed suit like a motorized snake. All the while, the rearguard M1 is nearly running into the back of Martens's Humvee. "Every time we stop and go, which is a typical accordion effect in any convoy, the tank is creeping close enough to make you panic. You haven't lived until you've sat in the back of a soft-skinned Humvee, while a young Marine with very little nighttime-NVG [night-vision goggles] driving experience is steering an M1 Abrams through a darkened city right behind you as you're trying to talk to aircraft and read a map under red lens. Nobody realizes how tall these tanks are, so when I'm looking behind me, I'm looking up at the front of this tank screaming closer. They are not the nimblest of vehicles, and driving them on pavement is hellacious to boot."

The pre-mission planning had established pre-assault fires, but these were not being directed by any of the air controllers in the convoy. As soon as the force turned on Route 7, the F-15s overhead conducted a strike on some barracks buildings, whose targeting was based on sources and intel well above the paygrade of those in the convoy. "When I say barracks, I don't mean the kind we have in the states on a DoD post; this was an entire city block sized building, which appeared to be fifteen stories high, which was being utilized by the insurgents for staging and command and control." Once the precision-guided bombs impacted this structure containing high numbers of reported insurgents, the entire building was on fire, the single biggest blaze any of the men had ever seen. "Just as I was registering this image, it hit me once again that Iraq was quite unlike Afghanistan."

Near simultaneously, Martens looked towards the hospital, which was illuminated by floodlights and streetlamps. Just like any modern hospital complex, Nasiriyah's had backup generators. Whoever coordinated to shut down the electrical grid for the entire city didn't take that variable into account.

Besides CAS and air-power integration, the single greatest advantage Coalition forces had when fighting in Afghanistan and Iraq was the darkness—thanks to night-vision optics and infrared capabilities, American and partner forces owned the night. But between the 15-story building that had been struck in the pre-assault fires package, and the backup generators for the hospital complex up and running, the rescue force no longer claimed that advantage. This myriad of circumstances, from departing the release point to reaching the canal bridge had taken less than ten minutes. As the convoy approached the bridge, the lead M1 notified the force over the team channel that insurgents had set up barricades across the bridge, using cars and other detritus. Prior to this mission, the Marines who were responsible for Nasiriyah had been fighting to get across this bridge days before the rescue mission, and each time had been repelled. "That should give an idea on the tenacity of the enemy we were facing in this city: U.S. Marines couldn't break through this bridge due to the intensity of the incoming fire during daylight incursions. The barricade would serve as the nighttime security for the Fedayeen forces in the city."

During infil, Martens was the restricted operating zone controller, meaning he had priority of fires with all aircraft. In addition to his primary control, another TACP was flying on helicopters with Bravo Company, 1/75, holding aloft at the edge of the city and waiting for the call to set in the western BPs. There was also an Air Force CCT, and a third TACP collocated with a quick-reaction force of Marines at the outskirts of the city, on call to enter the urban area. In the stack, several aircraft were qualified to release munitions, including a Marine F/A-18 who was an FAC–Airborne. There was more than a half-dozen controllers all vying for time on the net during a highly complex raid, which was further complicated by the mission being deep in enemy dominated territory. "The net was congested to say the least. This is a significant point because up until mission, I don't believe the air controller community writ large—TACP, CCT or otherwise—had sufficient training for a multi-controller mission set in a congested environment."

"When you're the controller on the mission, you are the conduit of all air-to-ground comms and coordination. Every important piece of information passes between your ears, and it's your job to convey ground truth to the air, and air truth to the ground, without creating a gap in situational awareness. When you have that many different puppet masters passing information back and forth, it complicates the monster. And we're all beholden to our ground commanders, each of whom has their own mission objectives. Sharing is something we don't do particularly well. I don't want to sound as if I'm shitting on any particular group of controllers, whether they are conventional or special operations, but I think that if there had been any less-experienced and proficient forward air controllers on this mission, it would have been a problem. But as everyone who was supporting this mission was either special operations, or the aircrew being highly proficient, we set our egos aside and respected each other's autonomy within the mission segments. The comprehensive planning, the contingency planning in addition to that, mitigated much of the complexities. We didn't get into a huge gunfight either, and if that had occurred, obviously things would have been more of a challenge, but at our level (higher echelons not accounting for the backup generators at the hospital notwithstanding), this mission was planned down to a 'T.'"

As the convoy started crossing the bridge under the shadows of the structure fire, the lead M1 bulldozed into the barricade at 55 miles per hour, tossing car hulks and debris everywhere. As the rest of the vehicles passed through the blockade, drivers were banking and jiving around the detritus, the collective mindset of the operators were meager hopes and prayers none of the vehicles flipped or blew a tire.

"I can see the hospital in detail now, just off our nose to the right. The official narrative is that there were no shots fired during this mission. That is not true." As soon as the lead tank crossed the bridge, it began to receive tracer fire upon breaking into the open zone on the southern bridgehead. This engagement continued as each subsequent vehicle passed through the field of fire. To the men in the trucks, most of whom had now experienced gunfights up close and recently, it was evident this wasn't an errant insurgent taking pop-shots like most had already seen in Afghan ambushes. These were prepared, hardened firing points set up on fields of fire overlooking main avenues of approach with designated kill zones. "I remembered thinking to myself, 'I'm in an open-back Humvee, and we are seconds away from passing through this field of fire.' The helicopter pilots were on their shit that night, and engaged that machine-gun nest once they had a good fix on the location, it was no more than 30 seconds before we passed into the kill zone."

With the entire convoy over the river and into the urban sector south, they picked up speed, moving east along the frontage road, with only a few turns remaining before they approached the pre-planned BPs. The M1 in the lead continued to its pre-designated intersection, while the SF Pandurs broke off to begin the assault and clearance of the hospital. Martens's element made a buttonhook onto the east side of the complex moving south, finding themselves hemmed in by high walls on both sides of the road. The lead Ranger vehicle hit a last turn, but this only served to double back the convoy, which was now facing north. "To my right I see the lead vehicle heading north, we are the last vehicle still heading south, and at the turn, I see a Ranger M240 turret gunner get launched from the top of the Humvee when that truck hits a bump in the road. I can see all of this clearly as we are now in the illumination of the hospital floodlights. This ranger rolls a couple times, barely missing the third truck, and just takes off running to where one of the BPs was supposed to be."

The trucks finally halt, with Rangers dismounting and moving to occupy hardpoints. Martens stood next to a young Ranger lieutenant, who took a knee between bounds to cover, and yelled, "Hey, sir, we probably shouldn't stop, I know we're bounding but we should probably just sprint to the street corner." One of the truck gunners called out armed movers in one of the courtyards to the east—exactly where the force was anticipating the reported Fedayeen to originate from. "I have the AC-130 under my control, as the assets were split off to various controllers for this phase of the mission. Due to the congestion of buildings, I had no chance of doing a fixed-wing gun run or employing heavy munitions, so the gunship was the best option I might have utilized here. Getting the gunship talked on took a bit of time, because we're fighting the urban canyon effect—if we're looking east at these guys who are peeking over the compound wall with weapons, I can't engage if the gunship is in the eastern hold of its wheel because that frag is going to come right at us. I can't employ from behind us as that would send frag into the building they came out of, and we couldn't confirm if civilians were inside. It's complicated, sorting the circumstances that arise during these precious seconds. I had approval from the A Co commander to engage, but ended up advising the commander to use the Mk-19 gunner on one of the trucks."

"This was a very important lesson for me: sometimes CAS employment just isn't the answer to every tactical problem. It goes back to our 'air-mindedness': we want to utilize airpower to keep the ground force safe, but there are times where CAS isn't appropriate. Air controllers needs to have the awareness and judgment to tell ground commanders that. All this work in coordinating and planning and integrating, and, in that moment, Ranger solved the problem with a 40mm."

Alpha Company soon received word Lynch had been located and secured, and, a few minutes later, looked up to see the medevac land on the roof to take her to safety. "We didn't know if she was unharmed or otherwise, which is obviously something we were all deeply invested in. Across the force, the concern was that as soon as her guards heard helicopters, they were just going to kill her for fear of her treatment being reported to the world. But the important thing was that she had been recovered." As soon as the Rangers saw Lynch's rescue helicopters depart, they received a FRAGO (fragmentary order) with their next objective. The team had recovered several deceased individuals from the morgue, presumed to be Americans. One of those recovered remains would end up being an Iranian, to the confusion of the operators. But the remainder of Lynch's team was assessed to be buried in a shallow grave in one of the hospital's southern courtyards, close to Alpha Company's blocking positions.

Finding and recovering the remains of Lynch's squad mates would be the next and final objective on this mission. Because they had left Talil rapidly to make mission timelines, Alpha Company had stripped the trucks of everything deemed non-essential; this included pioneer kits and shovels, everything stripped from the trucks in favor of speed. "We found the grave easily and tragically enough, but we were forced to start moving dirt with hands and knives. I think someone found a shovel from a nearby house. But that was a painstaking, macabre endeavor. There is a distinct smell that you never quite forget from recovering human remains. Thank goodness we were able to find the missing individuals, and we packaged them up as reverently as we could, returning them to Talil for the dignified transfer home after we returned."

***

"We hit several more objectives following the Lynch rescue. We secured Objective *Grizzly*, a staging area for follow-on forces in northern Tikrit, after we had passed through Haditha Dam where Tommy Case and Eric Brandenburg had stolen the show for an early chapter in this war. *Grizzly* was an important site because we wanted to show Saddam that there was nowhere he could go that we wouldn't be coming after him or his sons. Saddam was from Tikrit, so our taking of this objective was essentially a signal that the noose was tightening around him. The only thing that stands out from that mission is the amount of munitions that were left unsecured for people to steal—piles of AK-47s stacked as high as a pickup truck; those had been left there as a fallback for the Tikrit militias to regroup and stock up on once the Iraqi Army had fallen. Another unit had already broken open the base, and our job was to roll in and properly secure those immense weapons caches until conventional forces could relieve us and actually hold the facility."

"Following Objective *Grizzly*, our next mission was taking Tikrit Air Base, also known as Al Sahra Airfield. The strategic assessment was that, following the successful Coalition push into Baghdad, and breaking the main force, … Saddam would marshal his remaining resources in Tikrit and make his last stand there. But if we could rapidly take Tikrit airfield and military base, that alone would serve as a huge blow to their morale and ability to mount and sort of final defense. It was on this mission that I became an expert in Type II and Type III controls, where I would be using CAS on targets that I wasn't directly observing. The regiment was built for seizing key terrain and, following that, close-with-the-enemy raids, and ambush fighting, so much of what we had been doing was Type I controls: I see the enemy, I know where my friendlies are, and I make that physical assessment of the aircraft at weapons release before giving clearance. Pretty straightforward CAS, and utilizing Type II and III was simply a more complex dynamic for employing aerial fires."

"We get to the airfield, and it's time for the air show. I climbed to the roof of a building overlooking the airfield, while Ranger was doing Ranger business by clearing buildings, rooting out any resistance and establishing a hard point. I would occasionally be able to observe aircraft servicing targets but, for the most part, I'm working from targeting data on the enemy who were literally all over this base trying to oust us from the hard point. I had a constant stream of new aircraft checking in but, of all the assets, I was most impressed with the B-1 bombers and their ability to mass fires on a single objective in order to neutralize the threat."

"I'm posted on the roof, and I have my map laid out with a detailed sketch of the airfield alongside. The ground commander's intent for the airfield was simple: the only limit on effects was the runway itself—we couldn't crater it as it would be a critical resource for the air train in the coming days. But everything else along the flightline and the military base, so long as it was verifiably the enemy, was fair game. And this base was bursting at the seams with everything the Iraqi Army had left. There were guard towers all along the perimeter, occupied by Iraqi soldiers, and many extenuating logistical and tactical support apparatuses to ensure they were equipped for a protracted, dug-in fight. When I tell this story, this is often the part where I see people struggling to believe the extent of what we did with CAS that night. My final BDA [battle-damage assessment] from the mission into Tikrit read as follows: three companies worth of Iraqi armored vehicles destroyed, 24 manned guard towers neutralized, five military aircraft, and an additional 25 armored personnel carriers. Now technically, because I was elevated above the ground when I directed those airstrikes against the Iraqi aircraft, I think that makes me an ace by proxy."

"We did that as a company-plus of Rangers, taking an airfield from a ground-assault package, and fighting against an entire military base that was well-prepared for the defense. That's the kind of influence that air superiority and air integration can have on the battlespace. This wasn't all high fives and war stories from this mission, however. It was on this very mission, not long after we had essentially wrapped up these pre-assault fires around Al Sahra Airfield where Scott Sather—a combat controller from Fort Bragg—was killed. Scott was embedded with the RRD team that was working with us to locate targets for CAS, as well as shaping and observation work that would enable follow-on operations once we had taken the airfield and base. Scott would be the first U.S. Air Force casualty of the Iraq War. So that sets a pall over the incredible things we were able to achieve in short order, despite being outnumbered, deep in enemy territory. His sacrifice and coordination with the work the rest of us air controllers [were doing] nearby would ultimately eliminate what remained of the Iraqi Air Force and enable the rapid seizure of Tikrit. And of course, Saddam was captured less than a year after we had stormed into his hometown."

PART III

Evolving the Machine

Worlds Apart, 2004–2006

The cause is eternally right.
George W. Bush

CHAPTER 15

Building a Global Architecture

TACS/AAGS: Theater Air Control/Army Air–Ground Systems

In order to support requirements for a two-front war across multiple time zones and a new joint paradigm, integrating the diverse assortment of Coalition actors in the airspaces over Afghanistan and Iraq needed a comprehensive, responsive, and complex network for command and control. This system would have to allocate and distribute air-power assets needed to support the ground forces engaging enemy combatants across three time zones and thousands of square miles of air space. The system needed to sort through air-support requests from ground units in the preparatory phase of mission planning, as well as rapidly source immediate requests from forward-staged units who were "troops in contact," or "TIC," a term ubiquitous with firefights in the War on Terror.

This architecture needed to be located in a relatively centralized location to provide oversight across the two primary battle spaces and overcome the tyranny of distance for communications, data sharing, and management of airspace for routing and safety of flight. For nearly the entirety of the Global War on Terror (GWOT), the Combined Air Operations Center was located at Al Udeid Air Base in Qatar, where it remains as of this writing. This combined-operations function would support the maneuver plans for all ground forces in both theaters with the available air power and prioritize the assignment of aircraft based on mission necessity as directed by higher headquarters. This ever-expanding apparatus went by a variety of monikers, but by doctrine this system is called the Theater Air Control System/Army Air–Ground System (TACS/AAGS). The system fused command-and-control functions between the Army and Air Force, fomenting the uniquely "joint" DNA the GWOT demanded.

The unified combatant command CENTCOM (Central Command) serves as the joint force, led by the joint-force commander (JFC) who presides over all operations and ensures the force is organized and equipped to achieve national military strategy as defined by grand strategy—in the case of GWOT, defeating terror networks affiliated with the attacks on September 11, 2001—by dictating the prioritization of all systems in theater. The JFC deputizes the ground and air elements of the joint force via the joint force's air-component commander (JFACC) and land-component commander (JFLCC). At the direction of the JFC, the senior-most levels of the TACS/AAGS system develop *apportionment*, which is the percentage or priority of the total air effort that should be devoted to various air operations or geographic regions as recommended by the JFACC. Among the apportioned missions include air superiority (counter-air and air interdiction), airlift, theater ISR (intelligence, surveillance, and reconnaissance), electronic warfare, and special operations. Following apportionment, where percentages of all available aircraft are assigned to cover missions or areas, the JFACC directs the *allocation* of assets, where aircraft are divided into specific missions or flights and arranged in a daily report called the Air Tasking Order (ATO), which is disseminated across the joint force. For those aircraft apportioned for close air support (CAS), the allocation of those assets is organized and tasked by the ATO as recommended by the JFLCC.

Theater Air Control System

At the highest level of the TACS is the Air Operations Center (AOC), which is the senior deployable TACS element and develops/distributes the ATO/Integrated Tasking Order (ITO) across the force. Within the AOC are various planning and coordination functions: the Combat Plans Division, which actually produces the ATO on a 24-hour cycle for pre-planned missions; the Combat Operations Division, which coordinates aircraft execution of the ATO; the Combat Intelligence Division, which centralizes and distributes all air-related intelligence; and the Wing Operations Center, which possesses the aircraft and personnel tasked to fulfill the requirements of the ATO. The most active and integral component of TACS is the Air Support Operations Center (ASOC), typically aligned with the corps-level land component, which coordinates and directs air sorties based on prioritization emanating from the AOC as directed by the JFC. The ASOC is primarily responsible for reacting to immediate CAS requests from ground forces, those requests that were not part of the day's ATO cycle based on a TIC or unanticipated priority target. Afghanistan and Iraq would each have ASOCs subordinate to the CENTCOM AOC.

TACS is driven by the tactical air control party elements aligned at every level of the supported Army maneuver elements from the battalion to the corps. Battalion-aligned TACPs develop and submit the Joint Tactical Air Request (JTAR, or DD Form 1972) to the next highest headquarters for processing. This is the pre-planned air-request method for aligning available air support with the priorities of the various aligned ground forces, whose missions are processed for prioritization by ground component higher headquarters through the ASOC to the AOC. So long as the requesting joint terminal attack controller does not receive a denial from the next higher headquarters, it is presumed the requested mission would be supported along the pre-planned CAS allocation process. Such CAS requests are generated by specific, anticipated requirements of the maneuver-force commanders, who direct their forward air controllers (FAC) to request CAS against foreseeable times and missions. Any higher headquarters element involved in this process has the authority to deny a JTAR, based on higher-order priorities within various ground-force headquarters or known air priorities not always available to lower echelons of the TACS.

Once those requests are processed to the AOC, the various planning and coordination components collate all approved requests and generate the ATO/ITO. Within the AOC, a planning element generates the Airspace Control Order (ACO), which dictates routing and safety of flight for all aircraft in theater and is developed in tandem with the recurring ATO, although many safe-flight corridors for logistics and transit remained unchanged throughout the war. The ACO also included critical airspace-control measures (ACM) such as restricted operating zones unique to each FAC for their specific mission—these ACMs could and did often change daily, and sometimes hourly, depending on the prioritization of the JTAC's supported mission. When aircraft are allocated from the Wing Operations Center to fly sorties, the ATO directs specific callsigns/aircraft tail numbers to specific missions and particular locations; the ACO ensured safe transit and routing for those aircraft into and out of the airspace.

The ATO is a multi-day preparatory ordeal for sorting, prioritizing, and populating, based on standard constraints like aircraft available due to maintenance, aircrews, and mission requirements. The daily ATO is released over secure internet portals across the joint force, where any appropriate JTAC is able to retrieve and view it, special instructions, ACO, and other relevant air-power procedural control measures to conduct operations on a daily basis. Often, FACs conducting multi-day operations would not know if their requested VULs (vulnerability times) would be supported due to being out on missions. For such unknowns, controllers would contact the ASOC via the joint air request net (JARN), a satellite frequency (although initially reliant upon HF frequencies in the early years), to receive updates on pre-planned CAS requests. The JARN would ultimately serve a much more important and time-sensitive function: immediate CAS requests.

FACs and their supported ground forces who found themselves in need of immediate air support—unforeseen circumstances like a TIC, priority target, or change in mission—contacted the ASOC via the JARN. The ASOC fills those requests as able by diversion of pre-planned sorties via coordination with the AOC, interpretation of the ATO, or through rerouting of pre-planned sorties at various points in the ATO in order to provide timely and immediate CAS in time-sensitive circumstances. The ASOC's only purpose is the coordination of CAS missions, therefore intelligence/surveillance/reconnaissance, airlift, electronic warfare and other air-power missions are outside the control authority of the ASOC. The ASOC is populated and executed by various TACPs, airspace manager, and aircraft-liaison officers to fully integrate capabilities for supporting the joint force.

Other critical elements within the TACS regarding air-power integration include the Air Mobility Element/Center for airlift and logistics, as well as the tasking of aerial refueling tankers in order to extend the VUL times of assigned sorties in theater. The Control and Reporting Center/Element (CRC) provides radar tracking and airspace management for aircraft transiting across the airspace, in addition to providing the basic air-defense functions for the joint force. The CRC is extended and collectively managed by the near-persistent presence of the Airborne Warning and Control System (AWACs) E-3 aircraft, known for its massive radar dish aboard the four-engine platform, and the now retired Joint Surveillance Target Attack Radar System (JSTARs), another platform with ground-focused aperture radar to track and sort moving targets. Finally, Tactical Air Controllers–Airborne and FACs–Airborne aircraft, fighter jets with terminal attack control-qualified pilots, would extend the command-and-control apparatus for the execution and responsiveness of the TACS architecture.

Army Air–Ground System

The TACS architecture sources and allocates air support to enable the ground forces' missions. In order to do so, those ground forces must also conduct prioritization of their subordinate task forces and mission priorities in order to generate a coherent picture to ensure effective integration of air power. Further, the land component of the joint force must effectively interface with the Air Force's to maximize joint-force capabilities. To do this, Army/land components are organized under the Army Air–Ground System.

Parallel to the AOC, the AAGS staffs and manages the Battlefield Coordination Detachment (BCD), which processes requests from subordinate land forces for support, while interpreting the broader ground maneuver plan for the AOC. The BCD contains multiple critical sections which enable the translation of the ground picture into actionable planning for the air component—the Air Defense Artillery Section, the Plans Section, Intelligence, Airspace Management (which deconflicts Army surface fires and rotary wing aircraft from fixed-wing systems and contributes to ATO development), airlift coordination, and various liaison officers who provide joint-force integration as representatives for the AAGS and JFLCC.

The AAGS is represented at every echelon of the Army's maneuver force, from the battalion, through the brigade, division, and corps levels. The corps is the primary Army force for a theater of operations and executes current campaigns or major operations while planning and sourcing subordinate units for future operations. The division serves as the basic Army unit of combined arms and functions, and also provides the basic framework for combined or joint forces. The brigade is the basic unit whose purpose is to close with the enemy through the use of maneuver and firepower. The battalion is the basic maneuver element consisting of a headquarters and headquarters company, three rifle companies, and a support company, with some variation depending on the type of unit (airborne, mechanized infantry, etc.). At each of these echelons, AAGS is represented by the Command Post (CP). Within each CP is the basic hierarchy of the force command structure: the G-2/Intelligence Section; G-3/Operations (organizing and executing plans, operations, and training); G-3/Air (processes the air-support requests through the pre-planned process); G-4 (logistics/mission support); the fire-support coordinator/officer, who advises and is responsible to each echelon's commander on surface fire support and integration of all fire support (including CAS); and the Army Airspace C2 Element, which is part of the ACO execution apparatus.

Each element of the TACS/AAGS system and, over the intervening years of the GWOT, many other elements of command and control, were fused into a living ecosystem which transplanted information across multiple networks, languages, and dozens of major operating bases and hundreds of combat outposts for 20 years. But at the functional level, TACS/AAGS became the lifeblood of one of the most complex warfighting mechanisms ever contrived. Neither half of this architecture could function without the assorted air-power experts—both Air Force and Army, and later from across the entirety of the Department of Defense and Coalition—synergizing their efforts to provide timely, effective air support to the ground forces taking the fight to the adversary.

The concept of joint warfare has long been a foundational component of the United States military, synergistic effects and economy of effort being long-standing principles of warfighting that dictate the arrangement of forces. But until the GWOT, "joint" operations were still largely simultaneous affairs of segregated capabilities operating in proximity to one another, not wholly fused. America's longest conflict was the first to truly employ integrated networks of the internet age to their maximum potential.

The FAC community and the doctrinal network and organization of command-and-control architecture would put the "joint" into joint operations.

CHAPTER 16

"The insurgents turned that place into a meat grinder"

Scott Loescher would have the distinct achievement of invading Iraq twice and, in both cases, entering Iraq via the invasion route from Kuwait. He would comment during his interview, "My downrange career began in Kuwait, and it would end there as well," owing the terminus of his TACP career to his role as the Base Command Chief Master Sergeant at Ali Al Saleem Air Base in 2017, the same location from which he would enter Iraq as an airman first class in 1991, and again as a technical sergeant in 2003.

After entering Baghdad with the invasion force in 2003 alongside the 3rd Infantry Division, while stationed at the 10th Air Support Operations Squadron from Fort Riley, Kansas, Loescher had been part of the security package at Tikrit Airfield in northern Iraq. He would stand on the air-traffic control tower at Tikrit, overwatching the Special Forces raid that captured Saddam Hussein. Following those tumultuous events in the earliest chapters of the war, he would return home, and then PCS[1] to Friedberg, Germany, in the spring of 2004 to support the 1st Armored Division.

This was around the time the insurgency had started forming; most notorious among the extremist groups were the Sadr militia, who had turned Baghdad into a bloody warzone. Amid this upheaval in sectarian violence, the 1st Armored Division had been ordered to extend their 12-month deployment by another three months in Iraq. This would end up being the longest deployment of any U.S. Army unit since World War II. With TACPs in Baghdad, Loescher was told upon arrival to his new unit that he would be sent in to relieve those forward air controllers in place to cover the extension.

After arriving in Baghdad, with only two days in country, the division's air liaison officer told Loescher, "There is a big operation cooking in Karbala, and I need a senior TACP to go down there to manage the air mission." He sorted a flight from Baghdad to the 1st Brigade, 1st Armored Division (1-1AD), headquarters in Karbala. The unit would lead the partnered operation, supported by a mechanized infantry brigade from the Polish Army. There were also Special Forces (SF) teams who would participate in this massive clearance, supported by another TACP named Kevin Davis.

At this time, no Coalition forces could enter downtown Karbala, as it was completely controlled by the insurgency. The division had checkpoints all around the city perimeter, but every time Coalition forces transited the city, they were ambushed, including the imposing M1 tanks and M113 Bradley infantry fighting vehicles. "The insurgents we were fighting didn't care about destruction or damage to civilians, and they didn't care how many casualties they took."[2] There are some places during the Global War on Terror (GWOT) whose names carry a dark omen for how insurgents would throw bodies at the Coalition, who were simply trying to stabilize and retake territory—Helmand in Afghanistan, Fallujah and Sadr City in Iraq, to name a few. "Karbala would join those as locations where the insurgents turned the place into a meat grinder."

The division planned for both brigades to clear out insurgent footholds in the city, all the way to downtown Karbala, while the SF teams went after key targets simultaneously. It was a straightforward clearance, and they spent two days planning and rehearsing, working through priority of fires, sequencing of units, phasing, and key calls. This operation came at a particularly sensitive time, roughly one year after President Bush had proclaimed mission accomplished" Large-scale missions of this magnitude were being back briefed directly to the Secretary of Defense (SECDEF), Donald Rumsfeld.

The night when the operation kicked off, all forces were staged to their start points, the Brigade Headquarters C2 element was staged at the edge of the city to conduct overall command and control, with Loescher as the primary airspace controller and fire-support officer for the regiment-sized assault force. "We had an

Downtown Karbala after insurgents had ransacked the city ahead of Coalition force reclamation in 2003. (Photo provided by Scott Loescher)

"THE INSURGENTS TURNED THAT PLACE INTO A MEAT GRINDER" • 161

AC-130, F-16s, an MQ-1 Predator, and plenty of CAS requests to backfill those initial sorties. I was co-located with the Brigade TAC [Tactical Command Post], with a ROVER IV [remote-operated video enhanced receiver] video downlink system, which would enable us to watch live feeds of the aircraft's sensors. The ROVER was a brand-new system, which required a receiver that looks like a black manpack radio with manual input buttons on the front plate, antennas for both C-, S-, and Ku-band frequencies, and a lot of wires and cables. The video feed was streamed on a Panasonic CF-19 'Toughbook' [a ruggedized laptop computer]."

There was a multitude of technical necessities, which none of the controllers knew about with using this system, which they had to figure out on the fly. One issue was due to how antennas are mounted on many Coalition aircraft—on top of the fuselage; when the aircraft turned away, or was not pointed towards the ROVER antenna, the signal was lost. "It's tough to imagine for later generations of TOC-dwellers [tactical operations center], but for us, even with this live feed, we'd sometimes lose the video entirely, and have to recapture and re-correlate the targeting information."

"We had everything laid on for this massive mission; an American brigade is almost 3,000 soldiers, a third of which is purely combat power, and we had several hundred more of our Polish brothers, and dozens of Special Forces operators. As we're waiting to initiate, the word comes down through Baghdad, from Lieutenant General Ricardo Sanchez, who was commander of U.S. Forces–Iraq at that time, who told 1st Armored Division commander, Major General Martin Dempsey, that the mission had been canceled. We didn't get a reason. Though we all suspected it was a political decision. Who knows. But we certainly didn't get an explanation, just a SECDEF-directed 'stand down.'"

"Our brigade commander spoke for all of us when he said 'Fuck!' to no one in particular, and then notified our Polish partners of the change. 'We can't do the op,' and the Polish brigade commander tells him 'If we don't do this operation tonight, I'm taking all of my forces and I am pulling them out of the city.'" But the operation would be salvaged thanks to the insightful contributions of the Air Force TACPs, whose responsibilities, among controlling close air support (CAS) missions, included understanding the nuances of rules of engagement. Loescher thought they could still do the operation, and said as much to the brigade staff. The brigade commander demanded a more detailed explanation upon hearing this, and Loescher answered: "Sir, there are the rules of engagement which we are obligated to follow; and if our forces are engaged by the enemy, then we have the right to escalate lethal force as necessary to deter the threat to protect the force." The TACP suggested a repeat of the same patterns which the insurgents already knew well and had been doing for months: send out the patrols towards the city center. "We already have the pre-planned sorties on station. As soon as those advanced friendly forces are decisively engaged, which we know will happen as soon as they approach those insurgent checkpoints, we'll have the air assets on station and the remainder of the force is ready to execute the operation. But it's self-defense." The JAG[3] was standing next to the commander and heard the entire plan, and concurred: "Technically, the ETAC is right, sir."

This put the 1-1AD brigade commander in a difficult position: proceed with the operation and take a major city from the insurgents or pull back and risk being thought a coward when the rules technically supported his continuation of mission. It recalled for Loescher the situation in World War II, when General George Patton took the city of Trier in Germany in early 1945, after General Eisenhower at SHAEF (Supreme Headquarters Allied Expeditionary Force) told him to wait to take the city "because it would take four divisions." Patton had already taken Trier on account of his spiteful rivalry with Bernard Montgomery, the British field marshal, and his reply to SHAEF's orders was "Have taken Trier with two divisions, what do you want me to do, give it back?"

They sent patrols into Karbala, as they had done for months. But this time, there were simply more patrols—an entire brigade's worth of patrols. Once they became decisively engaged, there already just happened to be CAS—a lot of CAS—on station, and the TACPs responded in self-defense of the force with overwhelming firepower. "We sent the F-16s home with no munitions remaining, we did the same with the AC-130. It was pointing and shooting via the ROVER every time a patrol became decisively engaged with the enemy. We had a higher level of situational awareness than any of the observers with the forward elements, so I had control of all aircraft over Karbala while working from the Brigade TAC. What was cool about this mission, and I don't believe anyone had started this TTP [tactics, techniques, and procedures] yet—although it became a standard practice later in the war—is that we would key up the ROVER to the MQ-1 sensor feed, and use the Predator to locate the insurgents or 'hunt,' and that would queue the fixed-wing or gunship onto those enemy very quickly; you can pull a useable grid location right off of the Predator feed and, boom, immediate vector for the gunship, F-16s, AH-64s, and prosecute."

The first convoy from the brigade rolled out on patrol, just like any other day, and upon closing with the first known insurgent checkpoint, took six RPGs in rapid succession. This first encounter would open a citywide clearance and continuous CAS engagements for the next eight hours. "We absolutely evicted the insurgent presence, to the point that, the next morning, the American and Polish brigade commanders did a 'victory parade' through downtown Karbala, standing up in their tank turrets and waving—all of the tropey shit." The Iraqis—the civilians of Karbala, who were still living in the "meat grinder"—poured out onto the thoroughfares and byways to see the Coalition driving armor through the city. "They didn't want to be living under the rule of the Sadr militia, they knew what kind of monsters those insurgents were. Later years of the war and the deepening

Karbala's skyline as Coalition aircraft uproot insurgents within the city. (Photo provided by Scott Loescher)

insurgency would prove those fears valid too. But they were ecstatic to see Americans and Poles driving through their city."

"That was an impactful deployment for me, even though it was such a short tour. We had Combat Camera out with us during this operation, and they captured some pretty incredible images from the city after the fight was over. One picture, which is hanging on the wall at 1st Brigade Headquarters in Fort Bliss, Texas, shows a huge building in downtown which had been used by the Sadr militia as their main C2 site, which I had decimated with delay-fused 500-pound bombs, and there is a 1st Armored Division Tank parked right in front. I ended up getting a Bronze Star from that ordeal, which isn't that big of a deal, but one more example of air power enabling the ground force in ways that no other capability can."

***

"So, there I was in February of 1991, and I was a bad airman. I like to start this story off by telling people that. In the TACP community, where did leadership put the bad airmen? Up at the brigade level—processing air requests from the controllers down at the battalion and company levels, the ones who were trustworthy to be the lone Air Force representatives for the maneuver Army. This was so the bad airmen could be supervised by the TACP NCOIC (non-commissioned officer in charge). I was deployed with 2nd Brigade ("Blackjacks"), 1st Cavalry Regiment (2-1 CAV), with the Brigade Tactical Air Coordination (BDE TAC) cell. My brigade air liaison officer (ALO) was a weapons safety officer—a "Wizzo"—from an old F-4 Phantom. We left in the fall of 1990, staging in northern Saudi Arabia, waiting for the air war to kick off. Basically, we sat around in the desert sucking at life. We really had next to nothing out there, just a formation of soldiers, trucks, tents, living in about as austere of circumstances as you can imagine."

"But I was the 'bad airman,' stuck at the brigade with the ALO that nobody liked. So the air war kicks off, and we are circled up just north of a site called KKMC, 'King Khaled Military City' right where Iraq, Kuwait, and Saudi Arabia's borders coalesce into a veritable no-man's land. There was a massive wadi system along the contiguous border, with riverbeds shooting off into all three nations. While we were awaiting the air war, General Schwarzkopf decided that he wanted the big western hook from an organized force to make Saddam Hussein think that we were going to push straight north from Kuwait, straight up through the Iraqi sector of the wadi system. 2-1 CAV was tasked with the feints north and west of the tri-border area, about two weeks before the actual invasion force would disembark for Iraq proper. So we were the ones who blew up 'the Berm,' opening our advance with more than 270 multiple-launch rocket system salvoes. Two days after that barrage, we entered Iraq with a platoon of M1 Abrams tanks, the BDE TAC, which consisted of a handful of Humvees, an M113 Bradley—the Vulcan variant, which was a self-propelled anti-aircraft gun, for air-defense—and a scout platoon, which consisted of a few more Humvees. That was our 'feint' package, and we pushed more than twenty kilometers into Iraq in order to conduct this deception maneuver."

"We did not have an actual, qualified forward air controller, no ETAC, it was me, a radio operator, maintainer and driver, and the ALO. That was the air-controller task organization. I had the full radio suite—an ancient GRC-206 radio pallet in that truck which included the HF, VHF-Low/FM, and VHF/UHF—all set up in our assigned M113, sandbags on the floor for mine-protection, and a 1:50k map pinned to the map board on the wall. Once you get all of that equipment into a vehicle cavity that isn't much bigger than a household bathroom, you run out of space quickly. The first place we hit on this maneuver was about fifteen kilometers over the border, deep in the wadi system. The tank platoon was transiting inside the actual washout, while the scout platoon trucks and the BDE TAC were up on the high ground overwatching the tanks. Our first contact was a small group of Iraqi soldiers, manning this tiny outpost with a trench network, who engaged us with AK-47s, but nothing significant. They didn't hold up to the 25mm from the Bradleys for long and surrendered. Well, prisoners of war wasn't something we had rehearsed and, remember, this story is from 1991, not 2003, so things like care of transfer and personnel containment was just different than what people think of from personnel detention in the GWOT era."

"Since we didn't have room for these guys, we tied them up and strapped them to the front of the M113s to bring them back with us and held our position. The idea was that the loss of this checkpoint and the interruption of their surveillance comms should have been enough to achieve our objective of making the senior Iraqi commanders believe that the invasion thrust was us. Plenty of time for spotters to set up a decisive counterattack. It was only about 45 minutes later that we had our answer on whether or not this worked."

"We were on a slight rise, the M113s moved to the actual crest, and the Vulcan was about twenty meters to my left, when it stopped suddenly, erupting smoke with the cargo ramp halfway down. What the hell is going on over there? So the brigade sergeant major jumps down from his truck and walks over to the Vulcan. And bear in mind, we are all decked out in our Mission-Oriented Protective Posture gear, chem-suits, the whole rig—fears of chem/bio attacks in 2003 reflected our fears in 1991, the possibility was just as worrisome in both invasions. Sergeant Major climbs into the Vulcan, and hops right back out, yelling at us, which we can't hear over the din of the engines, but we can see that he is covered in blood. The Vulcan had taken a direct hit from a 100-mm recoilless rifle, right at the seam of the top hatch and the body. Killed the TC [truck commander] and gunner instantly, tore up the driver pretty badly."

"As soon as the formation realizes what has happened, maybe thirty seconds after Sergeant Major started yelling, a shitload of artillery starts falling all around us. There is no feeling on earth more helpless than being on the receiving end of incoming artillery. Even with the engines roaring and the tracks spinning, you can hear the rounds falling. It's like that scene from *Band of Brothers*, where they are standing in the tree line before the world is blown apart all around them. The air is so thick that you can't hear anything and then, suddenly, you can't hear anything else but those rounds falling."

"This barrage was overwhelming, we had a round land right next to my truck, which embedded shrapnel all along the side of the M113, much of which penetrated the armor, missing the back of my HF radio inside the suite by an inch. I didn't see this until we made it back to Saudi Arabia, but had that radio been damaged, we would have been completely cut off for long-range comms. I opened the hatch, trying to assess where the fire was coming from, and look down at the ALO who is supposed to be my boss—I'm just an airman first class after all, and a bad one at that—and he's curled up on the floor, piling the sandbags over him to protect himself.

"I think to myself, 'Well, shit, I need to do something useful,' so I used a pencil and filled out a paper DD1972 Air Request form, which I had pinned to the map board, and I called the Air Support Operations Center [ASOC] on the JARN [joint air request net] using the HF radio. The initial response I received from the ASOC was 'Yeah, we aren't doing close air support right now because the air war is underway, are you under fire right now?' So I keyed the mic and said, 'Fucking listen to this' then held the mic out the hatch to catch the sounds of the artillery landing all around us. 'That's incoming artillery on my position,

I need CAS right now.' One of my good friends, a guy named Angel Mendoza, was at the division headquarters, monitoring the JARN and heard everything, and coordinated to have a six-ship of A-10s vectored to my location. I should mention there was still a low cloud deck, probably no higher than five hundred feet, so observation from the air was completely obscured, but off to the northwest we could see the line of artillery pieces and make out the flashes which matched up with the round impacting soon after. While I'm going back and forth with Angel, he tells me to fill out some attack briefs while awaiting the A-10s to check on, and the whole time I was waiting for those birds to show up, you better believe I had attack briefs for everything nearby—paper briefs written with a pencil, using my protractor on the map board and all."

"Those aircraft showed up and checked in with me and, I'll be honest, I didn't ask for the ground commander's approval, the aircraft were here, it was time to return fire. We were all pinned down anyway, or at least were bobbing and weaving to make ourselves more difficult to hit. I told the A-10s that this would be Emergency CAS, which the flight lead acknowledged, 'Copy, we're gonna take care of you.' The first two A-10s rolled in, below the cloud deck, I passed approval to fire, and they both fired AGM-65 Mavericks right above us, which streak towards the artillery pieces like laser beams. The first impact must have been an ammo truck, because it wasn't just a single explosion, there were secondary effects lighting up the sky. Second Maverick hits, another explosion. Once those A-10s had a fix, which I confirmed from my hatch, they went to work. The BDA [battle-damage assessment] I received after they completed their engagement assessed that we had been engaged by a corps-level artillery element, likely either the IV or VII Corps of the Iraqi Army. The invasion headquarters would end up diverting air-war sorties over the next three days to shred that corps-level force, whose location remained concealed from intelligence until we had stumbled across it during this feint operation."

"One of the tanks would end up hitting a mine, and we would ultimately scrap the tank along with the M113 Vulcan, as we didn't have the ability to recover either vehicle with our force capabilities. As soon as air came into our piece of the fight, we hauled ass back to Saudi Arabia. Once we got back, the brigade commander marched over to our truck and asked who controlled the initial air strikes, which I answered for. 'Airman Loescher, if you weren't here, we all would have died today. You saved the lives of every man in this force.' That was a turning point in my life, I thought to myself 'This job is pretty badass, so I need to make sure from now on that I am the best possible TACP I can be, because people are depending on me to do my job.'"

"I turned 21 years old on that deployment. Barely old enough to drink legally, can't rent a car, hardly old enough to be considered a mature adult. But those are who are entrusted with the power and responsibility to change the outcome of a major battle."

CHAPTER 17

In Iraq's Shadow

Warzones within a Warzone

In previous eras of American warfare, certain battles took on near-mythical reputations. The strategic significance of those sites served as the foundation of many unit identities. Iwo Jima, where "uncommon valor became a common occurrence"; the Chosin Reservoir, one of the darkest and most brutally unforgiving days in the history of the Army and Marine Corps; "Hamburger Hill" in Vietnam, controversial for its intense bloodshed by American and South Vietnamese forces, only to be abandoned a short while after its seizure. In Somalia in 1993, the consequential Operation *Gothic Serpent* would dramatically change the manner in which the special-operations community organized and trained its forces in urban and low-intensity conflict following the fateful "Black Hawk Down" mission.

These battles imprinted a legacy of endurance and resilience on the units who participated in the events, and only serve as a sampling from across the diverse experience of America's armed forces. What these historical battles further exemplified were pivotal moments that, for good or ill, signaled a major transitional episode in the age of warfare and its execution. In many cases, these ethos-forging battles were harbingers of the end of a bloody conflict, while others were harsh lessons learned in blood and sacrifice, ultimately reshaping American fighting forces and doctrine. But this would be a small comfort to those who paid the ultimate sacrifice, which future generations of service members would learn in later years.

Afghanistan would offer its own such iconographic locales, notable for both their intense combat, fundamental shifts in task organization, equipment, tactics, techniques, and procedures (TTPs), and fomenting genetic imprint on many of the units and personnel who would serve in them. Scant attention is paid to the significance of the western reaches of Afghanistan, where few resources of the Coalition were devoted owing to the comparatively sparse insurgent presence and extended distances to overcome in order to conduct operations of any major scale. The north, despite the historical significance of the CIA-led Northern Alliance in the early phases of the war to oust the Taliban, was relatively passive for several iterations of the war, gaining tactical and operational importance in later years after the Taliban resurgence demanded changes to the Coalition force posturing.

The east and south in Afghanistan, however, would receive the lion's share of both media attention and Coalition efforts for the duration of the war. The two Afghan regions, most recognizable as "RC–East" and "RC–South," were made staples of the cyclic rotations of American combat troops from a multitude of units who would be forever bonded by names such as the Pech Valley, Nangarhar, the K–G (Khost–Ghazni) Pass, Panjwai, Helmand, and so many others. Veterans of any previous rotation would achieve immediate legitimacy and prestige among new unit members when rumors of the former's time in places like "Korengal," or "Arghandab" spoke volumes. Even a rivalry of significance for the time spent at such places could only be resolved by combat veterans who might have, and many often did, spent time in both locales at the height of combat operations.

The two regions of Afghanistan are rightly considered warzones within a warzone, as the systemic and institutional challenges of Afghanistan were nearly identical, albeit with unique facets of security and functional challenges that made for two similar but distinct microcosms of the war. In the south, particularly in Helmand, the Coalition would face the impossible challenge of the rampant opioid industry which served as the main source of Taliban revenue for the duration of the war. Opium production in Afghanistan in fact provided the lion's share of the world's opioid supply, vastly exceeding that of the "Golden Triangle" in Southeast Asia and all other hubs of opium growth. Further, Kandahar was the seat of the Taliban's power, and a bastion of Taliban forces who remained in the country after the allied invasion, and many of the new TTPs used by insurgent forces across the theater would be tested in the south. Kandahar also hosted what would become the second-largest airbase (KAF) in Afghanistan at its peak, only exceeded by Bagram in terms of size and volume of traffic. Thus, in the middle years of the war, Kandahar would host a sizable inventory of both ground and air forces, serving as a decentralized extension of the Afghanistan war command and enabling the force projection.

Bagram Airfield (BAF) would serve the same function as Kandahar, surpassing KAF in size only because of its longer lifespan as a hub of American war infrastructure, while providing the overall operational-level command site for Coalition forces in Afghanistan. The political and strategic function of forces command was located approximately forty miles south, in the capital city of Kabul, commanding a sizable component of Coalition resources. BAF would serve as the support hub for all operations in RC–East, augmented by super-forward operating bases (FOB) such as the smaller airbase at Jalalabad ("J-bad") in Nangarhar, where many battalion-level ground forces would headquarter for deployments. Air-power components such as fixed-wing close air support, fleets of ISR (intelligence, surveillance, and reconnaissance) platforms, and rotary wing support would hail from BAF, as well as KAF, which would serve a similar function in the south, augmented again by the addition of many smaller FOBs hosting ground forces across provinces of renown like Helmand, the Panjwai, and Shorabak.

Those locales would become forever etched in the institutional memory of countless units, roots running deep into the annals of the Global War on Terror's history. Between 2003–05, Afghanistan became a forgotten war, lost in the shadow of the invasion of Iraq, which had taken the preponderance of air, ground, and logistics infrastructure necessary to defeat a peer force. Meanwhile, in Afghanistan, provincial reconstruction efforts, bare-bones parliamentary elections and a feeble federal government in Kabul were pressured by the earliest inkling of the Taliban-led insurgency. These were further enabled by the sustained presence of extremist groups sheltering in Pakistan and elsewhere, while Coalition forces attempted to build upon the success of the 2001 invasion with limited resources.

Afghanistan in 2004 saw a constitution, drafted with Western assistance, laid at the floor of Afghan society by a new 502-member parliament intended to represent the diverse tribal demographics of the war-ravaged nation. This development would be praised internationally and, by the end of the year, elections took place despite promises of extreme violence and bloodshed by the Taliban. For the first time in four decades, a national ballot would select Hamid Karzai as the freely elected leader of the Republic of Afghanistan. The Coalition presence during 2004 focused on securing polling sites, deterring insurgent attacks, and enabling the fledgling democratic process—one that was marred by accusations of fraud and the kidnapping of three United Nations election-assistance officials by a militant cell. The most wanted man in the world, Osama Bin Laden—whose escape from Tora Bora in 2002 would fester in the souls of the service members who pursued him in those early days—would surface via telecast mocking the West's efforts in Afghanistan.

Those efforts, particularly in the east and south, would set the tone for the Coalition's next 15 years in Afghanistan. The hinterlands provided insurgents and violent extremist groups with safe passage into Pakistan, where they would make annual migrations around the warm weather "fighting seasons" of spring and summer. Coalition operations would engage in a clockwork-like cycle of targeting, raiding, and expanding intelligence assessments on terror cells, insurgent networks, and facilitation spiderwebs in both regions for the duration of the war.

But forward air controllers would be forced to contend with expanding insurgent networks and a loss of total resources, aircraft, intelligence and reconnaissance, and logistical support. Air operations were largely conducted out of Bagram in the east, Kandahar in the south, and Mazar-i-Sharif in the north. These locales, warzones of renown within a new and complex warzone, would become lost in Iraq's shadow before demanding Coalition soldiers return to these hallowed places again, and again, and again.

CHAPTER 18

"You can't politely ask permission to finish a war"

Forward air controllers would hail from every component of the U.S. military, both active duty and National Guard. Greg Kassa, among many others who helped meet the demands of America's longest war, would hail from the latter, the Washington State Air National Guard. What follows is an account of the earliest years of the war in Afghanistan immediately following the rapid takeover of the country and, in detail, recount the chaotic and largely unorganized movement of forces—specifically Air Force ETACs—throughout Afghanistan to support ground-force units. Unlike later years of the war, where manning decisions, personnel allocation, and force alignment became major muscle movements and dictums of the colossal personnel-management apparatus, 2003–04 Afghanistan would be anything but well-coordinated. Despite this, air-power integrators still found ways to support the suddenly unclear mission in Afghanistan as the world—and the critical resources necessary to achieve security—turned its eyes to Iraq.

The secrecy and smoke surrounding America's entry into Afghanistan would see men like Greg Kassa spun up for deployment and wait to depart the United States for war. And spun up again, only to wait longer. The invasion would occur while many forward air controllers (FAC) were being requested to support various maneuver components, after theater commanders had begun collating battlefield damage assessments from FACs during the early months of the war. Though public awareness of the usefulness of close air support (CAS) remained largely ambiguous, senior leaders began to see its utilitarian value at an early stage.

In the weeks after September 11, the ops phone rang at the 116th Air Support Operations Squadron (ASOS) at Camp Murray, near Fort Lewis, Washington. Kassa and his peers were told by the squadron commander "someone, somewhere was looking for volunteers," for what, precisely, went unsaid. Mustering Guard TACPs to align with Army units was an arduous ordeal, complicated by so many units requesting FACs. In late Spring 2002, Kassa traveled to Fort Bragg, where the Army's Special Forces (SF) groups were running a highly compressed training program to integrate Air Force controllers into the teams' standard operating procedures. "That took about thirty days, and the intent was for all of us volunteers to complete the training and immediately disembark overseas. Of course, that didn't happen according to plan."[1]

August 2002 would arrive, with operations in Afghanistan reaching a lull, when Kassa headed downrange to replace other TACPs already in country. At this early phase of the war, the architecture simply wasn't in place to facilitate a clean, organized relief-in-place. "By now, almost a year later, we knew that we were heading to Afghanistan. In the absence of a solid report date and means of getting there, I shamelessly utilized the 'bro network.'" The guardsmen would integrate with a variety of joint-force units and commands, crisscrossing the continental United States when and where they could. "We even trained with some Marines down in California which, as rare as it is today for Air Force and Marine ground units to train together, it was nearly unheard of in 2002."

After Thanksgiving, the group traveled to Volk Field, Wisconsin. The TACP National Guard Command had organized a massive exercise, with every Guard ASOS represented by members who would be augmenting Army SF teams. "Two weeks of very intense work—shooting, CAS training, full-mission profiles, ruck marching, of course, because TACPs love to carry heavy rucks everywhere—it was an oddly familiar kick in the pants for something that many of us had not experienced before. On the topic of ruck marching, I think some in leadership positions got a little overzealous on the initial reports that had come back from the invasion folks, so they took a few things like that to extremes."

By Christmas, Kassa's group finally secured paper orders and assignments, with a rough timeline in place. Six would deploy from the Washington State National Guard. They left on January 22, 2003. "My orders stated: 'Length of duty, 120 days.' I would return to Washington State almost a year later." It took five days to get from the United States to Afghanistan, transiting through Incirlik Airbase in Turkey, Karshi–Khanabad (K2) in Uzbekistan, and then finally landing in Bagram.

They landed at night, sleep deprived, and unsure of what came next. "They had some transit barracks where we dumped our gear, but amidst the weather, snow, and rain, it was a worse downpour inside than it was outside. When I say barracks, I don't mean insulated structures, these were barely clapboard shacks that didn't keep a lick of weather out. We ended up strapping our ponchos over our individual bunks just to keep beds dry." Once again, the crew would be waiting for processes to materialize that would send the controllers forward to their teams. In this lull, they trained on new GPS equipment and studied rules of engagement and use of force.

"By the time we got there in early 2003, we weren't late to the show, but we came for the end of it. The war paid no mind to the belief that it was supposed to be over. I was there when we lost two TACPs in combat, Jake Frazier and Ray Losano.[2] So, despite the fact that Iraq's shadow would hang over this deployment, it was still very much a warzone." They spent another week at Bagram, waiting for the special-operations task force (SOTF) to decide which outstation each controller would depart for. The logistics of travel from Bagram to the various outstations would present another challenge, "all of which was very on-call, dynamic decision making. Nothing was pre-coordinated, there weren't manifests with an Air Force guy going to team X or anything like that."

The only task organization they had, based on guidance received while back in the U.S., was that they would go as two-man teams with their assigned Army A-teams. CJTF-180 (Combined Joint Task Force) opted instead to disaggregate the controllers to the lowest level and distribute manning from there. "The guidance was 'Okay, cut your manning plans in half, figure out what you need as individuals, and we'll get you any missing equipment as we can.'" Kassa originally paired with another TACP, who laid out their team equipment in one of the tents, and piecemealed their individual loadouts based on what they had brought.

Kassa was assigned to a team that was still in K2, prompting him to pack everything up, and fly right back to Uzbekistan. "Two days on the ground looking for these guys, and when I finally did track them down, they informed me that they were leaving for a different mission in another part of the world entirely, and that I would be of more use back in Afghanistan." Kassa returned to Bagram, where a liaison officer at CJTF-180 told him to find a flight west into Bamiyan, as there were multiple teams in place training local militias who needed air support. "I'm at the airfield, waiting for a flight that was heading that direction—we didn't do air mobility requests back then, you simply waited on planes to land, figure out what their route was, and hope they would stop somewhere that you needed to go." In the terminal, there were two National Guard SF soldiers from the 19th Special Forces Group whom Kassa recognized from the spin-up training done six months before. "They asked where I was headed, and I told them about my verbal orders to Bamiyan, and coincidentally they were among the SF teams posted there. They asked which team I was going to be aligned with. I gave a name, and my buddy said 'Bullshit, I've already trained with you, so you're working for me when we get there.'"

This is a small glimpse into just how disorganized, but organically flexible, the whole construct of personnel management in Afghanistan was at this time. There was no manning document laid against a formal request-for-forces posting; it was a generic call for more enlisted terminal attack controllers (ETAC) from the Army. With rare exception, the Air Force provided FACs and, in most cases, simply figured out the rest on the ground. "I was supposed to go to one team, got bounced around for a couple weeks, and through some horse trading (and a literal log of tobacco being traded as compensation for stealing the ETAC), I ended up deployed with a team that I already knew."

On the flight, Kassa sat next to his newly acquired team sergeant, alongside the medic, and one of the weapons sergeants. This team had just finished training a company-size element of the Afghan National Army (ANA) in Bamiyan, giving the outpost a cohort of just over a hundred local Afghans who were deemed reliable, loyal, and vetted.

When the helicopter arrived at the mountain camp—which never received an official designation or evolved into a major forward operating base (FOB)—Kassa was recognized by the rest of the SF team, who welcomed the Air Force controller gladly. The camp had a small airfield, where a contingent from the 82nd Airborne was building a small encampment. On the far end of the airfield, opposite this build-up, the A-teams had a safehouse overlooking the valley. "From my bedroom window, I could see the remnants of the giant stone Buddhas in the valley wall which the Taliban had destroyed in early 2001. Talk about an experience. We (the Americans) did not know much about it, other than bits you heard translated from the local people. Years later, I came to understand the significance of what those sites meant, and their place in history. We were kicking over rocks that Genghis Khan and Alexander the Great had trodden upon. It was overwhelming."

The first week at the camp was an abrupt adjustment in a deployment already full of changes. The outpost rested at 8,000-feet elevation, and despite Kassa having been away from Washington State's sea level for several weeks, it took time to acclimate. Despite the impending spring thaws, the Koh-e Baba mountains in Bamiyan, 230 kilometers west of Kabul, remained covered in dense, wet snow. During the day, temperatures reached 30 to 35 degrees Fahrenheit, but at night dropped below zero. "I was unaware of this during that first week, but the A-teams had been preparing the Afghan National Army contingent for patrols and reconnaissance operations deeper into the valley. They had developed local HUMINT [human intelligence] sources, who worked with the A-teams' intelligence sergeant, and these sources

The view from Kassa's bedrom—in the distance the vacant crevices where the Bamiyan Buddhas once stood. (Photo provided by Greg Kassa)

were sifting through the villages surrounding the valley, looking for information on insurgent groups and any residual Taliban presence." While the team commander and intelligence sergeants managed their Afghan cohorts, Kassa had fallen in with the weapons sergeant, where they would take the ANA through daily weapons training, small-unit tactics, and other basic-soldiering skills.

The A-team would establish the foundations of the future provincial reconstruction teams (PRT), to be taken over in the future by Coalition partners, including New Zealand and Canada. Bamiyan served as a pilot for the Afghanistan New Beginnings Program (ANBP), which fell under the broader Disarmament, Demobilization, and Reintegration program set forth in the terms of the Bonn Agreement[3]. The ANBP sought to disarm the scattered and highly tribalized militias—which bore the main burden in the overthrow of the Taliban just two years earlier—and reintegrate them into a new national-security apparatus for Afghanistan. This program would function in tandem with the Coalition-managed PRTs in the near future but would be stymied by the financial resources and tribal loyalties deeply laid into Afghan culture. The Americans at this remote outstation would face the challenge of molding these militiamen into professional troops while carefully managing delicate relationships with local leaders.

Ramadan—the Islamic holiday which lasts 20 days and consists of daytime fasting and reduced activities—would arrive during these early days at the mountain base. "We would link up with the local provincial commander, who invited us to celebrate Ramadan with his household. That was a fascinating experience, my first time conducting a key leader engagement. His generosity stood out; he was more concerned about our comfort and wellbeing than his own troops; if we wanted a cold Coke, and didn't have one, he'd snap his fingers and someone would bring us a drink." This provincial leader—in truth a warlord—was a uniquely accurate representation of American interactions with their national hosts. When the Russians invaded Afghanistan in 1979, they offered the warlord a choice: fight against them or fight with them. He chose the latter. The Russians sent this Afghan to their military academy, where he became fluent in Russian, Farsi, Pashto, and Dari. "This guy was sharp, he knew his stuff when it came to fighting, and he knew the local environment well, and was a tremendous resource for us trying to pacify and stabilize this valley."

For the next two weeks, the team prepared for a major clearance operation directed by CJTF-180, pushing deep into one of the connecting ravines north of their outpost in search of residual Taliban fighters. From the camp, it was about a four-and-a-half-hour drive. There were already some American SF near this ravine, supported by National Guard TACPs from Washington States' 116th and the 118th ASOS (North Carolina National Guard). Those forward-staged teams occupied a remote camp looking into the target valley, no more than a compound which had been purchased from a local. "It was quite literally hanging over the edge of a cliff." All told, there were about eighty ANA soldiers living in tents, while the Americans—a hodgepodge of 19th and 20th Special Forces Group teams—had the small compound edged by concertino wire.

The intel driving Kassa and the other A-teams to this remote valley ravine indicated there were several cells of Taliban fighters in a remote village. Kassa's team was shocked at how austere and rugged the valleys and surrounding terrain were. The first attempt to enter this valley was on horseback. That element made it roughly one-third of the way up the mountain pass before the snow became waist deep, too much for the horses to traverse. They attempted a second push into the valley using trucks, which took two full days just to get as far as the horses did. "One of those other TACPs had built some rough graphics of the valley, really a detailed terrain sketch, so when I went in with the truck convoy, I hadn't done much planning for it." The force finally made it into the target village over the mountain pass and, after a frigid night spent on the side of the mountain, heard locally sourced intel that the Taliban were planning an ambush. "Things on the intel side would of course improve over the years of the war but, in 2003, the intelligence reaching the forward teams always seemed a day late and about one dollar short."

They entered the objective village, finding cheerful villagers celebrating the arrival of Americans and uniformed Afghan soldiers. It turned into a two-day-long party. "They led us to some weapons caches, which we reduced with explosives,[4] but nothing of significance on my very first mission. That's how things in Afghanistan had turned, at least in the more extreme reaches of that place. This wouldn't be the norm for the rest of the trip, but it forced me to learn some hard lessons about how I conducted myself as a forward air controller for multiple Army teams."

One of the strategic shortcomings of Guard TACPs integrating with special-operations forces (SOF), at least in those early days, was the more nuanced aspect of mission support—this included aircraft requesting, intelligence analysis, and team support. "The tactical stuff, controlling aircraft in a gunfight, we had those processes down pat. I had fallen in on the CAS plan by the previous TACP who made the first attempt into the valley, but I hadn't done the coordination, requesting of assets, or any of the other myriad 'support—plan, advise, and assist' functions of my job. This was my first time going on an actual mission with real consequences and, as such, I didn't have a baseline beyond training done in the States. You don't know what you don't know and, just like we had no structural allocation and distribution for getting guys to the teams, we didn't get a strong baseline for our jobs when it came to knowing how to request CAS."

Kassa adjusted quickly, each day finding new ways to support and enable his Army counterparts, whether that was conducting hands-on training with Afghan soldiers on battle drills, assisting the medic with trauma intervention, or the comms sergeant with programming radios and loading crypto for the entire team. "Bottom line—don't repeat mistakes. That pre-mission planning aspect is something that we often take for granted. Having failed at my mission planning on this first patrol made me realize that if things had gotten hairy, it could have been truly traumatic." The lack of assets available for Afghanistan meant FACs had to be very deliberate with mission planning, even SOTF didn't always get what was requested.

This particular team had already been in Afghanistan for months and was preparing to rotate home, the valley clearance operation being their final hurrah. Leaving the mountain camp, the team commander was anxious to make his flight home, prompting them to plan a lengthy convoy to Mazar-i-Sharif—the northern base would offer a better chance of catching a flight than Bagram. The drive from Bamiyan to Mazar-i-Sharif would upend Kassa's deployment once again, but not on account of the enemy. On the route, the lead truck (with Kassa in the back seat) missed the turn at a bridge checkpoint, thanks to a sleep-deprived driver, and the truck ended up nose down in a wadi. "I ended up with shredded shins and a nasty cut on my scalp from when I was thrown through the turret opening from the passenger rear seat. These injuries would send me back to Bagram for treatment and a few days recovery."

While recovering from injuries at Bagram, Kassa passed the time giving basic CAS instruction to the incoming SF teams who were headed into Afghanistan, averaging four classes per day over the course of two weeks.

Kassa would be cleared for normal duties in early April 2003; once again in search of another team, he reported to CJTF Headquarters, spending several days at the strike desk, managing asset requests and battle tracking live operations. This provided an opportunity to learn the nuances of requesting CAS, "doing the planning, and advising which I had not done well during my first stint up in Bamiyan. I would also make my way to the ASOC [Air Support Operations Center]. That was an enlightening experience, seeing the gears turning behind this massive air-support machine that was responsible for all of Afghanistan."

Kassa had intended to re-connect with the Coalition SOF team whom he had trained in K2, this time linking up at the embassy in Kabul. But his efforts to transit from Bagram to Kabul would be swept under the tide of tumultuous events. "We coordinated with them to make the journey from Bagram a few days later. On the day this trip was planned, we requested a vehicle from the CJTF HQ, and were denied. 'You don't understand, these Coalition team guys requested us by name today for a specific event.' 'Negative, no personnel are allowed to leave,' we were told." Kassa and another TACP walked over to the dining facility (DFAC), ruing the chow hall offering when they could have been enjoying superior embassy food at Kabul with their British colleagues. Seated at a bench, they noticed the TVs on the DFAC wall were showing American forces pushing north from Kuwait and Saudi Arabia. "We weren't allowed to leave that night because the Iraq invasion had just kicked off. So now, and for the rest of this rotation, we found ourselves living in the shadow of Iraq."

After a week in Bagram, Kassa connected with another Army SF acquaintance, whose team was posted to Asadabad, in Kunar Province. That team's captain was glad to have a TACP and told Kassa to link in with the team sergeant to get situated. "This is when I would come face to face with my first resistance from the Army, a team sergeant who said, 'We don't need an ETAC.' I respectfully notified this senior NCO [non-commissioned officer] that the team leader wanted me along, and if they weren't going to employ me then I would need to know so that I could find another crew. Grudgingly, I was admitted to the team, and would fly to Asadabad with them, where I would stay through May." This would not be the first time, and certainly not the last, when Air Force controllers received a less-than-warm welcome from their counterparts.

The camp at Asadabad had one A-team, a contingent of 2/75 Rangers from Fort Lewis, 82nd Airborne soldiers with a 120-mm mortar crew, and a SEAL team. Asadabad was still in early construction, and the mass of bodies on such a small compound made for cramped conditions on the narrow perch overlooking the imposing valley beyond. On May 1, 2003, they listened as Defense Secretary Donald Rumsfeld declared that combat operations in Afghanistan had ended, "and wouldn't you know it, Asadabad took five rockets from insurgents." The service members on the FOB would joke that the Taliban obviously hadn't watched the Armed Forces Network and missed the memo about the end of combat operations.

Just as odd, the coming weeks would see a surge in patrols across Kunar, movement to contact in pursuit of a growing insurgent network. "We started with local patrols and the like, but the missions got gradually more aggressive and pushed deeper into the surrounding valleys, sometimes an overnight patrol where we would RTB [return to base] to Asadabad the next day."

An early mission into Kunar's hinterlands would bring Kassa into contact with the enemy for the first time. "We got shot up by some insurgents who took issue with our freedom of maneuver. This was my first time getting shot at, very surreal, and my impression was 'Is this really happening?' In retrospect it's amusing, because I recall the turret gunner in our truck asking, 'Did you guys hear that popping sound?' 'Nope, we don't hear anything.' After this happens about three times, and he's nudging me in the back seat with his foot about noise." Kassa rolled down the window of the HMMWV door, and immediately heard the sharp "clink" of a round glancing off the door frame. "Yup, that's gunfire." The driver asked what the "Air Force dumbass" thought of that, and Kassa nodded sheepishly, recognizing the self-critiquing moment. But this incident would uncover deeper problems they would face which required resolutions. "It was a bit of a fiasco too. I jumped on the JARN [joint air request net] to request immediate CAS, and the ASOC informed me that I was beyond the X-CAS coverage area.[5] Re-rolling a pre-planned sortie would have aircraft on station in roughly forty minutes."

This delay in reactive fires was a frustrating reality, and learned at an inopportune time, especially for the remote location, far away from support hubs and surrounded by a stubborn adversary. Kassa would seize an opportunity to integrate with the 82nd Airborne 120-mm mortar team, doing something that was uncommon for TACPs at that time, relying on organic mortars before CAS. "I broke the ice with the gun bunnies, going to their TOC [tactical operations center] with a handful of humility and asked them to teach me everything I needed to know about integrating organic mortars into the fires plan." This was a whole new science of firepower, and the soldiers instructed Kassa and his team on everything related to mortars and artillery—ranges, loads, altitude variation, setting baseplates, and all manner of how to pass an attack brief.

When executing CAS, the controller thinks of the battlespace in three dimensions, communicating and interpreting so that ground and air understand what each other is doing, and where the enemy is. For the most part, it is all target or friendly centric descriptions and vectoring. Artillery is different and, when used efficiently under the control of a forward observer, it is positively devastating. "This is something that TACPs and other TAC-qualified personnel didn't become competent or experienced with until later years of the war. Many forward air controllers never even have the chance to control artillery in combat, and few even do it in training."

CAS is controlled using nine-line or five-line calls for fires, where the controller briefs the target by type, its location, the friendly location, and the ground commander's desired effects. The brief includes targeting data, restrictions, and other critical data, all organized to vector the pilot or guided bomb from a remote location in the sky to a specific point on the ground. Artillery call-for-fire (CFF) is a different animal entirely. With CAS, the controller is typically communicating with a human who can help vector those munitions based on the ground controller's descriptive capabilities. With artillery, the observer is telling a fire-direction cell (FDC) the same kind of information, but the latter cannot visually acquire the target in most circumstances, "and hoping to hell that you were correct because physics—the physics of a projectile being hurled across the battlefield—is not going to be vectored any more than your CFF brief dictates. 'Big sky, little bullet' is an analogy which means when that round goes somewhere up into the sky and is beyond anyone's ability to control or change once it leaves the mortar tube, it's a risk to aircraft, albeit a statistically unlikely one. You don't want to be the guy that hit an aircraft with a friendly artillery round because you didn't deconflict."

For artillery, the CFF has three radio transmissions. First is the observer ID and the WARNO (warning order)—the observer (or FAC) telling the FDC to receive the target location, and what kind of fire mission this is: "Adjust fire" (target location is not precise and will need correction based on first round impact), "Fire for effect" (needing effects immediately and with confidence in the target location), and "Immediate smoke" or "Immediate suppression" (some form of suppression or obscuration near the target). The second transmission is the target location, which the FDC reads back to ensure accuracy. Third, and finally, the observer describes the targets, "Enemy personnel in rock outcropping," followed by method of engagement and method of fire and control. Method of engagement dictates additional information like type of adjustment, trajectory conditions (particularly impactful data in Afghanistan), if the target is already marked, type of munition and fusing, and distribution of rounds.

Method of fire and control passes the final categorization and any additional restrictions on surface fires. Unless the observer states "At my command," the FDC will fire the first round once the transmissions are complete and the tubes are laid on the calculated azimuth and trajectory. The observer call also states "time on target" or "time to target," if they are sequencing artillery fire with aircraft passing near the target. "That's the real graduate-level artillery/CAS integration: combining aircraft and artillery, which became a common practice by forward air controllers years later."

Once all of the data is compiled by the FDC, they transmit to the forward air controller a "Message to observer," declaring the unit to fire, any needed changes to the CFF, number of rounds, a target number (for the mission), time of flight for the round from tube to target, ordinate altitude (highest point of the rounds' trajectories for altitude deconfliction). Once the rounds are fired, the observer must be prepared to adjust those rounds from a known point or target location—"Adjust north five-zero meters"—and once the ground commander's intent is met, the observer passes a battle-damage assessment and states "End of mission" (with the target number).

For Kassa, this new tool in the firepower inventory fundamentally changed his appreciation for the joint-force weapons inventory. "This is a truly three-dimensional calculation and requires the gun bunnies and FDC to pay close attention, and it requires the observer to be precise and accurate with target data."

After several days of instruction, and some training rounds fired to produce tangible feedback, Kassa was prepared to utilize mortars. His intent was not simply reactionary assets, but to completely dominate the valley and forays beyond the walls of Asadabad. "I worked with them to develop TRPs [target reference points] all across the valley surrounding the camp, based on where we regularly took rocket fire from." This would come in handy a few days later, when the FOB took rockets from nearby one of the established TRPs, enabling the TACP to immediately send two mortar missions on that location, which effectively ended the incoming fire. The Air Force controller and the mortar team would develop a strong relationship, to the point Kassa would often use mortars first, while requesting aircraft if they needed expanded fire support on a mission.

Kassa perched alongside the mortar firing point above Asadabad's valley. (Photo provided by Greg Kassa)

Not only did this integration of assets improve local security and reduce attacks on the FOB, but it also provided a significant morale boost for the Army mortar crew, who had seen little action to this point. "They appreciated my aggressive use of their abilities to support our missions. Even on days when we weren't on a mission, I could bring over the SF guys, who would train to call in mortars whenever the mortar team needed to reset the baseplates for each gun."

With the late spring thawing out passageways in the steep mountains and the fighting season approaching, the teams at Asadabad saw more missions approved. The base received incoming fire and patrols were consistently engaging the enemy, soon occurring on every mission. As a result of this uptick in enemy activity—"end of combat operations" becoming a farcical memory—the ASOC began to allocate X-CAS sorties just to support the Asadabad teams with immediate assets. Kassa and his A-team would continue patrols through June, at which point that team was also queued to go home. Once again, Kassa returned to Bagram looking for work.

While volunteering another shift at the CJTF fires desk, Kassa was asked if he wanted to go to Kandahar. "I said that I did, so a few calls were made, and I was notified of a flight in two days, and that I would have to work my own transportation from Kandahar airfield to the SOTF compound." The flight from Bagram stopped in Jalalabad, where the aircraft picked up a SEAL team with their embedded combat controller and continued on to Kandahar Air Base (KAF). "I sat in KAF for two hours, because the guys who I was supposed to link up with forgot I was coming in that day."

Kassa would finally arrive at the SOTF compound, which would go on to become Camp Brown, just off the flightline's western end. There were no fixed billets for the Air Force personnel assigned to support the A-teams at the camp, resulting in Kassa and two other TACPs needing to acquire improved bedding for the next few months. "We were adjacent to the hard-shell building that the SOTF personnel were using for a gym. After a few weeks of getting warm and fuzzy with the ops sergeant major, he managed to get us moved into our own little building in the back corner of the compound. We felt kind of like the lepers of the camp, being so far away from everyone else, but it was certainly preferable to a tent." Their quarters were old Russian barracks with no bathrooms, but at least there was a door and windows. Fortuitously, this building just happened to be next to the far corner of the camp where CJTF stored all its construction materials. With a little ingenuity and scrounging materials, they built a loft, recreation room, and a place to store all their mission equipment. "We even found an old couch and a small TV to keep in that recreation room and called it the 'TACP lounge.'" There are countless versions of this kind of handyman-ship throughout the war, and those rooms hold a special place in every veteran's recollection; this one never failed to bring back fond memories for the three TACPs.

On Camp Brown, there were three Army SF A-teams with their Company Command ODB (Operational Detachment–Bravo), and the SEAL team relocated from Jalalabad. Each team had to plan for their own missions, and whichever team wasn't on target on a given night provided a quick-reaction force (QRF). It was in constant rotation, hitting sensitive areas all around KAF. They would do unilateral missions, but often two A-teams or an ODA–SEAL combined force would conduct raids. Whichever one of the TACPs wasn't out on target would sit in the camp's operations center and provide command and control, coordinating with CJTF and the ASOC at Bagram for additional assets. These last few months would be the busiest of the entire deployment. "And it wasn't all sexy, but it certainly wasn't boring either. Every day was different, and as we got our processes in place, we would extend those missions to two, three, sometimes four, days. You'd get back from one of those long patrols, refit while being QRF for another team, and then go right back out."

Kassa's previous time spent in the CJTF Joint Operations Center would prove beneficial to the joint-force component, utilizing the variety of hard lessons learned from his two previous outstations. The SEAL team that came from Jalalabad had a combat controller providing fire support for the Navy special operators, whom Kassa would seek out to bolster their collective capabilities. "In the TACP community, we always bash the controllers, but that's usually until you actually meet them, and we came to respect the hell out of each other. We were planning a joint op with the SEALs, and instead of him doing his own thing for requesting CAS, we worked together on filling out the DD1972 [the joint tactical air request], and learned from each other."

This was the early era of requesting pre-planned requests, where the community developed certain catch phrases and buzzwords to massage the asset-allocation process. "You can't specifically request aircraft by type. If you wanted an A-10, you wouldn't put that in the aircraft remarks on the request form. Instead, we'd say 'request low-altitude, extended loiter time, forward-firing 30mm anti-armor capable aircraft. Weapons required: precision munitions capable of penetrating cave complexes.'" Small details such as this were the result of Kassa having spent time seeing the air-support architecture at work. "I'd help get these requests submitted through the proper channels, 96 hours prior to the mission, so that they had plenty of time to make it into the 72-hour pre-planned mission allocation process."

Being the TACP who knew the ASOC and knew the teams handling the requests was Kassa's chance to help the entire cohort, instead of bickering over rivalries. Rivalries would mar the relationships between FACs in many separate instances of this war, but not here. "Since we're all going out together on this mission, I didn't see it that way. I saw everyone as those I needed to enable just like my own team. If another team called up troops in contact, we'd start working the immediate CAS requests. Or sometimes a target would pop up at one in the morning, so while one of us is jocking up to get in the trucks, the other guys would head to the ops center and start processing the CAS requests with what little information was available."

This entire deployment and mission planning was wholly different from the TACP standards the community had grown up knowing. Before 9/11, they were trained as "TOC monkeys," controlling the big CAS fight over a large area, with a dislocated role in the planning, coordinating, and requesting process. In Afghanistan and Iraq, they were still coordinating at operational levels, but wholly integrated at the individual team and platoon level. "I had reached the point where I was giving training to the teams during our downtime, things like map reading, radio use, and aircraft capabilities just like an infantryman would lead the team in a shooting drill or the medic teaching first-aid interventions."

With the pivot in Iraq, fighter jets like the F-16 and A-10 became an extreme rarity in the skies over Afghanistan. The FACs began to see more B-1s and B-52s, which was not an easy adjustment. For one thing, back then, bombers couldn't track or utilize MGRS (military gridded reference system] grids from a map—everything else had to be passed in latitude/longitude. That takes a long time, and it was something the controllers at Camp Brown had barely trained on—if they had ever trained on it. "Those are things that your Army counterparts don't think about, or even know to think about, having to convert map coordinates from one type to another. And it was my job to do that and make it appear seamless. It takes time to build credibility with your partners, but we got better by necessity."

In August, the Camp Brown teams would plan two major operations far from the security of the air base. "The first one took us five days to plan. For big missions like these wide-sweeping clearances, we would do full rehearsals using austere mockups. Often, two teams come up with a plan, brief each other, then critique each other's concepts and fit the 'good' pieces together. Doing so would produce some comprehensive operational concepts by letting the cream rise to the top." Updated maps were a tough get; Kassa could get the big 1:250,000 maps, which covered a huge area, but were not detailed. The company level element had a map imagery printer, from which the teams would print 1:50,000 maps with greater detail but smaller cross-sections. "When the team sergeant had finished printing his products for the mission, he had a small phone book that he would have to flip through based on where we were on a given day. Lesson learned—sometimes the comfortable tool isn't the best-suited tool for a job."

Kassa's team left KAF in convoy, with American flags fixed to the antennas; the team wasn't planning on going around quietly, but trying to draw the insurgents towards the patrol. In the first objective village, they rolled up six insurgents and a large weapons cache with AK-47s, ammunition, and RPGs. They used demolition charges on the pile of weapons in a dry wadi and continued on. They also mistakenly blew up two anti-aircraft cannons belonging to the local provincial governor. "After some repayment for damaged goods, we pushed on to the next objective, setting up a remain-overnight site and observing a village while we had overwatch elements set up containment positions in the surrounding terrain." A B-52 checked in and, based on an unexplained increase in activity through the villages, Kassa brought the bomber in on a low pass over the village, to discourage anyone from pushing into the high ground. "There is nothing quite like seeing that behemoth swooping in at five thousand feet, it's a tremendous sight. That's a lesson you can only learn being in that scenario: just because we had CAS, and because there may have been a threat in the village, that doesn't mean we need to drop bombs. You innovate ways to utilize aircraft to achieve the commander's intent." This was often true in places

Navigating the "Registan," the Great Red Desert south of Kandahar. (Photo provided by Greg Kassa)

like southern Afghanistan: it's wide-open country and ambushes are unlikely with such lengthy visibility, forcing controllers to be judicious with overhead aircraft.

At the end of this five-day mission, their clearance had pushed up into the mountainous areas north of Kandahar, with one final insurgent hide site remaining. A reconnaissance team had been sent into this valley days prior, where they had seen weapons being transferred between multiple locations within the village. When Kassa's team arrived, those buildings correlating with the recon team's reports were packed to the roof with munitions; "It was like the insurgency supermarket." They moved to isolate the village, setting up a perimeter with the trucks breaking off into different blocking elements. Kassa remained at the truck with the team leader while the rest of the team went in to clear, which immediately escalated into a verbal altercation with some of the men in the village—several of whom were assessed to be part of the insurgent cohort responsible for transferring the weapons back and forth.

"The captain asked me if there was anything we could do to massage the situation. In this phase, there wasn't a credible threat or obvious enemy, so using aerial-delivered munitions from an airplane is out, but that's not the only thing of value CAS provides. We had F-16s on station for once, whom I had assigned to keep overwatch on our security team in the high ground. The situation between the team guys and the adult males in the village was escalating, and the team guys called us saying we needed something to happen because this was spiraling out of control. I advised a show of force to the ground commander, which he approved, and directed the F-16s to make a low-level pass over the village, north to south, separated by ten seconds."

The nimble fighter jets came in at 4,000 feet above the ground, popping flares as they passed over the southern end of the village, then hitting afterburners. They were low enough that some of the flares bounced off the ground before igniting. A few seconds after the roar faded, one of the operators notified the team leader that the antagonistic villagers had begun moving the contraband weapons from the storage buildings to an open field for demolition. "We managed to persuade them without ever dropping a bomb or starting a gunfight."

August would end with another huge clearance. By this point, Kassa had worked with six different SF teams, and another would be arriving at the SOTF compound at Kandahar. This short-cycle construct was the norm for Army SF teams, making the deployed TACPs the only constant in many of these battlespaces. With so much rotation of personnel, one such team was driving from Kandahar to Bagram for their transit home. The day after leaving Kandahar, using the Ring Road,[6] they became stuck in a three-day ambush. The SEAL team at Camp Brown provided initial QRF, but their attempts to reach the beleaguered A-team turned into their own intense gunfight, forcing Kassa's team to be the next relieve-in-place. "We expected to spend 48 hours on the ground and didn't return to KAF for 12 days."

Kassa's convoy would pull into the ravine just short of where the first team was bogged down, trying to establish a new base of fire before counter-assaulting the Taliban positions. They spent the next four days living on a rock outcropping overlooking the valley, waiting for the insurgents to emerge. Like so many other instances, the enemy disappeared into the nooks and crannies and never materialized in force. "We had AC-130 overhead, and I would use them to search for groups of personnel moving towards or near our blocking position. Back then, the Army guys had a general understanding of what the gunship could provide, but not explicit knowledge. My employment in an offensive manner was something of a novelty, as the gunship was primarily considered a defensive, friendly centric device."

Kassa's command element occupied an observation point about four miles deeper into the valley from the company command post, with a sniper element another 900 meters higher in the terrain for observation—another "sensor" for the FAC. They could hear the Taliban chattering on handheld radios, Pashtun voices echoing from the rocks in the night, expecting the insurgents to cross over the ridgeline separating the beleaguered team from the relief force. The gunship called Kassa to confirm that all friendlies were marking themselves with infrared GLINT (gated laser intensifier tape) patches, which was confirmed after multiple checks on the team net. "Not everyone had IR [infrared] strobes back then, so we used GLINT to reflect IR light, theoretically making all friendlies visible to aircraft using IR sensors." With this assumption, the gunship identified a group of individuals with IR reflections moving in a place where there shouldn't have been any friendly forces, who were all stationary in the darkness. "The Taliban had somehow acquired GLINT and were mimicking our TTPs [tactics, techniques, and procedures], moving from cover to cover, which is why we hadn't seen them to this point—they looked like another group of good guys." After multiple confirmatory calls across the force, with key personnel at each known element turning on an IR strobe to double-check all friendly locations, Kassa prepared to engage this group of Taliban with the AC-130. But as the shot was lining up, one of the blocking positions identified and engaged the insurgents with small-arms fire. "After that, it was nearly impossible to tell who was who, and we were unable to engage with the gunship. That led to a heated debrief after the mission: don't move around the battlespace without giving a front-line trace, the air controller and ground commander can't use air power effectively if we can't keep track of where friendlies are." After several more days of cat and mouse, the Americans were able to extract all forces and return to Kandahar.

Kassa's final mission airlifted multiple teams on three CH-47s, clearing three villages in an eight-kilometer square area. They landed at sunrise on the first target and cleared it. Some quick intelligence collection on the ground led them deeper into the valley, which correlated to historical Taliban bed-down locations. This mission was another hodgepodge of personnel from different cohorts, with two A-teams serving as the assaulters, while the command and control was done by the company's headquarters. Kassa coordinated the relocation of one of the assault troops deeper into the valley on a single CH-47, while directing AH-64s to hunt ahead of the ground force. The gunships quickly identified a group of nine insurgents with weapons exiting the village for higher ground. "Our assault team immediately pursued these guys, because if they made it over the ridgeline into another valley, we would never get them, and we'd have to return to this valley at a later date, except now they knew we were hunting them." The insurgents entered a tree line, which shielded them from the ground force's line-of-sight.

With the AH-64s overhead, the lead pilot called Kassa with an enhanced talk-on; "I've got this group dead to rights in the trees, and can take the shot with rockets." Kassa was prepared to approve, but only if the pilots could eliminate this threat in one pass. While setting up the attack, he continued coordinating with the assault team, telling the soldiers the approximate insurgent location. "Be ready to push in to get these guys, because I'm going to engage with the Apaches, but if we don't get them on this first go then they are all yours, take a knee and standby." But the complexity of melding air and ground was not something the ground forces had experienced at this proximity to date. "The captain was working the C2 piece, but he just couldn't wrap his head around the fact that I was talking to the aircraft, the assault team, and that we could pull off this attack as long as the assault team didn't move until I gave the go-ahead. This guy just froze up." Not wanting to lose this opportunity, Kassa called the company commander back in the first village miles below, who approved the strike. After making one last confirmatory call to the assault team on their position, he cleared the gunships on the target. Two rockets later, the enemy force had been neutralized as they were setting in an ambush for the approaching ground force.

"It takes a unique mindset to really understand coordinating these kinds of three-dimensional battlefields and, in that instance, I was working for a guy who couldn't process those kinds of moving pieces. You can call in airstrikes, close to friendlies, without the wrong people getting hurt, but it requires a high degree of understanding, comprehension, and confidence to do it successfully."

***

"I spent nearly all of 2003 in Afghanistan. I would return exactly a year later in 2004 for another rotation. When I left in 2003, we had near absolute control of Afghanistan. Sure, there were dustups and skirmishes, plenty of which I was a part of, but we could go anywhere and move around largely unimpeded in most circumstances. The remaining threat from the Taliban was residual, most of them taking refuge in Pakistan. At the end of 2003, we transitioned to NATO operations, and that is where I think we went horribly wrong. We brought in a lot of people—I mean all the different organizations, the contractors, the sub-contractors, and countless different aid and development agencies—the pot of money was tipped over. Everybody who jumped on the bandwagon was paid to play, and the U.S. Government footed that enormous bill."

"Places I had helped secure in 2003 were back in Taliban control a year later, or, if not the Taliban explicitly, it was other insurgent groups, or corrupt governmental cohorts who were siphoning money from that overflowing pot. That was a level of frustration I wasn't prepared to deal with, knowing that I had spent blood and sweat to stabilize this war-torn nation, and a year later I can see from the bird's-eye perch these places becoming safe havens for extremists. What the hell are we doing if we aren't going to remain aggressive in pursuing the enemy? And, of course, there is a limit to that aggression, you can only push so far before you stop being liberators and become conquerors. But in my experience, the Five Eyes partners—us, the Brits, Aussies, Kiwis and Canadians—we were willing to push the aggression to its necessary limit, but once we introduced NATO into the mix and all of the hangers-on that came with it, we stopped being capable of fighting a war against a ruthless adversary."

"A place like Afghanistan isn't a place where you can politely ask the battlespace to conform. I think after 2003, politics—domestic and international—got in the way of pressuring the Taliban to their ultimate breaking point and removing that threat. And what really compounded this reality was the detour to Iraq. All the resources we had and needed to achieve that pressure left. We worked with a skeleton of resources to try and stabilize an entire country, and we nearly did it anyway. It's like Afghanistan suddenly decided to stop being a war on the heels of NATO taking over, and no one told the enemy about this change."

"And still we rotated our guys over there again and again. As I was preparing to leave for home, I got a call from the ASOC telling me to pick up two guys at the airfield who would be my replacements. I'm standing on the flight line, and the plane lands. The guys who picked me up in Bagram when I first got into Afghanistan walked off the plane to replace me. They had gone home, deployed to Iraq, home again, and now were replacing me in Kandahar. That whole time I had been bouncing all over Afghanistan. That's when the rotational deployments had begun, and we would spend entire careers sending our people back over and over."

CHAPTER 19

"Our targeting was incredibly deliberate"

House of Bones

In May 2003, the Coalition Provisional Authority would disband the Iraqi military and intelligence services, sending scores of able-bodied men, formerly of the diverse Iraqi state apparatus, into the streets with little to no hope of a future in their country. Already, the Ba'ath Party of Iraq's former ruling elite had been summarily evaporated by a similar administrative order. The summer of 2003 would be highlighted by the hunt for Saddam Hussein, and his sons, Uday and Qusay, as well as many other priority targets on the "deck of cards," setting the groundwork for the man-hunting architecture that would define the next 10 years of conflict in Iraq.

The United Nations would begin expanding its presence as the Coalition looked to rebuild Iraq in a Western, democratized image, suffering tragedy when a suicide bomber killed 23 delegates, including special envoy Sergio Vieira de Mello. The remainder of 2003 would be ensconced in the search for key Iraqi leaders, chiefly the "Ace of Spades" (Saddam), as well as the former military personnel who had since faded into the shadows of Iraq's boiling pot of sectarian violence. In December 2003, the highly publicized capture of the former president of Iraq—buried in a fabricated hole in the ground and "willing to negotiate"—was lauded as a turning point in the violence. The hope would quickly erode.

The new year of 2004 would begin with the admission by the Bush Administration—following an administrative commission to analyze the faulty, non-existent intelligence that prompted the war—that there were no weapons of mass destruction in Iraq. But nearly a year post-invasion, with that justification for toppling a state regime in the heart of the Levant now defunct, American forces were still widespread across Iraq and faced with a renewed threat from a well-known adversary—Al Qaeda, now led by Abu Musab al-Zarqawi, who had fled Afghanistan and disappeared into the extremist underworld, waiting to return to the foreground. Al Qaeda in Iraq (AQI) would seize upon the instability fomented by the eradication of the Iraqi state and the apparent loss of strategic initiative by Coalition forces, utilizing suicide bombings on holy sites in Baghdad and Karbala. In this mire of foreign fighters and violent extremists flooding into the new low intensity and urban battleground, AQI would serve as the new targeting deck for the growing Coalition war machine. The objectives were simple, but incredibly difficult: find, fix, and finish these emerging threats before permanent damage was done to the fragile Iraqi state, with hope of achieving some measure of stability that would allow the birth and growth of a stable nation.

Abu Ghraib would severely undermine the legitimate efforts of the Coalition whose operations removed scores of terrorists, murderers, and threats from Iraqi battlefields, cities, and hinterlands. The atrocities committed by American personnel in the prison located just west of Nasiriyah would result in an increase in violence, kidnappings of American contractors, and another round of domestic criticism within the United States for the Coalition's increasingly unclear purpose in Iraq. Several cities throughout Iraq became insurgent strongholds, while countless smaller cells throughout Baghdad continued to undermine stability, harass Coalition patrols and forward operating bases (FOB), and strike fear into the civilian populace ahead of the delicate national elections planned for the end of 2005.

The coming year saw expanded Coalition military operations across Iraq, hoping to degrade insurgents and terror-group operations deeply enough to allow for a new Iraq to emerge on the back of legitimate, democratic process. But the sectarian violence, widespread insurgency well on its way to permeating the entire country, and enemy strongholds—notorious among them being Fallujah in Anbar Province and Sadr City to Baghdad's northeast—would require the Coalition to deepen its commitment to Iraqi security; the fledgling Iraqi security forces were utterly incapable of widespread stability operations.

Fitting close air support (CAS) into this environment was a difficult, dynamic, and complicated endeavor. By 2005, the command-and-control architecture that allowed forward air controllers (FAC) to request pre-planned sorties for asset coverage was fully integrated into the Central Command (CENTCOM) machine, and enough Coalition resources had been invested into Iraq that assets were a near-constant presence in Iraqi skies. But unlike the invasion two years prior—where the enemy was on one side of demarcation, and friendlies the other, with civilians largely on the sidelines—targets for Coalition operations were now in the buildings, homes, and sometime rooms next door.

This would fundamentally change how FACs—now titled "joint terminal attack controllers," or JTACs by updated Joint Publication and the CAS Memorandum of Agreement signed by NATO militaries in 2004—employed assets to enable the ground scheme of maneuver. This new paradigm of ground forces transitioned from targeting entire forces, bases, or key strategic sites, to targeting small groups, cells, or specific locations. Airstrikes would be constrained by this highly urbanized construct, congested passageways, and obscuration for sensors, as well as the heightened scrutiny on all sensitive operations conducted in urban locales.

The use of overwhelming firepower at a grand scale faded with the swell of martial pride for having toppled Saddam Hussein's regime. But this would not reduce the role of JTACs; rather, these joint-force enablers would see their roles expanded as a whole-of-force integrator of information, communications, legal understanding, and battle tracking for commanders at all levels of the force—from the strike teams, platoons, and company-size elements to the higher echelons of operations centers with constant live-video streaming and intelligence collection and dissemination.

At the locus of all these capabilities—constant overwatch from the skies above, to the ground and the joint-force commander's objectives and requirements, the intelligence machine and its constant churning of raw data into actionable mission directives, to the expanding global observance on the complex environment equalized by air power—was the JTAC.

Rebuilding in Ashes

The following interview with Chris Spann examines a scarcely reported phase of the War on Terror: post-invasion, pre-surge combat before the insurgency had reached its fullest destructive potential and the Coalition remained mired in the early phases of unclear strategic vectoring. The volume of airstrikes decreased in the years between the initial invasion and the 2007 surge as the Coalition attempted to oust the rising insurgency and bolster the fledgling Iraqi Government amid increasing sectarian violence.

Chris Spann is a well-known name in the JTAC community, noteworthy for being one of the first American JTACs on the ground during the Afghanistan invasion in 2001 with Army Special Forces (supporting the 3rd Special Forces Group on the east side of "The Whale" during Operation Anaconda*). Of note, his cousin, Mike Spann, was the first American to lose his life in the War on Terror in Afghanistan in November 2001.*

Chris would spend most of his career in Special Operations, regularly deploying to Afghanistan and Iraq, seeing the rise of insurgencies in both locales while embedding with multiple Army Special Forces commands. By the time he retired after two decades in service, he had seen more of both countries than most military personnel.

Spann would deploy in March 2005, based out of Fort Lewis, Washington, and aligned with 10th Special Forces Group's Crisis Response Force (CRF). The CRF was a modular unit based out of Stuttgart, Germany. It would work under the CENTCOM CJSOTF–I (Combined Joint Special Operations Task Force–Iraq), which provided command and control for all special-operations teams in country.

CJSOTF–I presided over two advise-and-assist missions labeled Task Forces (TF) *Viper* and *Raptor*, where American Special Forces (SF) teams embedded alongside Iraqi special units, conducting multi-lateral operations with American and Iraqi operators, worked hand in hand as the latter developed their TTPs (tactics, techniques, and procedures), operational capacity, tactical prowess, and professionalism. Spann would enter the theater alongside several other TACPs, who would be split between *Viper* and *Raptor* as advisors/enablers. Spann's team would enable *Viper* on the coming rotation.

Task Force *Viper* would be the Iraqi Special Operations Direct Action raid force, modeled after the U.S. Army's Ranger Regiment; *Raptor*, however, would be more like an American SF team. This Iraqi element was comprised of highly mobile units with a smaller footprint whose operational construct focused on much more precise, smaller-scale operations. "I was happy to go with *Viper*, but there was plenty of work for both Iraqi units, and only a handful of U.S. special forces teams, so if any of the elements within each task force was going out, we were by necessity out with them. There was a lot of crossover between the advisor elements by necessity."[1]

The present state of the Iraqi military was not renowned for its soldiering skills, but CENTCOM had taken a group of the very best they could find, and aligned them under these two assault forces. *Viper* was nominally the 36th Commando Battalion, comprised of roughly 350 personnel, recruited and elevated from the Iraqi security force apparatus. The 36th was broken up into several companies, which were segregated by ethnicity to depress any sectarian rivalries or ethnic tension—something Iraq was far from overcoming. "One company was entirely Shias, another were Sunni, and another Kurdish. You can rightly presume that targeting—what target would be hit and where it was—was influenced which company was assigned to conduct the raid. For example, there was no chance in hell we were going to send the Kurdish Company into Sadr City, that would have been a bloodbath, and precisely the reason we were there as advisors." Rounding out the 36th Commando Battalion was a special-reconnaissance company. While the entire battalion was deemed by their American advisors to be generally solid and reliable, the reconnaissance scouts were a cut above; "really excellent soldiers. What may be surprising, especially where this story fits in the historical timeline and the social dynamic that is Iraq, is that most of our scout troops were female."

That difference would prove instrumental in *Viper* and *Raptor*'s successes. In Iraq, males who were affiliated with government forces could be spotted or "made out" quickly by insurgents. But a female operator, especially in a highly traditional, conservative culture, when dressed in traditional garb, could approach a principal—the high-value target—with relative ease, in most cases ignored completely. "Those female scouts could stare the target right in the face and never worry about being compromised. Those women took incredible risks and never batted an eye."

Task Force *Viper* and the 36th Commando Battalion were posted to Camp Justice, in the northernmost part of Baghdad. The FOB rested on the last curve of the Tigris River before it runs out towards Taji. Justice was an Iraqi intel facility before the invasion and it bore evidence of darker times. "It was still an odd, eerie sensation being on this base. Even though the invasion was two years prior, there were still scars and signs of the old regime there. In the basement, there was an 'interrogation center' with hooks on the ceiling, and the smell was awful. Obviously once the Coalition had gone through, they had collected any and all valuable items and intelligence, but you'd find interesting bits and bobs of what used to be a functional torture facility. This was a weird time to be in Iraq in general, not merely the haunting location we occupied." In January, just prior to the team's arrival, parliamentary elections had been held, a defining and momentous occasion and the first free elections in Iraq in over three decades. January was when Iraqis had chosen their 275-seat congressional body, executive committee, and other federal bodies. But swearing in those newly elected leaders would last an interminable time—Iraq simply did not have a functional government to do so effectively. Only a select handful of military functions—such as the 36th Commando Battalion—resembled the products of a functional state, and Iraq's security force enterprise was the most evolved of the state's ecosystem. "We—the coalition of 29 member states at this point—were still heavily involved in all military and all other security operations."

Task Forces *Viper* and *Raptor*'s American advisors would have no respite from combat, and this rotation would prove to be one of the busiest of Spann's career. "In those days, we were on four-month rotations, it was closer to about one hundred days on the ground. We'd typically hit between

Chris Spann during a daytime clearance in northern Baghdad, 2005. (Photo provided by Chris Spann)

150–170 targets on those cycles, very often going out on multiple raids in a single period of darkness. We never had a single, entire night off. With these Iraqi SOF [special-operations force] units having multiple maneuver companies and strike forces, but only our single team with TF *Viper*, and another team advising TF *Raptor*, there was no break. *Raptor* was only slightly less busy than we were." On a typical "day," after sleeping off the night before, the team would wake up around the middle of the day, eat and work out, then head to the operations center. There, the Americans would collate and analyze the intelligence-collection packages and tip-off reports gathered from the HUMINT (human intelligence) networks being run by other government agencies or the scouts within the 36th Commandos. Based on which intel offerings seemed most promising, the advisor teams would develop the assault plan and timeline for that night's raid. During this process, Spann and his fellow JTACs would work asset coordination with CJSOTF–I, determining which aircraft would be available to support which team, and route those requests for support. "Most of the time, we had AC-130, but rarely did we ever get fixed-wing fast movers."

Iraq had a few advantages over Afghanistan in 2005, primarily consisting of infrastructure for the technological networks and proximity to major logistical support. They also developed TTPs to overcome the dense urban environment. Among those TTPs was the gridded reference graphic (GRG). JTACs would build GRGs for nearly every pre-planned target, and send those graphics to the aircrews who would be flying for them each night. "We didn't have that in Afghanistan until years later, it was still largely map and compass over there, and shitty maps to boot. Everything we did on this rotation was deep in the urban jungle, and having those common graphics made talk-ons with aircraft so much easier. I'd print out the GRGs, laminate them if I had the supplies, and tuck them into a quarterback sleeve on my forearm." Using GRGs to correlate aircraft sensors would become a standard operating procedure (SOP) for all JTACs in the coming years. "I could tell the gunship, 'Look at building Alpha-Five, a group of squirters[2] just left that compound and headed south, track that group.'" The teams would utilize aircraft sensors to vector the Iraqi SOF units on every target, and although the use of aerial-delivered munitions decreased dramatically, the JTACs were still on the radio for eight hours non-stop—managing sensors, queueing the assault force towards points of interest, looking for threats, all refined tasks that became genetic to JTACs. It was a productive rotation, despite the lack of bombs being dropped. "I lost count of how many insurgents we rolled up and sent to Abu Ghraib."

Most missions were conducted via ground-assault force (GAF), and only occasionally did they utilize helicopters. "We had a whole fleet of trucks for this purpose, specially configured for fast assaults. HMMWVs ["Humvees"] without doors so you could egress quickly once you hit the release point near the target. We also had Humvee-chassis trucks with skids on the side and horizontal grab-bars. Our Iraqi SOF would stand on these skids and hang on to the grab-bars, and we'd roll through the city like that. IEDs [improvised explosive devices] were not as prevalent as they would be in the near future."

The 2005 deployment would produce another change for the JTAC community: the increased scrutiny and public awareness of what teams were doing thanks to embedded journalists. "There is a video floating around on the internet somewhere, taken by a Combat Camera crew, of one of our Iraqi strike units in these trucks, with the theme song to *Team America* playing in the background. Media crews went with us fairly often, it wasn't uncommon for Combat Camera—military media and public affairs—to go with us, but sometimes we had proper news crews." *Viper* would take a CNN crew with them on a compound raid, on a notable high-value target. "I would say this wasn't the right time for those guys to join us, we had been preparing for this particular target for some time, as we were conducting a raid to capture some truly evil people—key facilitators and some residual hardcore Ba'athists who were part of the foundational insurgency. We knew this was going to turn into a fight, but CNN came anyway." Unfortunately for *Viper* and the CNN crew, if something was going to go wrong, it would be this night.

The mission started with comms issues; every time the trucks left camp, Warlock signal jammers in the trucks were turned on to counter command-detonation IEDs, which are activated by hardwired cell phone or radio receivers. The SOP on these missions would have the JTAC establish good two-way comms with the aircraft—usually an AC-130—and, once that occurred, the gunship would keep one sensor on the convoy, and the other sensor scanning the route according to the mission brief. If there was a threat, the gunship would shine the sensor's infrared spotlight on the lead vehicle to halt the convoy. Jammers would be switched off, and the JTAC would control aircraft as needed before the convoy set off again.

As the GAF approached the first of three pre-planned compounds, the jammers switched off, allowing Spann to coordinate with the aircraft. As soon as he checked in with the gunship, the pilot notified Spann they had been re-tasked to another mission, leaving *Viper* without sensor coverage. "Now I'm just a regular rifleman with seven extra batteries and really long antennas." The first house turned out to be a dry hole, neither the targeted individuals nor any useful intelligence was there. This pushed *Viper* to the next compound but, without aircraft looking ahead or assisting with navigation by marking key intersections and turns, the convoy soon was lost. "The interior of Baghdad, to put it mildly, is a labyrinth, and we were completely turned around. We ended up bypassing a section of the city using a drainage dyke, but the lead vehicle got caught up in some randomly placed concertino wire, which we ended up having to cut away before anyone could turn around. In short, we looked like a complete bag of dicks, with a CNN news crew watching the whole thing."

They spent the next few hours weaving deeper into the city, into insurgent-dominated urban zones. During various short halts, Spann kept checking in with the Air Support Operations Center, telling them to be ready to re-roll aircraft on short notice due to the increased risk. By the time they reached the third compound, they had already exceeded normal mission timelines which required them to begin exfil under cover of darkness, but the significance of this target dictated they waive normal mission parameters. With the final compound in sight, the blocking forces moved to the outer wall, setting containment, and entering the buildings. "There were multiple armed insurgents inside, but our Iraqis were well-trained, and we had the compound secured fairly quickly." But there was still no sign of the primary target. "I'm helping with securing the prisoners when all of the sudden a string of gunfire erupts on the other side of the courtyard from us. The Americans all reacted immediately, I grabbed the nearest Iraqi soldier and handed him the insurgent I detained, and moved towards the ensuing gunfight a few feet away."

Outside one of the opposite buildings, two American operators were on each side of a broken window, systematically tossing flashbangs into the room, preparing to breach. There was one insurgent in the corner—*Viper*'s high-value target—who had hidden behind detritus to avoid capture. "One of our Iraqis had broken the glass with his AK-47 a moment before the gunfight broke out and, strangely enough, a negligent discharge was the first shot fired. He thought that he was being engaged. If it weren't for that 'accident,' we might have never found the TI [target individual]."

While no airstrikes were conducted on this mission, the raid was thematic of the entire rotation. This timeframe was one where teams were hesitant, to the point of over-restricting themselves, to call in any airstrikes. "Everything—our targeting—was incredibly delicate, so we purposefully exhausted every option before escalating to close air support. There was ambiguity across the battlespace, not within our unit, but between security operations and the human domain. CAS engagements were highly constrained, especially inside the city. Even a shaping measure like containment fires[3]—which became a dirty word in a few years' time—was a no go. We would use CAS to put effects on the ground to keep squirters from escaping into open ground, especially if they had a big lead on us trying to chase them down on foot. A few rounds into the empty dirt a few hundred meters ahead of them—only if the aircraft critically sanitized the area of collateral risks—would usually turn them back and we'd catch them." There were many occasions where they could have employed such aerial fires, with no collateral risks, to prevent losing targeted individuals, but because they were in or near the city, they lost several objectives because the strategic guidance, "that perception environment, simply wasn't conducive to doing so."

Tensions remained extremely high on the ground for both the Americans and their Iraqi partners. On one mission halfway through the rotation, *Viper* raided a typical objective to capture known facilitators with nothing seemingly untoward. The gunship was calling out movers, helping *Viper* avoid contact with civilians and mitigating risks to both the force and the locals in a highly congested part of the city. Spann was standing next to his truck with the ground commander, when suddenly the Iraqi soldier in the turret of their truck began firing the M240B. "For those who don't know, when that 7.62mm machine gun opens up, it is loud, and even more so when you aren't prepared to hear it go off; quite simply, it will scare the shit out of you."

The turret gunner was reacting to an unseen individual who came out of his home brandishing a pistol, not knowing that an entire company of Iraqi Rangers and American SOF were parked on his street, capturing his neighbor who was aiding the insurgent network. This unfortunate civilian had been dealing with people regularly breaking into his garage, usually around the same time of night that *Viper* raided the compound next door. "He obviously assumed we were the next burglar, came out of his home brandishing a pistol, and our turret gunner reacted. Fortunately, it was only a minor injury to the dude's hand, but that exemplifies the kind of 'wild west' environment that was Iraq in 2005: it was not pacified or stable."

Another mission took *Viper* to the edge of the city, this night using Air Force MH-53J Pave Lows—behemoth helicopters that dwarfed even the MH-47 Chinooks. They took nearly an entire company—roughly 120 Iraqi soldiers—on this target due to the space afforded by the airlift, and once again Combat Camera recorded the force at work. They landed at a short offset, as the helicopters were simply too big to land right next to a compound. The landing zone distance to the target was approximately four hundred meters. The pilots opted to lift off and pass right over the target compound, for reasons that Spann was never able to discern. "When this happened, apparently the surface-to-air warning radar teed off on both birds, causing them to pop flares right there." This immediately blinded the entire assault force, who were sprinting towards the compound using night-optical devices.

After a few seconds of total confusion, the assault force reset their front line and closed the gap to the compound. Spann was in constant comms with the gunship overhead, going back and forth with each of the two sensor operators. The assault force split the objective, meaning he had two maneuvering groups he needed to help relay target data for, as well as track their positions. As the *Viper* units set isolation and containment, Spann continually asked the gunship about any movement, to which they replied all was quiet, no movement, no heat signatures, nothing. Inside the compound were multiple buildings evenly spaced around a large courtyard in the middle. As they entered the compound, the entire courtyard floor moved like a wave. "There were entire families—six in total, multi-generational families—laid out sleeping on the ground." Somehow, the gunship missed that mass of humanity during near-constant scans.

"Things like that made us so hesitant to employ CAS in the city. This wasn't the wide-open spaces of Afghanistan where it's you and your team on one ridgeline, duking it out with the Taliban or Al Qaeda in the rocks on the terrain opposite your position. Sure, there were urban locales in Afghanistan, and villages aplenty. But the work we did in Iraq on that rotation was all urban, and the civilians were the environment."

The misconception that reigns about Iraq is likely rooted in the volume of missions that were undertaken; when observers combine those repetitions with the civilian dynamic, the appearance is that more mishaps occur. The increased publicity of missions and raids only exacerbated this perception as well. "Because this was war, and the entire power construct in Iraq had been removed only two years prior. Nothing was stable, and discerning civilians from the enemy is almost impossible, even with robust intelligence collection in place. But our targeting and execution of operations was incredibly deliberate."

Viper would raid a mosque, which had lost its protected status after significant intelligence collection—primarily from 36th Commando Battalion scouts, as well as a diverse cohort of other HUMINT—revealed it was being used as a major staging node for the insurgent network. This mosque was deep inside Baghdad, and the intel driving *Viper* there had been vetted repeatedly. Only Iraqi commandos would enter the holy site, no Americans. "They went in and blew the doors off this place—not kicking the doors in, literally blew the doors with C4 on breach—and they successfully interdicted the cell that was abusing this protected site."

It became the standard in Afghanistan and Iraq later in the war for offensive operations to be partnered, but the early years of that war were American-led with limited Afghans integrated into the force. *Viper*, and *Raptor*, would be partnered and closely integrated from the onset. "There were times where we may not brief our Iraqi partners on the target location or target individual until it was time to load up and head to the objective, but that was on a case-by-case basis. It was extremely rare that we [the American teams] went out on unilateral operations, and those were under explicit and unique circumstances. We did one solo raid on a high-level financier, drove right up to the car lot that this individual owned and pulled him right off his chair." That mission was a particular rarity for the American team, to be out there without Iraqis doing the assault and clearance.

***

AH-64s controlled by Spann overhead Camp Justice during a daytime attack. (Photo provided by Chris Spann)

Even though the Coalition had been on the ground for two years and had taken the preponderance of resources from Afghanistan, support was not the challenge the advisor teams faced, nor was it training and enabling their Iraqi partners. The challenges came from within their own command-and-control network. Camp Justice was attacked once, which was a shock to the Americans staged there—that an insurgent cell would be foolish enough to attack a relatively obvious American-held post with a large contingent of special operators and a highly-trained Iraqi cohort on hand as well. "We had rehearsed our attack-reaction roles regularly, so when the incoming fire started, we all moved to our assigned spots to return fire. My place was on the roof of the TOC, spinning up assets and getting ready to move sensors and help vector our response. I had AH-64s pushed to me from the ASOC, who quickly identified the insurgents maneuvering through alleys and foliage along the river." Soon after AH-64s were deep into coordination with Spann, F-16s checked into the airspace. This was an unexpected development, as Spann had not requested fixed-wing aircraft, who were poorly suited to this kind of engagement. "The Apaches were doing everything I needed. I called back to the ASOC and asked why I had gotten F-16s. The fire duty technician at the ASOC told me that they had confirmed that the F-16 was indeed working with a JTAC at that location. But it wasn't me."

Across the river, less than a kilometer away, a different SF team (not affiliated with Camp Justice) was in a totally separate gunfight with insurgents, unbeknown to those defending the camp. Another TACP named Mike Prout, a close friend of Spann's, was controlling the F-16, completely unaware Justice was under attack and that AH-64s nearby were under Spann's control.

"That scenario encapsulates a lot of the headaches we had to deal with, at least on the task force side of the operation. The conventional forces were much more adherent to the flow of information and battle tracking by higher headquarters, but our work had us far more deeply embedded with our partner forces, keeping us a little out of the loop. The air-integration component—for the most part—helped track where friendlies were across the battlespace, but it wasn't completely coherent."

CHAPTER 20

The Birth of Digital Close Air Support

Ex Id Aer Pro Id Terra

The efforts of forward air controllers (FAC) to integrate aerial-delivered fires into the ground scheme of maneuver had proven to be a herculean challenge, but one the community of innovative and daring men effected with tireless obsession.

But this war began with men and machines operating on outdated and inaccurate maps, compasses, and loosely established communication procedures that, in most cases, worked by luck or tenacity. In other incidents, such as those addressed in the introduction, mishaps occurred because of equipment failing at a time when it was needed the most. There are too many instances where FACs did everything correctly, only for an unforeseeable circumstance to induce risk. But equipment—battlefield technology and its limitations—proved to be the most common contributor to losing situational awareness, as was overreliance on equipment.

The role of close air support (CAS)—digitally aided—would go on to shape the future battlefields of Afghanistan, Iraq, and Syria. From 2001 to 2004, no such capability existed on this modern battlefield that could truly enable ground controllers to integrate their targeting systems with the acquisition sensors and queuing capabilities of aircraft in real time. The software simply did not exist, as this capability had never truly been actualized, scarcely even theorized. The closest comparison in American military hardware would be the innovative use of laser target acquisition and laser target designation which began in the Vietnam War. In that conflict, hundreds of air sorties were flown against the "Dragon's Jaw," the bridge at Thanh Hoa, which facilitated countless quantities of personnel and materiel into South Vietnam from the north.

Targeting this key infrastructure had been largely unsuccessful, as weapons queuing and delivery was still limited to pre-set mil tickers on physical bombsights, slaved to the archaic head-up display in the cockpit. As noted by Steven Coonts and Barrett Tillman, who both served in Vietnam and published extensive books on air power and operations from that war:

During Operation *Rolling Thunder* in the Vietnam War, from 1965 to 1968, F-105s typically scored 5.5 percent direct hits, with a circular error of probability (CEP) of 450 feet. Later, technique and equipment cut the previous CEP in half, to a still unsatisfying 365 feet.

The mil setting the pilot put into the bombsight was a number derived for the middle bomb in the string, or if an even number of bombs were dropped in one pass, the average of all of them. If one bomb in the string was a bull's-eye, all the others in the string missed by varying distances. The average miss distance of all the bombs in the string, divided by two, was the CEP (circular error of probability), or the distance from the target at which half the bombs fell inside.

Still, any way one approached the problem, there were a lot of bomb craters scattered all over the landscape, with precious few bull's-eyes.[1]

The Air Force, lamenting accuracy and precision shortcomings for its bomber fleet, moved ahead with developing the Pave system, an electro-optical laser-guidance pod to designate an aimpoint for a laser-energy-seeking nose kit mounted to a free-fall bomb. In 1972, the first successful "precision" weapon was dropped on the Long Bien bridge, proving the system's effectiveness. These weapons would be used to eliminate the Dragon's Jaw too, at the time the single most heavily defended piece of terrain on the planet. F-4 Phantoms employing nine 3,000-lb laser-guided Mk-118 bombs destroyed the bridge, which was further reduced by unguided munitions after the precision munitions had scored direct hits. Less than a dozen bombs had done what thousands dropped on previous missions had failed to do.

Laser-guided munitions were merely the first generation of precision-guidance systems, which would evolve into the complex joint-fires engagement panoplies of the War on Terror. As previous chapters have shown, FACs employed both ground-based laser-designated weapons and devised the tactics, techniques, and procedures (TTPs) for utilizing GPS-guided weapons on targets in austere terrain. Providing that targeting still required laborious map reading, target correlation, and redundant steps in the CAS briefs to make these weapons work as intended. But, functionally, work they did, which is one key component of how and why CAS broke the Taliban and Iraqi regimes in both invasions.

Yet a disconnect endured between the machines above and the men below, at least in such a manner as to fuse these targeting capabilities with one key component of safe and effective CAS: friendly battle tracking. Situational awareness of the ground forces, maneuvering through rugged mountains and dense urban environments, remained solely at the mercy of the FACs speaking on single channels to all aircraft in the stack above. Even now, augmented by situational-awareness technology, knowing where all friendlies are, and effectively relaying this critical data to the pilots, is the single greatest challenge for an FAC.

In 2005, with insurgencies and uncertain future strategy already undermining the Coalition's raison d'être, improving the situational awareness of the increasingly critical CAS mission was not only necessary, but singularly important to legitimizing the role of air power going forward. No piece of technology can ever replace the ingenuity and perspective of the men on the ground in a gunfight, but innovators of air-power integration would put their diverse skillsets to the challenge of improving this shortfall in the CAS inventory.

"War, and life, is about seconds and inches"

Matt Schleich spent more than two decades in the Air Force, deploying multiple times as both an active-duty service member and defense contractor. Schleich would be a pivotal actor in institutionalizing cohorts of the TACP career fields into the Air Force Special Tactics community alongside combat controllers and pararescue whereas, previously, TACPs had been sourced to joint special operations on individual or special assignment. In addition to his singular shepherding of the 17th Air Support Operations Squadron into AFSOC (Air Force Special Operations Command), Schleich, like so many others in this book, would participate in strategically pivotal episodes of the war. He was among the first Americans to go into both Afghanistan and Iraq during the invasions and would return to each several times over the course of his distinguished career.

In addition to his contributions to career-field organization, he was a key member of the team that would design, test, and implement the very first iteration of ground-based situational-awareness targeting and battle-tracking systems. In later years, these systems would go by a variety of names and labels: Killswitch (KSE), TACP–Close Air Support Suite (TACP–CASS), Android Tactical Assault Kit (ATAK), Digitally Aided Close Air Support (DaCAS), and others. Schleich would assist in developing, and would test in combat in 2005, a toolkit simply known as Battlefield Air Operations, or BAO, which his team colloquially referred to as "Bareback." The effort took more than three years from conceptualization to implementation.

BAO was never catalogued for mass distribution, as the Air Force's Air Combat Command was simultaneously developing the TACP–CASS software and hardware suites. But the efforts of creating a field-proven prototype resulted in a formal Air Force and Joint Program of Record, which would produce the advanced situational awareness technologies of later years, are credited with saving countless Coalition and civilian lives.

After invading Iraq, Schleich would receive orders and transfer to the 720th Special Tactics Group based at Hurlburt Field, Florida, to take over the previously vacant fire-support non-commissioned-officer-in-charge (FSNCOIC) position. He was tasked with joining an innovation team on developing a new system—hardware and software—for improving battlefield situational awareness and target acquisition. While at the 720th, he would report to then-Captain Mike Martin who, in later years, would serve as the operations officer for United States Special Operations Command, as a lieutenant general. Martin's guidance to Schleich was to the point: identify where and how to improve the quality and proficiency of special tactics (ST) FAC programs wholesale. "There were FAC-programs within each of the ST units, but not a program manager at the 720th to preside over the unit-level standards and programs. We were starting from scratch."[2] Schleich spent nearly a year standardizing the TTPs across Air Force Special Operations Command (AFSOC), working with Todd McCabe, J. J. Salsberry and other joint-fires experts to improve controller proficiency.

Schleich would join a team of several combat controllers (CCT), working most closely with Phil Freeman, who would later stand up the JTAC Weapons Instructor Course at Nellis Air Force Base in Nevada, institutionalizing JTACs as a weapons system alongside the existing F-15E and A-10 weapons schools. Further, Schleich would partner with Alan Yoshida, a CCT who had been embedded alongside Army Special Forces during the 2001 Invasion of Afghanistan, and received a Silver Star. Yoshida was at Shawali Kowt in December 2001, when the GPS-guided bomb tracked onto faulty coordinates briefed by another FAC and nearly killed Hamid Karzai.[3] At the time, Yoshida had not been on the radio, but had seen firsthand the devastation caused when equipment and situational awareness failed to prevent a CAS mishap. When Schleich arrived at Hurlburt to join this initiative, Yoshida was still recovering from his injuries sustained during the mishap, including a still-immobilized right arm.

"Alan was there that day, and his mindset from then on was 'Never again, we must figure out how to prevent this. We must ensure the friendlies have a way of knowing where all the friendlies are and prevent the risk of bombing themselves.' In addition to my job as the new group FSNCO and overseeing the ST fires program, Freeman and I would be assisting Alan Yoshida in developing a system for improving situational awareness and targeting for the guys out forward while standardizing JTAC programs for ST." The first challenge lay in the disparate communications networks through which aircraft received targeting and mission data, as well as situational awareness queues in their flight systems. The Navy primarily used VMF (variable message format), while Air Force aircraft employed both Link-16 or SADL (situational awareness downlink) networks, depending on the aircraft. The different systems performed similar-enough functions, but the radio signals and data bytes did not cross streams, and no ground system existed to provide similar situational-awareness capabilities.

The Air Force's Air Combat Command (ACC), the primary provider of all combat air forces to the service, would be simultaneously developing a digital-CAS capability, but it was met with a variety of technical setbacks and dogged iterative development. Yoshida and Schleich's team, bent on creating a holistic solution to the situational-awareness problem, worked simultaneous to the ACC's effort to create such a capability, though not collaboratively. They simply achieved battlefield results first.

Creating a bridge system to speak across air-coordination networks, driven by ground coordination, was pivotal in advancing the air-integration capabilities of the joint force. The initial concept was called Battlefield Air Operations, originating from a single integrated kit with one purpose: preventing fratricide. Neither Schleich nor Yoshida, however, were programmers or hardware developers; they were operators, experts in controlling joint fires. But somewhere in their mandate—train, test and evaluate (TTE)—they would find a way to overcome this lack of functional knowledge and fuse it with their battlefield prowess, from conceptualization to TTP development and doctrinal standards.[4]

The prototype for this system would be hosted on a Panasonic CF-34 "Toughbook," a ruggedized and slightly slimmer version of the better-known CF-18 laptop from the same manufacturer. But starting from scratch meant the software simply did not exist; they would have to innovate to create a way for radios, computers, and battlefield-tracking devices to crosstalk. Exploiting their diverse Air Force network, they connected with a captain at Wright-Patterson Air Force Base named Lou Pochet. "Lou was an engineering nerd, super intelligent, and he could write code on the fly, which was perfect for us literally building this software and its required capabilities … on the fly." Schleich and Yoshida sat down with the young captain and explained their vision in detail: "We need to be able to digitally talk to an aircraft, while that same platform is simultaneously looking down at the ground and can 'see' where we are at, we can see where he is at, and we need to see where his sensor crosshairs or 'sensor point of interest' [SPI] is pointed." The system also needed to have comprehensive failsafe protocols to redundantly remove the possibility of fratricide by errant correlation.

More than a year into the testing-and-evaluation phase of this project, their work had drawn interest from other special-operations contingents. As they continued iterative development, three more TACPs, who were serving AFSOC personnel at Pope Airfield, North Carolina, became involved in requirements generation and system refinement. Having investment from elements of the AFSOC community would only increase the chance of this revolutionary capability becoming a program of record and, thus, garner congressionally appropriated funding for long-term sustainment and improvement.

Compatibility across the different software languages would prove to be the most challenging hurdle in this system's development—foreshadowing many future Department of Defense programs of record which continue to the present day. "How do you make these disparate systems talk to each other so that you can rapidly employ bombs on target? I spent most of 2003, and all of 2004—which is the only year of my GWOT [Global War on Terror] career that I didn't deploy—at Nellis Air Force Base helping create this capability." Over this period, more FACs from across the community assisted testing and development. This meant more inputs and feedback, and more experts asking questions which Schleich and his team crafted solutions for.

Just as critical to making this concept a reality for ground forces, staging the program at Nellis enabled the team to test their software and connectivity with the cadre of aircraft from the A-10 and F-15E Strike Eagle weapons-school units (the 66th and 17th Weapons Squadrons respectively). A ground system that could not communicate with aircraft systems would be pointless, and this collaboration provided a fount of joint-fires experts enabling the system's development by soliciting the pilots' perspective. "Every time we went to the range, while conducting advanced proficiency CAS training for the guys getting ready to go downrange, we tested integration with our aircrew partners. I was also standing up and standardizing the AFSOC joint-fires program, writing and maintaining records, and wrote the first iteration of the SOCOM 350-5 Joint Fires JTAC training manual."

The prototype for this emerging software would become known to the test team as "Bareback" and, for all intents and purposes, it was very similar to modular software applications found on the secured end-user devices years later. "Once we had the software fairly refined, we could take different equipment—the radio, computer, laser range finder—and the bytes would translate back and forth. Then we configured hardware so that the devices could be connected to man-portable radios to transmit to external receivers, from the ground to aircraft in the stack." Their first radio suite tested was the Enhanced Position Location Reporting System (EPLRS), a computer-controlled and jamming-resistant unit which also provides secure frequency hopping UHF capability. The EPLRS was too unwieldly for operators to carry in their rucks, but it was a minor and necessary iteration in ensuring the software on the CF-18 could be transmitted and received through the more-common PRC-nomenclature radios carried by JTACs (like the PRC-117F).[5] The CF-34s, being an older generation of the small wearable computers, were replaced after about a year once the CF-18s became available. "We finally got the software to the point where we could write nine-line briefs on the laptop for digital transmission to the aircraft. We would connect a hand-held laser range finder like the old Mark-VII using a wireless dongle and range a target. This would calculate a coordinate based on distance and azimuth from the user's GPS signal, which would upload to the Toughbook. From there, we would upload the target data into high-resolution imagery software, which would allow us to geo-rectify a mensurated grid for the target." Mensurated grids are refined coordinates plotted on one location, viewed from two separate imagery "plates"—or the same site captured from two different satellite captures in orbit. The rectification of those two images at different angles splits the difference of terrain relief, ensuring the most accurately calculated impact achievable.

On the test range north of Las Vegas, this would be the first time in history an FAC could calculate a fires brief in a fully digital format, while broadcasting their ground position to the aircraft in support. But the system was not finished or pristine; the data rates were "horrible, the connectivity was shit and the system crashed all the time." It was frustrating and laboriously slow work and, despite their incredible initial achievement, they still had to answer the burning questions in every operator's mind: "How am I going to shoot-move-communicate with a laptop, a GPS, a big-ass

Mk-VII laser range finder, and cables going everywhere? How do I convince the shooters that they need to carry all this crap, because it's good for calling in fires?"

Even if the system could not reliably connect and communicate with aircraft, the team had achieved one revolutionary and useful capability: determining and mensurating coordinates from a forward position. While Bareback and its unwieldly harness was not suitable for dismounted operations, it provided ground forces with an ability to "generate balls-on coordinates." Operating the equipment itself wasn't the challenge, rather, it was "getting all of the components plugged in, and simply getting them to 'talk' to one another."

The seriousness of the team's endeavor did not eliminate occasional levity, however. While Donovan Huss was providing feedback to Schleich's team, he relayed one explicit request for software manipulation: "Dude, if you can just code a button, like, a magic button, to get the equipment to talk together in the software, that is all I want." Captain Pochet would indeed code a "boot-up/connection" function into Bareback, and it would live forever in this digital CAS prototype as the command prompt "Donovan's magic button."

Another variable would be introduced into this capability in 2004; other select special-operations teams had been utilizing first-generation small unmanned aerial systems (sUAS), such as the RQ-11 Raven, Puma, "BatNav," "POINTer," and other variants. Alan Yoshida was also heavily involved in the advent of these portable, recoverable aerial sensors designed to provide more eyes in the sky for the ground force. "We were taking these aerial systems, snapping pictures of a planned target, uploading the imagery onto Bareback, correlating on our CAT-1 imagery, and still employing them as a traditional ISR [intelligence, surveillance, and reconnaissance] sensor for building nine-lines."

The year for proof-of-concept was 2005; Schleich and another FAC named Andrew Martin deployed to Afghanistan with prototypes of the new targeting system to field it in a combat environment. Like Schleich, Martin would utilize the prototype system on this deployment in multiple large-scale attacks with success. "After sorting issues with battery life and other technical details, we had this thing at about 80 percent of a finished product." They arrived at Bagram in September 2005, taking a few days to acclimate, ensure the equipment survived the transit to the other side of the world, and await travel to their outstations. Martin would go south near Kandahar, while Schleich would forward stage at Lwara, in Khost Province overlooking the Pakistan border. Lwara is north of Bermal and Shkin, two of the most notorious battlegrounds in all of Afghanistan. He would relieve-in-place a CCT and utilize the callsign *Jaguar16*. The village itself was named Lwara but, to Coalition personnel, the outpost was known as Camp Tillman; it was established near the location where U.S. Special Forces soldier and former NFL player Pat Tillman was killed in April 2004. Camp Tillman was surrounded by small observation points (OP) looking into the dominating mountains where Coalition forces conducted Operation *Anaconda* in 2002. This part of Afghanistan remained flush with major transit routes for insurgent forces sneaking over the Pakistan border during the fighting season.

On Schleich's first night at Camp Tillman, one of the OPs was being overrun by Al Qaeda insurgents and Taliban militias. "I figured that I would have the first night to break out the equipment, set it up and pinging before the work started; no such luck. As soon as I unloaded gear we got the call on the radio, I threw on my kit and we headed out the door to go help those guys on the OP." The outpost was occupied by a platoon of soldiers from the 82nd Airborne Division, and members of the Army's 3rd Special Forces Group team who staged out of Camp Tillman (Operational Detachment–Alpha 344). "The team commander told me to get everything overhead that I could, so I passed the brevity term for such a contingency: 'Tablecloth, Coalition OP is being overrun." That pro-word, "Tablecloth," is more referentially thought of as "Broken Arrow" from the movie *We Were Soldiers* starring Mel Gibson. Labeling aside, it produces the same result: all available aircraft are immediately re-tasked to consolidate above the ground emergency to provide immediate and overwhelming support.

Schleich would end up driving one of the trucks, and the quick-reaction force (QRF) faced immediate problems upon leaving the camp, including a truck breaking a trans-axle after hitting a rock obscured by darkness. By the time they arrived at the OP, the Taliban assault force had begun breaking contact and slowly withdrawing from the fight, thanks to a valiant effort by the small team at the OP. But since the Tablecloth call had upended the night's Air Tasking Order for the entire country, aircraft had already been checking into the restricted operating zone with Schleich preparing to execute the ground commander's intent for defensive fires. An AC-130 had been scrambled from Bagram Air Base (BAF), providing the most responsive asset in the U.S. inventory overhead. "But the problem was, with that emergency call, they had launched and immediately pushed south towards Khost." Normally, gunships would leave BAF and pass over a cleared firing range, performing a boresight, or "tweak," of their guns. Between missions, the targeting sensors lose alignment with the gun barrels due to vibration; these initial test fires realign the sensors and weapons for suitable accuracy.

Targeting a group of insurgents who were continuing to pepper the OP with small-arms fire, approximately 400 meters away, Schleich passed the call-for-fire to the gunship, which sent one round from its 105mm.

"The round impacted about 200 meters behind me, almost landing on the staging area where our relief force stopped short of the climb to the OP. I thought, 'What the shit just happened?' My first airstrike on this rotation and it nearly smoked friendlies." Fortunately, no one was hurt, and a quick radio conversation between Schleich and the gunship weapons officer discovered the technical cause which nearly produced a fratricide incident. Schleich would direct the gunship to "check fire" (cease all targeting and engagements) and proceeded to defend the OP with A-10s until the threat had been eliminated.

It was situations just like this one which instigated the team of FACs, led by Yoshida, Freeman, and Schleich, to develop a situational-awareness tool to avoid potential misidentification, errant targeting, and ensure safety of the force. A technical mishap like a misaligned gun sensor is not within the purview of these kinds of systems, but data-sharing software that could transmit weapons-readiness status in such a case, could very well have. "That moment just put more emphasis on the fact that this capability was important. And this wasn't necessarily the gunship's fault, if the pilot had told me right away that they weren't tweaked, we would have approached the target set differently. But he didn't brief, and I didn't ask. A JTAC can do every little thing right and then, in the middle of a gunfight, those little things can become major things. The immediacy of the emergency just accelerated the kill-chain and that small piece got missed."

This rotation based out of Lwara would be among the busiest and most demanding of Schleich's career. Their location, just over the border and west of Miram Shah (Pakistan), meant insurgent networks were constantly funneling personnel and materiel into the Afghan warzone. Following the gunship incident, lessons learned were captured in AARs (after-action reports). Once the dust had cleared from that first night, he settled in and established his new system in the tactical operations center (TOC), alongside the TACPs from the 82nd Airborne Platoon sharing the camp with ODA344. The static set-up was necessary as there were limited vehicles available, and none were capable of hosting a field-expedient jury-rigged Bareback system. Still, this enabled him to provide air-support coverage across the entire area.

In 2005, not every mission in Afghanistan would have dedicated CAS sorties, unless the mission priority dictated the allocation of limited assets. The early weeks of the rotation consisted of regular patrols into the terrain surrounding the OPs overlooking Camp Tillman. "We did a lot of KLEs [key leader engagement], went out almost every night, and on nights when we didn't make contact, we still encountered IEDs [improvised explosive devices]. The OPs and Camp Tillman were under near-constant harassment. But now, I had the BAO set up and ready to support. Everything ran off my CF-19 computer, set up next to the conventional Air Force TACPs (callsign *Hardrock*) supporting the 82nd Airborne guys in our clapboard shed that housed the operations center." From the TOC, they had fully integrated multiple-imagery software suites, including PSS–SOF (Precision Strike Suite for Special Operations Forces), DPPDB (Digital Precision Point Database), providing imagery as refined as 1.5-meter cuts (as accurate as possible in 2005). The only function BAO could not provide was digitally transmitting the nine-line briefs directly to pilots, due to the lack of radios capable of executing the transmission sequence (an SADL or EPLRS radio). Further, none of the aircraft in country were flying with a Link-16 capable datalink. The entire SADL concept was in its infancy and, without a satellite gateway for Link-16 systems, there was no way of transmitting over the SA network. But they were able to quickly develop and generate precision-attack briefs.

This was ODA344's third rotation to Lwara, and the intelligence sergeant on the team, Sergeant First Class (SFC) James "Jimbo" Oschner, had built a comprehensive and elaborate network of sources, contacts, and local support personnel to facilitate patrol priorities. Such relationships drove many of the team's missions and targeting, often more so than intelligence sourced from higher headquarters. On November 15, they would conduct a patrol eastward from Lwara, heading towards the Pakistan border, ostensibly to conduct a familiarization link-up with border guards from a nearby Pakistani base that overlooked the national boundary. On such missions, the team split between multiple vehicles, taking along a platoon of 82nd Airborne soldiers for additional security, as well as a platoon of the Afghan "Scorpions"; these special-forces-trained militias were some of the best-trained Afghans of the war. In addition to the platoon of Scorpions, the Special Forces (SF) team was supported by two platoons of "reconciliation forces," repatriated Taliban who had either surrendered to Afghan forces or simply approached Coalition forces stating their intent to defect. "There was an existing program to pay these guys as camp security, reintegrate into the Afghan Army and, in 2005, we were up to two total platoons worth of these guys. The Scorpions managed these personnel, we obviously didn't trust them for missions, but they were under close-enough watch to go out and man the perimeters."

The convoy departed Camp Tillman, passed through the village of Lwara, bypassing OP4 on their way towards the border. On the way, they came across two of their militia members, walking along the road away from the OP, which caused SFC Oschner to halt the convoy to ascertain why these two weren't at their post. A few minutes later, they came across several more of the hired Afghans departing the OP. Something seemed off to the Americans, and the Afghans' explanation—a relief in place and shift changeover—didn't add up. Oschner and Schleich would switch seats in the Humvee, the former moving to the back seat, while the JTAC moved to the driver's seat. Normally, Schleich would be in the back seat to operate radios and perform battle tracking but, in this moment, the conditions demanded the JTAC take the wheel for the intel sergeant to consort with his network on the unexpected change of personnel.

With Schleich behind the wheel, the team leader in the front passenger seat, Jimbo behind the driver, and JJ, the gunner, the truck roster was filled out by two Afghans in the bed of the truck, an interpreter and a Scorpion. No more than a few hundred feet down the road, they hit an IED with the back left tire, blowing the vehicle entirely off the road and tearing it in half. "I thought we had been rear-ended by another truck. The cab is full of smoke, and my reaction to the moment was to hit the accelerator to get out of the kill zone, not realizing we had been tossed in the ditch. The truck immediately dies, and we all began scrambling to get clear of the vehicle." It was somewhere in the chaos-infused moment that Schleich realized he was covered in blood, his own, and that of SFC Oschner, who was killed in the explosion. Schleich would lose consciousness multiple times over the next few minutes, due to a severe concussion and significant blood loss. While attempting to secure his ruck from the vehicle, where his portable radios were stowed, he discovered the UHF antenna on his radio had been sheared off in the explosion. Securing the SATCOM cable into the J6 port on his PRC-117F, he called the Air Support Operations Center (ASOC) at Bagram, notifying them of multiple casualties and coordinating for a medevac to recover the wounded.

As the team leader worked to get a QRF of 82nd personnel scrambled to secure the site, the ASOC had tasked A-10s to push overhead, and AH-64s had launched from Orgun-E to the south to provide immediate air support. Fortunately, no complex ambush would follow the IED strike—two anti-tank mines stacked atop one another in the ruts of the road—but the mission ended then and there as ODA344 would return to Camp Tillman.

Later that night, Schleich would continue to deal with severe concussion symptoms, including a stiffening neck, violent headache, and loss of consciousness. "I hadn't even showered, was still in the same uniform, and still wearing my baseball cap. We were still coming to terms with the fact that we had lost Jimbo, multiple casualties, and were trying to figure out about rehabbing equipment, but I knew something was wrong with me." Checking in with the team medic, his hat was removed, and congealed blood peeled away revealing shrapnel through his neck and the back of his skull. That prompted an immediate medevac to Bagram's hospital for emergency surgery to remove the debris. "War, and life, is about inches and seconds. I was sitting in that seat doing my job, and the circumstances forced us to switch seats, then a hundred meters later, the entire back of the truck was sheared off by that IED, taking good people with it."

After two weeks in Bagram, Schleich was allowed to return to light duty, meaning he would fly back to Lwara, but not yet able to conduct operations beyond the relative security of the camp, as he was unable to wear a helmet until his head and neck healed. It took no small amount of persuasive powers on his part to convince the doctors to allow him to return to duty under these restricted auspices. Ordinarily, this would be a significant degradation of air-power interdiction—except Schleich had spent the months before this rotation building out the BAO, and this was just the kind of situation where such a tool would prove useful. "The team was really constrained if I couldn't support them; yeah, they had the *Hardrock* JTACs on site, but those guys weren't embedded with the team. Having Bareback on hand, a system that I helped create, meant I could effectively provide air support even if I wasn't on the mission." He had to return to Bagram (BAF) one more time, to be fully cleared by the doctors to get back in the proverbial saddle and, upon his second return to Lwara, brought back 10 extra-large pizzas from the food complex at BAF for the camp, a gesture that endeared the airman to his Army brethren even further.

In early December, missions continued apace. As the year ended, between combat casualties and other problems, ODA344 was running short of personnel. "We lost Jimbo in November. Our senior 18C (engineering sergeant) had been injured in the IED that day as well, and the junior 18C started having seizures, so he was sent home. We suspected he had developed some kind of reaction to breathing in red-phosphorous fumes from a weapons cache we had detonated on a previous mission. In total, we were down to seven or eight of us from the team. We knew eventually the ODA was going to close up Lwara and relocate efforts to Shkin or Orgun-E." On, or very near, December 22, the degraded team would face its own mortality once again.

Schleich went to bed after a recovery day, no missions planned. Sometime in the sleep cycle, he woke up to use the austere restroom facilities adjacent to the plywood TOC. "It's kind of a funny story, I turned right from the 'Tillman hotel,' our hooch, and as I'm taking a piss into one of the tubes in the shitter, I heard a few rounds popping off. I didn't think much of it, we regularly took occasional pop shots." A few seconds later, the errant shots became a growing drone of incoming fire, prompting Schleich to shake off sleep, realizing they were under attack. Several 82nd Airborne soldiers were sprinting from the TOC, sounding the alarm, and the gunfire increased to a steady, overwhelming cacophony of bullets and rockets. One RPG round passed overhead and impacted 30 meters away, just inside the compound. "I ran back into the hotel, wearing some Jim Beam pajama pants and a brown t-shirt, and yelled at the team that we were under attack. One of the team guys shouted back 'Fuck you!' only to be answered with the roof of the hotel getting peppered with several dozen rounds." In just a few seconds, the camp erupted into a flurry of activity, men shouldering body armor, helmets with night-vision devices, and charging to the compound walls to return fire.

As Camp Tillman was under sustained assault, all four of the OPs were also in heavy contact. Only OP1 had Americans (from the 82nd), but they had retrograded from the outpost due to the intense assault. OP2 and OP3, manned by Afghan militias, had also given up the key locations due to the overwhelming fire. Only OP4 remained under friendly control. They would later determine through post-assault intelligence that OP4 did not receive a full assault as the Taliban assigned to that attack prong has mistakenly begun shooting at each other during the movement through the darkness. OP4 contained a Hughes Technologies AN/TPQ-36 counter-battery radar used to reverse calculate incoming mortar fire, while OP1 had a ZU-23/2—a 23-mm anti-aircraft machine gun. "The only thing that prevented them from turning that ZU into direct-fire mode onto Camp Tillman was an RPG projectile which had gotten wedged in the turnstile, and they couldn't swivel the guns around. If they had managed to do that, it would have turned us all into shredded cheese."

Taking to the wall, Schleich had already passed another Tablecloth call to the ASOC on SATCOM, notifying all Coalition aircraft of friendly positions being overrun. Firing back, he awaited the squelch break on the fires channel signifying aircraft overhead. "It had devolved to an all-consuming gunfight, nothing but shooting and being shot at. I called for the guys at OP1 to just shine their IR [infrared] pointers straight up in the air to mark themselves for the pilots to identify, there was nothing else they could do. The team sergeant was on our Afghans' DShK heavy machine guns, pouring 12.7-mm rounds into the high ground." Meanwhile, the team's 18B (weapons sergeant) was firing mortar rounds from the organic 82-mm mortar tube as fast as he could while under fire. An eternity of gunfire passed, at least it seemed as much to the men on the ground, when comm checks started coming through the fires net.

By the time aircraft had begun converging overhead, the front gate and a second spot on the compound wall of Camp Tillman had been breached, the first by a suicide bomber, the second through another explosion, though it wasn't known if the second breach had been with an RPG or other explosive. In both instances, the beleaguered American and Afghan defenders repelled the sudden rush of insurgent attackers with weltering machine-gun fire. The sound of aircraft—a B-1 bomber first, and an MQ-1 shortly after—immediately caused the bulk of Taliban to withdraw from Camp Tillman's perimeter, and from OPs 1 and 3. OP1 remained decisively engaged as the attackers tried desperately to bring the damaged anti-aircraft gun to bear on the forward operating base (FOB) below. An hour after the attack began, OP1 was retaken by Americans. Observing through their sensor, the aircrew could easily identify dozens of attackers, though exact numbers, especially in the dense scraggy undergrowth of Afghanistan, would be impossible to determine.

After breaking contact, the Taliban attackers consolidated in groups and moved south, straight into the curving ridgelines and rugged terrain, and towards the Pakistan border. The bulk of their force made it into a valley adjacent to OP1, where American personnel, having retaken the outpost, could occasionally make out their attackers breaking in and out of small terrain features and vegetation. Returning to the TOC with Bareback running at full capacity, Schleich continued to track the insurgent packs through the MQ-1 sensor. "At the time, the B-1s flying in country didn't have Sniper [advanced targeting] pods, so I was reliant on the RPA [remotely-piloted aircraft] crews who continued to feed me updated enemy positions. I utilized the imagery software in the BAO to build a fires box—four corner grids pulled from PSS–SOF—and passed those mensurated coordinates to the B-1." The bomber distributed six 2,000-lb GBU-31 JDAMs within the box, neutralizing dozens of enemy personnel. The MQ-1 continued to track and sort the remaining enemy, and another pass from the bomber would result in that aircraft going "Winchester" (all air-to-ground ordnance expended). But there remained more enemy maneuvering despite the overwhelming firepower.

A two-ship of A-10s would check in with Litening advanced targeting pods (ATP), Mk-82 unguided 500-lb bombs, rockets, and 30mm as the B-1 departed. Finally, Schleich was able to establish a clear video feed from the MQ-1, shortening his timeline for building targeting data with the BAO even further. The A-10s, despite the precise and accurate targeting data built from the RPA overhead and SA software correlation, could not locate the remaining enemy personnel maneuvering through the rugged terrain. This would prompt Schleich to attempt a TTP that had only been sparingly attempted in sterile training events, and never in combat.

"A new feature of the Litening ATP pod was a laser spot search and track (LST) capability; meaning another aircraft or ground-based laser could provide a target designation, and if the correct pulse-repetition frequency, or number of flashes per second, were programmed into the LST, it could immediately queue the sensor itself to the designation energy. We had tested this back in Nevada, among all the other Bareback capabilities but, to my knowledge, no one had ever used an aircraft-to-aircraft handoff like this. I directed the MQ-1 to put their laser spot on a group of enemy personnel, and told the A-10s to utilize their new LST function. Immediate tally target, just like that." This TTP would eventually become standard operating procedure for laser talk-ons. The A-10s quickly rolled in with Mk-82s and guns, followed by one last strike with the MQ-1's Hellfire missile.

A contingent of the ODA and 82nd soldiers went out the following morning to conduct post-attack analysis. Of the assessed 250–300 Taliban who attacked Camp Tillman and the surrounding OPs that night, only a handful would escape to Pakistan. "If there was any kind of validation for the BAO system, it happened that night. This was the culmination of years of trial and error, development, and testing. It worked."

Lwara would remain occupied by the platoon from the 82nd Airborne, but due to the attrition of previous missions, casualties and redeployments, ODA344 was down to five soldiers and Schleich, rendering them combat ineffective. That team would rotate out of Afghanistan, leaving Schleich looking for work.

Once they had recovered all men and material, Schleich would return to Bagram, and soon found himself supporting another SF team, ODA774, at Camp Wright in Asadabad (Kunar Province). At Asadabad, Bareback became a primary tool for Schleich, who installed the equipment in the back of a Hilux pickup truck. He had also begun flying a Raven sUAS ahead of convoys and while on the FOB. That tactic of imagery and live-video area surveillance would inform and evolve the integration of the Bareback system as well. "I spent hours tweaking and rehashing how the equipment fit into a vehicle, because it wasn't something you could readily throw in a backpack and walk around with. How best can I manage a Toughbook, radios, and cables, which make sense in a truck, but then what about jumping out to return fire? Or is it in the way of the gunner standing up behind the driver? A lot of missions I was the driver, just by necessity, so how do I utilize this SA tool while not driving over a cliff, which are seemingly everywhere near the roads of Afghanistan."

"I was utilizing the entire system now, correlating the ISR feed with PSS–SOF, I essentially had a full C2 [command-and-control] suite just on my set up alone. We were plotting CAS and artillery attacks in the high ground based on my live feed and targeting software, and it worked. We could pass gnat's ass coordinates to B-1s holding up at more than twenty thousand feet, build them a firebox, and they'd be astounded at how precise and accurate our coordinates were." The system, once refined and adapted to meet mission demands, instilled an incredible amount of confidence in the operator, and it significantly decreased the time it took to brief aircraft on the ground situation and various key locations across the battlespace. "It gave me the confidence knowing that I could pass a target coordinate and be certain that the bombs were going to hit exactly where I wanted them to. We still confirmed via talk-on in the necessary circumstances, but it was a fundamental change."

Schleich (right) during a KLE in Kunar Province with ODA774. (Photo provided by Matt Schleich)

The success of this early system caught the attention of special-operations forces (SOF) and the intelligence community operational teams who were in country at the same time, and those cohorts became invested in iterative systems that would build upon the success of Schleich and his team's prototype. Those entities were supported by their own, more exclusive ISR and C2 capabilities beyond that of the White SOF cohorts, but the concept of the SA tool Schleich had helped create would fundamentally evolve the CAS ecosystem. Bareback would fade into the annals of obscure military technological history, but the success of Alan Yoshida's conceptualization, Lou Pochet's engineering and programming genius, an entire ecosystem of other air controllers' inputs, and Schleich testing it in combat, would lead to the development of more advanced situational-awareness tools that would become a mainstay for nearly every JTAC by the end of the war.

***

"That deployment, and everything leading up to it, produced a system that worked. It wasn't flawless, it had many problems, and the development was not sexy: a lot of AARs, consolidated briefings on what worked, what didn't, how do we adjust the system and components to meet one requirement? But our success in utilizing the SA tool in 2005 garnered the awareness of other service components, so it started gaining traction, which meant funding, which meant real resource dedication towards making a functional tool to keep friendly forces safe on the battlefield."

"CAS wasn't effective initially, although we made it work. But because we had air supremacy and freedom of movement, we trained and trained until we refined it, and we did so quickly. It grew and evolved to meet the unique demands of the battlespace. That's all that forward air controllers did: we trained non-stop and dedicated ourselves to improving the systems, technology, and TTPs to adapt to the change. The CAS environment fundamentally changed the air inventory too. In the 1990s, we trained for the Cold War, high-threat/low-altitude, with aircraft avoiding surface-to-air threats using pop-up attacks. Then GWOT came around, and everything was medium altitude, talk-on driven attacks and constant coverage without fear of anti-air threats. Aircraft changed too; before GWOT, F-15E Strike Eagles only did air interdiction, they didn't even think about close air support. Then they became a mainstay of the CAS inventory. Every aircraft became some type of CAS platform to one degree or another. And it wasn't just the aircraft, but every component of the air-power enterprise became dedicated to dropping bombs close to friendlies: the maintenance, munitions, aircrew, everything became about CAS."

"If there was a reason for losing the war, it's because we left. And it really has nothing to do with winning or losing, but we just left all the same. You can't instill Western democracy into a culture that doesn't want it either. The ideals that make up our identity don't exist in places like Afghanistan and Iraq, it's just a different worldview that we didn't understand. And when we left, we took any incentive those people might have had to keep fighting for a future. Without us there, the Afghan and Iraqi people didn't have a good reason to keep fighting. Had we stayed, just like we did in Germany, in Japan, in Korea, maybe we could have learned to work within those cultures which are unique to Afghanistan and Iraq, but there isn't enough money and time to do that while you're also continuing to fight a war."

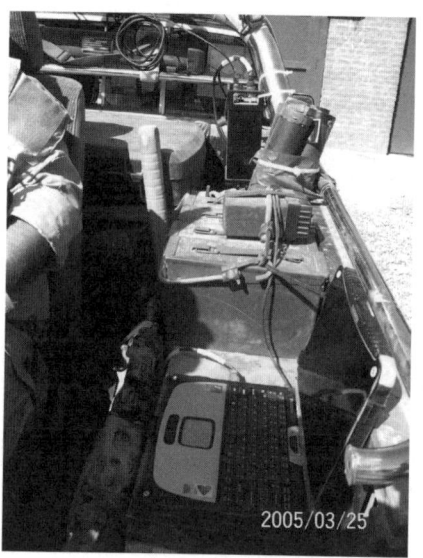

"Bareback" configured for use in the back of a Hilux. Schleich seated alongside. (Photo provided by Matt Schleich)

"It's like that line from the movie *Heartbreak Ridge*: 'Sergeant Major, you're 0-1-1. No wins, one tie, Korea. And one loss, Vietnam.' In GWOT, we're 0-1-1. No wins, one tie, Iraq. And one loss, Afghanistan. But we didn't lose that war. Our leaders lost that war."

Afterword

Scratching the Surface

If this book has captured the curiosity of, inspired, or otherwise astounded the reader for what this small community of men and machines achieved in the opening act of the War on Terror, then it has met the intent. But this is not the end of the story. The collective interviews, recounted missions, decisions, and influences of this story are but a taste of the saga that is still being told.

In this book, I have recounted the experience of men who were given an impossible task: break the enemy with new tools and procedures supported by limited resources, unclear architecture, and the variables of modern warfare against an enemy the greater strategic environment failed to understand in Afghanistan, and woefully misattributed in Iraq. And they did so, while the concept of "joint force" operations had not yet entered the imagination of tactical leaders, and certainly not those who commanded task forces or component commands.

So much of the doctrinal mission of close air support would change in the years that followed these accounts, but those changes were the product of the hard lessons these men learned in the crucible of warfare—not knowing any better in most cases, often acting in simple desperation—and an entire war would become defined by their actions and decisions.

At no point in the linear timeline of warfare, from ancient history to the battlefields of today, has an individual held as much power in their fingertips as did the forward air controllers of the War on Terror. No single entity was able to influence the outcome of a battle in the same fashion and, likely, this will never occur again.

I was only able to interview American air controllers for this first volume of the contemporary history of the war. In the volumes that follow, I will incorporate joint and Coalition forward air controllers who shared as much of the burden of coordinating air power as did their American brethren. These men comprise a truly global community who, not only by label, but action, put the "joint" into joint operations.

And herein lies a key point: the war changed how the Western Coalition of liberal states integrated with one another to fight a common enemy and, like so many other elements of this dark chapter of history, it was fused by the tactical element with little aid or contribution from the higher echelons of command. "Joint" terminal attack controllers, forward observers, aircrews, and maneuver commanders made up what would be known in military doctrine as the "CAS team," for indeed, it is a team effort.

This book began in darkness and the fog of war, and it ends at a time when the War on Terror lost sight of itself; but the demands of this war would send the men and women of our armed services back into the fog again and again, and the one constancy of this war was close air support. Everything else revolved around whether the ground force would be supported with "air" for the given mission. Intelligence collection, targeting, and developing the networks of our adversaries, became a fundamental pillar of this conflict too. But even the highly complex targeting and engagement cycle would only serve as added contextual and situational awareness for the men who spoke to the sky, on behalf of the ground.

And no war is complete without the ground forces themselves, for without those brave soldiers who move towards the sounds of gunfire to close with and destroy the enemy, the air-power experts have no purpose in combat. There are so many threads in this narrative that were critical in weaving together the story, but it all comes back to supporting those on the ground who do the actual fighting.

This project is my attempt at being a historian, but as I learned during an "historical methods" graduate course at Johns Hopkins University, the subject often becomes the focus in history, rather than finding where the subject fits into history. This is often referred to as narrative bias or contextual bias. I could not help but approach this project with some bias, because the subject was my own, and one I've endeavored to share with the world for its place in history. I won't apologize for that. This story needed to be told, in the voices of the men who did it, and it needed to capture their experience and narrative in a way that corrects the flawed public perception of this capability.

This concludes the first volume of the history of the War on Terror, as told by the men who controlled the most relied-upon tool of the war: close air support. But we are merely scratching the surface of this subject and its place in history.

Glossary

Alaska tent	A portable, quick-set-up range of enclosed weatherproof modular shelters used for accommodation.
ALICE	"All-Purpose Lightweight Individual Carrying Equipment."
AWACS	"Airborne Warning and Control System," a synonym of Airborne Early Warning and Control, a variety of different aircraft and radar antennas are used in this role around the world; the most recognizable is the USAF's E-3 Sentry with its rotating radome.
BDA	"Battle Damage Assessment," a judgement of the final effects of an aerial engagement collated and relayed to higher headquarters post mission, performed by forward air controllers.
Crypto	Cryptological encryption keys used to secure voice and data transmissions between coalition radios.
DAP	"Direct Action Penetrator." Specifically configured MH-60 Black Hawk helicopters equipped with miniguns, rockets, and Hellfire missiles.
DCUs	"Desert Camoflague Uniform."
FalconView	A mapping system, developed by Georgia Tech Research Institute for the Department of Defense, that displays various types of maps and geographically referenced overlays.
FIDO	(F)rom a known point, (I)n a direction, for an established (D)istance, to an explicit (O)bject.
GAF	"Ground Assault Force," a label for when an assault force uses ground vehicles to conduct mission infiltration.
GRG	"Gridded Reference Graphic," an image overlay containing maneuver symbols, building labels, and other key information, made by mission planners for high-resolution imagery to facilitate rapid talk-ons and unit vectoring.
HAF	"Helicopter Assault Force," used for when an assault force uses rotary wing platforms to conduct mission infiltration.
HMMWV	"High Mobility Multipurpose Wheeled Vehicle." The ubiquitous "Hummer," or "Humvee" was widely used for mounted patrols during the early years of the war.

ICS	"Internal Communications System," allowing operators to plug into the helicopter's radios and hear multiple channels simultaneously.
JDAM	"Joint Direct Attack Munition," a kit fitted to unguided (dumb) bombs to convert them into precision-guided (smart) munitions.
JSTARS	"Joint Surveillance Target Attack Radar System," an airborne ground surveillance, battle management and command and control aircraft, the E-8C was a modified version of the Boeing 707 airliner.
MGRS	"Military Gridded Reference System," the gridded overlay of kilometric blocks used on military maps to ascertain precise coordinates.
MOLLE	"Modular Lightweight Load-carrying Equipment."
PAVE	"Precision Avionics Vectoring Equipment"; LOW: denotes the helicopter's ability to fly at extremely low altitudes, at night, and in adverse weather using the specialized avionics.
ROZ	"Restricted Operating Zone," a three-dimensional block of airspace with a center point fixed to a target location, by which the forward air controller keeps allocated aircraft deconflicted from each other and from other active missions.
RPA	"Remotely piloted aircraft." Colloquially, a drone. An unmanned aircraft, capable of reconnaissance and/or weapons deployment, "flown" by personnel on the ground, sometimes from a location halfway around the world and nowhere near the combat zone.
SAW	"Squad Automatic Weapon."
STACK	Verbiage used by the forward air controller to denote the multiple aircraft under control above a target in a designated section of airspace.

Endnotes

Preface

1. "Senate Armed Services Committee Hearing on Afghanistan Withdrawal," 5:30:09, September 28, 2021, https://www.c-span.org/video/?514537-1/senate-armed-services-committee-hearing-afghanistan-withdrawal&live=.
2. "Statement from Senator Jack Reed (D-RI) office following the Afghanistan withdrawal," August 17, 2021, https://www.reed.senate.gov/news/releases/reed-statement-on-situation-in-afghanistan.
3. Andrew Roberts, *Leadership In War: Essential Lessons from those who made History* (London: Penguin Books, 2019), 13.

Introduction

1. Halimah Abdullah and Courtney Kube, "Pentagon Punishes 16 for Afghan Hospital Strike," *NBC News*, April 29, 2016, https://www.nbcnews.com/news/us-news/pentagon-punish-16-afghan-hospital-airstrike-n564826.

Chapter 1

1. Daniel L. Haulman and John Tirpak. "44 Hours: Operation Enduring Freedom opened with the longest bombing missions ever flown," *Air Force Magazine*, January 2017, https://www.airforcemag.com/PDF/MagazineArchive/Documents/2016/December%202016/1216hours.pdf.
2. Roger Connor, "The Predator, a Drone That Transformed Military Combat," historical accounting of the first use of an RPA in an offensive strike capability, *Smithsonian National Air & Space Museum*, March 9, 2018, https://airandspace.si.edu/stories/editorial/predator-drone-transformed-military-combat.

Chapter 2

1. The Fulda Gap was the presumed route to be utilized by Soviet forces in the event of a Europe invasion—the nominal World War III scenario of the Cold War. The "Gap" was geographically the quickest route for the consolidated forces of the Soviet sector to enter NATO-controlled Europe and spearhead its way towards the English Channel, with multiple key cities and industrial sectors along its route. Throughout much of the Cold War, the Fulda Gap scenario was the foundational concept for all US Army training, organization, and equipping of forces.
2. Interview with Steve Tomat, February 4, 2023 (virtual).
3. "Brown out" is the rotor wash from a helicopter stirring up a blinding cloud of dust and particles making the aircrew unable to see the ground during the final approach to wheels down.

Chapter 3

1. Steve Bowman, "Bosnia and Kosovo: U.S. Military Operations," *Congressional Research Service*, February 16, 2004, http://congressionalresearch.com/RL32282/document.php#:~:text=Bosnia%20and%20Kosovo%3A%20U.S.%20Military%20Operations%20In%20the,opposed%20by%20the%20Serbian-dominated%20Yugoslav%20central%20government%20in.
2. Susanne Chapman, "The War Before the War," *Air Force Magazine*, February 2004, https://www.airforcemag.com/PDF/MagazineArchive/Documents/2004/February%202004/0204war.pdf.

Chapter 4

1. Interview with Robert Zackery, October 7, 2022 (San Antonio, TX).
2. The ubiquitous American armored assault vehicle of the late 20th-century, the "Highly Mobile Multi-Wheeled Vehicle," light assault vehicle with four crew seats, a diesel V-8, and multiple mission-specific configurations.
3. Operational Detachment–Alpha, 5th Special Force Group, 4th Battalion, Team Two.
4. Enlisted Terminal Attack Controller. "Joint" in the namesake did not become doctrinal standard until September 2003 with the release of *Joint Publication 3-09.3 Close Air Support*.
5. Zakim Khan would contend with Pacha Khan (no relation), both from the Ghilzai Pashtun Dzadran clan, who vied for influence near the Paktia region of Afghanistan, among the many rival tribes being coordinated by American Special Forces and CIA teams to rout the Taliban. See Adam Geibel, "Operation Anaconda, Shah-i-Khot Valley, Afghanistan, 2–10 March 2002," *Military Review*, May–June 2002.
6. Operation *Jawbreaker* was the CIA program that served as the initial entry point for American forces into Afghanistan immediately following the attacks on September 11, 2001. See Gary C. Schroen, *First In: An insider's account of how the CIA spearheaded the war on terror in Afghanistan* (New York: Presidio Press, 2007) and Gary Berntsen, *Jawbreaker: The Attack on Bin Laden and Al-Qaeda, a personal account by the CIA's key field commander* (New York: Crown Publishers, 2005).
7. "Rope" is the brevity term indicating the controller uses a beam of infrared (IR) light pointed up into the sky to give the helos a point in the night to vector to. Typically, the pilots know the grid for the landing zone, but on short final in the oppressive Afghan darkness, they needed every bit of help. Once the pilot calls "Contact Rope, mark Touchdown point," the controller moves the terminus of his IR pointer to where he wants the lead aircraft to put wheels down.
8. The term "Middle East" is attributed to Alfred Thayer Mahan in 1901, was popularized by British parliamentarian Sir Mark Sykes, and further expounded upon in Edward Said's post-colonialist theory on Orientalism.
9. Recreational Equipment, Inc. A retail chain that sells outdoors equipment and adventures.

Chapter 5

1. U.S. Army. (1942). "FM-31-35 Basic Field Manual, Aviation in Support of Ground Force." Pg. 2.
2. Author suggests reading: David Halberstam, *The Coldest Winter: America and the Korean War* (New York, Hachette Books, 2007) and I. W. Toll, *Pacific Crucible: War at Sea in the Pacific, 1941–1942*. (W.W. Norton, 2012).

Chapter 6

1 Richard Kugler, "Operation Anaconda in Afghanistan: A Case Study of Adaptation in Battle," *Case Studies in Defense Transformation #5*, National Defense University Press (2007): 11–13.
2 Interview with Matt Achey, August 23, 2022 (virtual).
3 FAA regulations require all aircraft to monitor two standard guard frequencies: 121.500 (VHF/AM) and 243.000 (UHF/AM). These are emergency broadcast frequencies that all air–ground–maritime radios are capable of transmitting and used for emergency transmission.
4 *Bone*: B-One.

Chapter 7

1 "Visual Reconnaissance" is the identification of enemy targets such as tanks, armored personnel carriers, aircraft, and surface-to-air systems to enable reporting and mission requests for CAS.
2 Interview with Peyton Knippel, July 20, 2022 (virtual).
3 "Single Channel Ground and Airborne Radio System."
4 A thick piece of oval-shaped plastic that rolls up for transport and unrolls to accommodate an adult-sized human, or several hundred pounds of equipment.

Chapter 9

1 Interview with Lance Maguire, November 1, 2021 (Columbus, GA).

Chapter 10

1 CENTCOM. (April 23, 2001). "Investigation of Live Fire Incident that Occurred at Udairi Range, Kuwait on 12 March 2001." http://www.jointterminalattackcontroller.com/finaljumper/ud_range_compiled.pdf.
2 Air Force Tactics, Techniques, and Procedures Manual 3-3.JTAC.
3 Ibid.
4 Ibid.
5 Joint Publication 3-09.3 "Close Air Support."
6 Ibid.
7 Ibid.

Chapter 11

1 Interview with Tommy Case, November 17, 2022 (virtual).
2 Brevity term, all air-to-ground ordnance expended, only self-defense weapons remaining.

Chapter 12

1 Interview with Robert Zackery, October 7, 2022 (San Antonio, TX).
2 The bronze star device affixed to a paratrooper's jump wings, signifying the wearer had parachuted into combat.

Chapter 14

1. Interview with Abel Martens, December 17, 2022 (virtual).

Chapter 16

1. Permanent change of station.
2. Interview with Scott Loescher, December 16, 2022 (virtual).
3. Judge Advocate General—a military lawyer who advises every commander on the legal use of force and interprets the theater rules of engagement and special instructions to ensure compliance with international law and grand strategy.

Chapter 18

1. Interview with Greg Kassa, January 11, 2023 (virtual).
2. Jacob Frazier was deployed from the 169th ASOS, Illinois National Guard, supporting Army Special Forces teams in Afghanistan. After multiple successful reconnaissance missions producing highly valuable intelligence on insurgent networks, his convoy was ambushed by insurgents on motorcycles in Southern Afghanistan on March 29, 2003. Ray Losano was deployed as a ROMAD from the 14th ASOS, Fort Bragg, North Carolina, supporting the 514th Parachute Infantry Regiment, 82nd Airborne Division. He was killed in Paktika Province, Afghanistan, near the Pakistan border, on April 25, 2003. As soon as his convoy was ambushed, Losano called in an airstrike on enemy positions before being killed by sniper fire, along with Army Private Jerod R. Dennis.
3. "Disarmament and Reintegration in Afghanistan," *International Crisis Group*, September 30, 2003, https://www.crisisgroup.org/asia/south-asia/afghanistan/disarmament-and-reintegration-afghanistan//.
4. Many of the caves, including those related to the destroyed Buddha statues, were utilized by the Taliban for weapons depots and staging areas for harassing Coalition operations throughout the Bamiyan Valley.
5. X-CAS were pre-planned aircraft sorties that were active and flew day and night lines over Afghanistan but were not allocated to a specific mission. These sorties would be on-call to respond to troops-in-contact situations once called up by the controllers on the ground or the unit ground-force commanders.
6. "National Highway 01" or "NH01," the interprovincial highway built by the Soviet Union in the 1960s, is a contiguous two-lane highway that encircles Afghanistan, touching many of the provinces on its circuitous route around the entire country. It was commonly referred to by Coalition personnel as the "Ring Road."

Chapter 19

1. Interview with Chris Spann, December 14, 2022 (virtual).
2. A group of adult males who departed from a key building designated in the GRG.
3. Direct-fire munitions employed in open terrain to prevent insurgents from fleeing a given area.

Chapter 20

1. Barrett Tillman and Stephen Coonts, "First Laser Bombs bust the Dragon's Jaw," *Invention & Tech Magazine*, Summer 2021, https://www.inventionandtech.com/content/first-laser-bombs-bust-dragons-jaw//.
2. Interview with Matt Schleich, May 1, 2023 (virtual).
3. The PLGR–GPS incident discussed in the introduction of this book.
4. Bareback was one initiative under a family of programs built on SADL principles, while "Jockey" enabled the downlink to display on map imagery like FalconView. Bareback would be the lynchpin for integrating direct datalinks between ground users and aircraft in the SADL network.
5. AFSOC personnel had been able to determine the EPLRS radios could in fact "push" an air key to link SADL aircraft to ground segments, but only when working with Block 30 F-16 variants. The first time a ground component could queue an aircraft using a sensor point of interest was after Schleich's team integrated the Bareback/Jockey prototype into an SADL network.

Selected Bibliography

This lists only the interviews and official documents used throughout the book. Other sources are fully referenced in the endnotes.

Achey, Matt. Interview with author (virtual). August 23, 2022.
Case, Tommy. Interview with author (virtual). November 17, 2022.
Kassa, Greg. Interview with author (virtual). January 11, 2023.
Knippel, Peyton. Interview with author (virtual). July 20, 2022.
Loescher, Scott. Interview with author (virtual). December 16, 2022.
Maguire, Lance. Interview with author (Columbus, GA). November 1, 2021.
Martens, Abel. Interview with author (virtual). December 17, 2022.
Roberts, Andrew. *Leadership in War: Essential Lessons from Those Who Made History*. London: Penguin Books, 2019.
Schleich, Matt. Interview with author (virtual). May 1, 2023.
SIGIR. "A Final Report from the Special Inspector General for Iraq Reconstruction." (February 1, 2013). https://apps.dtic.mil/sti/pdfs/ADA587236.pdf.
SIGAR. "Lessons Learned: Special Inspector General for Afghanistan Reconstruction." (2019). https://www.sigar.mil/lessonslearned/index.aspx?SSR=11&SubSSR=59&WP=Lessons%20Learned%20Program.
Spann, Chris. Interview with author (virtual). December 14, 2022.
Tomat, Steve. Interview with author (virtual). February 4, 2023.
U.S. Army. (1942). "FM-31–35 Basic Field Manual, Aviation in Support of Ground Force."
Zackery, Robert. Interview with author (San Antonio, TX). October 7, 2022.

Index

Aircraft
  Fixed Wing
    A-10 xxiii, 116, 117, 122, 125, 126, 127, 128, 129, 130, 166, 182, 183, 202, 204, 207, 209, 212
    AC-130 xxi, 43, 64, 65, 66, 94, 148, 161, 162, 186, 193, 194, 206
    AV-8B 66
    B-1 4, 33, 34, 65, 66, 116, 149, 183, 211, 212, 213
    B-2 3, 4
    B-52 xxi, xxii, 4, 15, 18, 39, 60, 61, 66, 67, 76, 78, 94, 97, 98, 109, 116 183, 184
    C-5 70
    C-17 31, 108, 130
    C-130 70
    E-3 AWACS 156
    E-8 JSTARS 33, 156
    EA-6B 93
    F/A-18 20, 38, 62, 63, 64, 94, 96, 97, 98, 101, 102, 146,
    F-4 163, 200
    F-14 15, 94, 101, 112, 117
    F-15 38, 43, 61, 62, 109, 110, 122, 125, 144, 145, 202, 204, 214,
    F-16 xxiii, 27, 62, 104, 111, 112, 116, 122, 125, 126, 161, 162, 183, 185, 198
    MC-130 124
    MiG-21 4
    MQ-1 xxiii, 5, 65, 161, 162, 211, 212
    MQ-9 xxiii
    O-1A 49
    O-2A 49
    P-3 59, 60
    RQ-11 Raven (sUAS) 205
    Small-Unmanned Aerial System (sUAS) 141, 142, 205, 212

  Rotary Wing
    AH-1 74, 79
    AH-64 55, 57, 162, 187, 198, 209
    HH-60 65
    MH-47 10, 71, 72, 80, 122, 123, 124, 129, 130, 196
    MH-53 33, 196
    MH-60 117, 122, 124, 125, 126, 144
    Mi-6 34
    Mi-8 34
    Mi-17 34

Command and Control (elements)
  Air Support Operations Center 65, 73, 74, 75, 76, 115, 154, 155, 165, 177, 178, 181, 182, 183, 188, 198, 209, 211
  Combined Air Operations Center 4, 5, 9, 13, 14, 15, 21, 53, 60, 61, 90, 94
  Combined Joint Special Operations Task Force-North 90
  Control and Reporting Center 156
  Direct Air Support Center (USMC) 144
  Joint Operations Center xiv, 80, 109, 182
  Special Operations Command and Control Element 16
  Tactical Operations Center (Multiple) 59, 124, 161, 179, 183, 198, 207, 210, 211
  Wing Operations Center 154, 155

Command and Control (methods)
  Airspace Management
  Be-no Line 114
  Danger Close xiv, 21, 60, 95, 118
  Gun-to-target line 66
  Helicopter Landing Zone (HLZ) 10, 11, 34, 55, 64, 67, 71, 114, 140, 196
  Joint Air Attack Team 115
  No-Fire Area 76
  No-Strike List xxii

Restricted Operating Zone (ROZ) 66, 114, 146, 155, 206
Time-on-target 14, 180
Time-to-target 180
Procedural Control xxi, xxii, 7, 11, 20, 69, 81, 104, 114, 155
Airspace Control Order 155, 157
Air Tasking Order xx, 76, 154, 206
Tactics, Techniques and Procedures 64, 105, 109, 114, 162, 167, 168, 186, 191, 193, 200, 202, 203, 212, 214
Neutral Sensor Posture 110

Equipment
  Tactical
    AN/PEQ-1B SOFLAM 11, 12, 17, 20, 21, 40, 114
    AN/PEQ-2 IR 127
    AV-2125 73, 90, 110
    CF-18/19 Panasonic Toughbook 161, 203
    Combat Track II 4
    Enhanced Position Location Reporting 204, 207
    System (EPLRS) Radio 204, 207
    Falconview 95, 98
    GRC-206 164, 206
    Infrared Pointer 34, 103, 127, 129, 211
    KYK-13 90
    Link-16 63, 202, 207, 208
    Mk-VII Laser Range Finder 32, 205
    Mission-Oriented Protective Posture (MOPP) 123, 139, 165
    OE-254 78
    PRC-104 32, 72
    PRC-113 32, 72
    PRC-117 32, 57, 58, 71, 72, 73, 90, 204, 209
    PRC-119 72
    PRC-148 90, 123
    PSN-11 PLGR xx, 58, 59, 75
    PSN-13 DAGR xxi
    Precision Strike Suite-Special Operations Forces (PSS-SOF) 207
    Remote Operated Video-Enhanced Receiver (ROVER) 161, 162
    SEE-SPOT Infrared Optic 12
    Situational Awareness Downlink (SADL) 202
    SKEDCO 72

Functional Components
  Theater Air Control System (TACS) 153, 154
  Army Air Ground System (AAGS) 153, 154, 156, 157

Locations
  Afghanistan
    Arghandab River Valley xix, 168
    Bagram xiv, 34, 54, 65, 66, 67, 70, 73, 76, 80, 81, 168, 169, 172, 173, 177, 178, 181, 182, 185, 188, 205, 206, 209, 212
    Bamiyan 173, 174, 175, 177
    Camp Brown 181, 182, 183, 185
    Camp Tillman 205–212
    Camp Wright 212
    Chapchal 13
    Federally-Administered Tribal Areas (FATA) 26, 134
    Gardez 34, 36, 37, 39
    Ghazni 26, 36, 168
    Helmand 160, 168, 169
    Hindu Kush 26, 34, 37, 38
    Jalalabad 168, 181, 182
    Kabul xv, xxiii, 24, 46, 168, 169, 174, 177
    Kandahar xix, xxi, 5, 24, 168, 169, 181, 184, 185, 186, 188, 205
    Keshendeh-ye Bala 11
    Keshendeh-ye Pa'in 11
    Khost 26, 33, 36, 168, 205, 206
    Kuh-e Al Borz 16, 17
    Lwara 205, 207, 208, 209, 210, 212
    Marzak Village 56, 63, 64, 65, 66
    Mazar-i-Sharif 11, 16, 17, 19, 20, 21, 22, 23, 24, 169, 177
    Naqa Valley 36, 39, 40, 42
    Paktika 33
    Registan Desert 26, 184
    Shah-i-Kowt 39, 42, 53, 66, 67, 71, 72, 75
    Shkin 205, 210
    Shawali Kowt xix, xx, xxi, 202
    Takur Ghar 26, 56, 71, 72, 74, 75, 79, 80, 138
    Tora Bora 26, 169, 185
    Tiangi 16, 17, 19
    Zaraq 37, 38, 40, 44
    Zurki Khel 66

INDEX • 229

Iraq
  Al-Lasaf 141, 142
  Al Sahra Airfield (Tikrit Air Base) 149, 150
  Karbala 134, 159, 160, 162, 189
  Camp Justice 192, 198
  Debecka Pass 89, 91, 93, 94, 99
  Erbil 91, 93
  Fallujah 119, 134, 160, 190
  Kirkuk 93, 119
  Nasiriyah 137, 143, 144, 145, 146, 190
  Mosul 86, 93, 120, 134
  Talil Air Base 143, 148, 149
  Tikrit 134, 149, 150, 159
  Sadr City 120, 134, 159, 160, 162, 163, 190, 192
Key Sites
  Abu Ghraib 86, 132, 190, 194
  Al Udeid Air Base 153
  Ali Al Saleem Airbase 160
  Baghdad International Airport (BIAP) 108, 130
  Camp Bucca 86
  Diego Garcia Auxiliary Naval Station 4
  Haditha Dam 107, 108, 109, 110, 111, 115, 117, 118, 121, 122, 149
  Incirlik Air Base, Turkey 172
  Karshi-Khanabad (K2) 9, 31, 70, 172
  Tarnak Farms (Kandahar) 104
  Presidential Palace (Lake Tharthar) 121, 122, 123, 125, 130
  Qala-i-Jangi Prison 19, 22, 23
  Roberts Ridge (Takur Ghar) 67, 71, 75, 76, 78, 80
  Shrine of Hazrat Ali 19
  Udairi Range (Kuwait) 30, 74, 81, 101, 102, 105
  "The Whale" 59, 75, 79, 191
Other Locations
  Bosnia 5, 27, 29
  Israel 87
  Khe San, Vietnam 43
  Kuwait 29, 30, 32, 87, 91, 92, 101, 141, 159, 164, 177
  North Korea 25, 48
  Pakistan 19, 26, 33, 40, 69, 107, 169, 187, 205, 206, 207, 208, 211, 212
  Qatar 4, 9, 60, 87, 153
  Saudi Arabia 87, 108, 163, 164, 165, 166, 177
  Syria xii, xiii, xiv, xvi, xvii, xxii, xxv, 86, 100, 108, 119, 141, 199
  Turkey 87, 91, 172
  Uzbekistan 8, 9, 10, 22, 31, 40, 70, 172, 173
United States
  Barksdale Air Force Base, Louisiana 98
  Fort Bliss, Texas 137, 163
  Fort Bragg (Liberty), North Carolina 29, 30, 32, 40, 89, 120, 138, 150, 171
  Fort Campbell, Kentucky 8, 30, 31, 40, 70
  Fort Drum, New York 54, 62, 64, 69, 70, 71
  Fort Hood (Cavasos), Texas 91
  Fort Lewis, Washington State 38, 89, 120, 171, 178, 191
  Fort Riley, Kansas 159
  Hunter Army Airfield, Savanna, Georgia 138
  Nellis Air Force Base, Nevada 202, 203
  Volk Field, Wisconsin 172
  Whiteman Air Force Base, Missouri 3, 4

Munitions
  Aerial
    2.75-inch rockets 49
    20mm M61A1 Vulcan 62, 111, 112
    30mm GAU-8 Avenger 129, 183, 212
    40mm Bofors Cannon 65, 142
    AGM-65 166
    AGM-114 5, 6, 74, 212
    CBU-87 98
    CBU-103 97, 98
    GBU-12 62, 66, 96
    GBU-16 96
    GBU-31 xx, 60, 211
    GBU-32 xx, 96
    GBU-38 xx, 96
    GBU-43/B xiv
    Mk-82 96, 97, 101, 112, 212
    Mk-83 96
    Mk-117 97, 98
  Artillery
    HIMARs 118, 120, 121
    Javelin anti-tank missile 111
    Mortars 45, 56, 57, 58, 59, 60, 61, 63, 65, 72, 90, 93, 94, 95, 111, 141, 178, 179, 180, 181, 210, 211
    SA-6 (surface-to-air missile) 124

SCUD (missile, Iraq) 139
unexploded ordnance (UXO) 140
white phosphorus 49

Units
　Maneuverer
　　1/87 Infantry Regiment, 10th Mountain Division 54, 55, 57, 66
　　1st Brigade, 1st Armoured Division 159, 162
　　1st Special Forces Group 90
　　2nd Battalion, 75th Ranger Regiment 120
　　2nd Brigade, 1st Cavalry Regiment 163
　　3rd Infantry Division 110, 111, 120, 130, 160
　　3rd Special Forces Group 89, 90, 92, 191, 206
　　4th Infantry Division 91
　　5th Special Forces Group xix, 7, 8, 9
　　7th Special Forces Group 10
　　10th Mountain Division 53, 54, 63, 70, 71, 72, 73, 74, 78, 79
　　10th Special Forces Group 191
　　14th Air Support Operations Squadron 29, 30
　　17th Air Support Operations Squadron 138, 201
　　20th Air Support Operations Squadron 69, 76
　　23rd Special Tactics Squadron 9
　　36th Commando Battalion (Iraq) 192, 193, 197
　　82nd Airborne Division 120, 130, 138, 174, 178, 179, 206, 207, 208, 209, 210, 212
　　116th Air Support Operations Squadron 172, 175
　　118th Air Support Operations Squadron 175
　　173rd Airborne Brigade 91, 92
　　720th Special Tactics Group 201
　　Afghan National Defense & Security Forces xxi, xxii, 46
　　Alpha Company, 1st Battalion, 75th Ranger Regiment 139, 140, 142, 143, 144, 148
　　Alpha Company, 2nd Battalion, 75th Ranger Regiment 120, 121
　　Alpha Company, 3rd Battalion, 75th Ranger Regiment 108, 122
　　Bravo Company, 1st Battalion, 75th Ranger Regiment 144, 146
　　Bravo Company, 3rd Battalion, 75th Ranger Regiment xvii, 108, 109, 111, 113, 115
　　Combined Joint Task Force-180 173, 175
　　Crisis Response Force (10th SFG) 191
　　Fedayeen (Iraqi paramilitary) 143, 146, 148
　　Grande Armée xvii
　　Northern Alliance (Afghan, multiple) 8, 16, 17, 18, 19, 22, 167
　　ODA344 206, 207, 208, 209, 210, 212
　　ODA394 94
　　ODA395 94
　　ODA542 31, 33, 34, 36, 37, 38, 39, 40
　　ODA574 xix
　　ODA595 8, 9, 10, 13, 16, 20, 23
　　ODA774 212, 213
　　Peshmerga, Kurdish (Iraq, multiple) 91, 92, 94, 95, 96, 97, 98, 99
　　Task Force Mountain 53
　　Task Force Raptor (Iraq) 191, 192, 193, 197
　　Task Force Viper (Iraq) 191, 192, 193, 194, 195, 196, 197
　Flying
　　17th Weapons Squadorn (Nellis AFB) 204
　　66th Weapons Squadron (Nellis AFB) 204
　　160th Special Operations Air Regiment 10, 71, 72, 110, 122, 130
　　325th Bomb Squadron (Whiteman AFB) 3
　　393rd Bomb Squadron (Whiteman AFB) 3

Vehicles
　Armored
　　BM-21 (Soviet) 18
　　M1 91, 143, 145, 164
　　M2 91
　　M113 67, 131, 132, 160, 164
　　Pandur II armored personnel carrier 144, 147
　　T-72 (Iraqi) 139
　Tactical
　　highly-mobile multi-wheeled vehicle (HMMWV, "Humvee") 30, 70, 178, 194
　　Hilux pickup 33, 212, 214
　　light tactical vehicle two-and-a-half-ton (truck) 94
　　Zodiac (boat) 113